Not Counting the Cost

Jesuit Missionaries in Colonial Mexico—a Story of Struggle, Commitment, and Sacrifice

For alfred

JOHN J. MARTINEZ, S.J.

John J Martinez, SJ

JESUIT WAY

an imprint of

LOYOLAPRESS.
CHICAGO

an imprint of

LOYOLAPRESS.
3441 N. ASHLAND AVENUE
CHICAGO, ILLINOIS 60657

Interior design by Amy Evans McClure
Interior illustrations by Tracey Harris

Library of Congress Cataloging-in-Publication Data
Martinez, John J.
 Not counting the cost : Jesuit missionaries in colonial Mexico, a story of struggle, commitment, and sacrifice / John J. Martinez.
  p. cm.
 Includes bibliographical references.
 ISBN 0-8294-1555-6
  1. Jesuits—Mexico. [1. Mexico—Church history.] I. Title.

BX3712.A1 M36 2001
266'.272—dc21

00-044367

Printed in the United States of America
01 02 03 04 05 / 10 9 8 7 6 5 4 3 2 1

In memory of my parents,

John Martinez and Katherine O'Brien

CONTENTS

INTRODUCTION

The missionary work of the Jesuits in colonial Mexico (called New Spain at that time) was a 201-year effort that reached from Cuba and Mexico City to Arizona and included Baja California. It began in 1566, forty-one years before the founding of the first permanent English colony at Jamestown, Virginia, and well before the better-known work of French Jesuits in Canada and of English Jesuits in southern Maryland.

The work in New Spain was contemporaneous with the Jesuit work in Paraguay. The Paraguay missions—or the Reductions, as they are called—are very well known. There are many books about the Reductions, and there is a movie about them, called *The Mission*.

The Reductions were very successful, mostly because the Indians were completely separated from the Spanish. In New Spain, on the other hand, the work was more difficult because the Indians and the whites were in close proximity. Mining camps throughout the north of New Spain contributed to continual tension and general disorder between the Indians and the whites.

Working at the mining camps required many men to live apart from their families. The result of this, along with a get-rich-quick mentality, was often the exploitation of native labor, heavy drinking, gambling, drunken brawls, prostitution, and a disregard of any harm being done to the environment.

The work in New Spain involved not just evangelization but also the founding of many mission schools and the higher education of white mestizos (part European and part Indian) as well as the integration of Indians in Jesuit high schools and colleges. The work required learning the Indian languages and resulted in the publication of Native American grammars and catechisms, as well as reports about the geography of the different areas and the customs of Native Americans at the time when they first had contact with Europeans.

It is important to know about these efforts because our roots are not only in Europe and Africa but also on this continent. The development of agriculture in the New World and the first great North American civilizations were within present-day Mexico, and the roots of Christianity are there as well. New Spain was among the more important Spanish colonies in the Americas. Like Portugal's Brazil, it was a major location where Indians, Africans, and Europeans came together to form a new race, culture, and civilization.

The work of the Jesuits was often dangerous. Twenty-nine Jesuits were killed by Native Americans—for religious reasons or in insurrections—during the 201 years that the Jesuits were in Mexico. Their work ended in 1767, before the founding of the United States, when the Spanish king expelled them from all Spanish lands. During the expulsion from New Spain to Europe, 101 of the 688 Jesuits in New Spain died from maltreatment and disease.

In this volume, if the modern names of towns and rivers are different from the colonial names, then the modern names will be used. Places are located in modern Mexican States rather than in colonial provinces, and Indian nations and languages are identified and located. Only the more recognized villages and Jesuits are mentioned because their numbers are so great that the story becomes confusing. The founders of the different missions, however, are always included.

The book is based on an abundance of original documents that have been edited and published (many in English translation) in recent decades. Some of the documentary historians are Ernest J. Burrus, S.J. (prolific and now deceased); Félix Zubillaga, S.J.; Luis González Rodríguez; W. Michael Mathes; Froylán Tiscareño; Miguel León-Portilla; Theodore E. Treutlein; Charles W. Polzer, S.J.; Thomas E. Sheridan; and Thomas H. Naylor. Polzer, Naylor, and Sheridan have provided mostly military and civil documents, and the others have provided Jesuit documents.

I wish to thank Luís Verplancken and Charles Polzer, fellow Jesuits, who helped me get started on this project by recommending good sourcebooks.

I wish to thank the parishioners of St. John's in Dinwiddie County, Virginia, for helping me with the project, especially Joanna Kofron, Howel Wynne, and Matt MacLaughlin for their editorial help.

And I wish to thank my editor, Linda Schlafer, as well as George Lane, S.J., and other staff at Loyola Press, for their interest and commitment.

CHAPTER 1

John Segura, S.J., and Companions, 1540–1571

In 1540, Pope Paul III authorized a group of graduates from the University of Paris to form a new religious order, which they named the Society of Jesus, or the Jesuits. In 1541, the group took religious vows of poverty, chastity, and obedience and elected Ignatius of Loyola as superior general of the new order.

One of the founders, Father Francis Xavier, was missing at the election of Ignatius because Xavier had already left Europe with the Portuguese to begin the missionary work of the order in India, Malaysia, and Japan. Other Jesuits followed Xavier to the Orient, and in 1549, four Jesuits were sent to the Portuguese colony in Brazil.

During these early years, Ignatius was in Rome writing the Constitutions of the Jesuits and directing the order. Schools were started. The order grew rapidly; there were almost a thousand Jesuits when Ignatius died in 1556. Although the order had been founded by a Spaniard and had a heavy concentration of Spanish members, no member of the Jesuits went to the Spanish colonies in the New World at this time because of hostility toward the order within the Spanish government.[1] Some of the hostility resulted from Ignatius's acceptance of applicants who were converted Jews or Muslims.

It was only in May 1566 that King Philip II of Spain asked Francis Borgia, the third general of the Jesuits, for missionaries to Florida. In response, Borgia sent two priests and a brother. Father Peter Martinez was superior of the group; his companions were Father John Rogel and Brother Francis Villarreal.

Peter Martinez was from Aragon. Having finished his philosophical studies, he entered the Society of Jesus in 1553 at the age of nineteen, during the lifetime of St. Ignatius. During the early years of the order, the course of studies for seminarians was not well organized. Martinez did two years of novitiate, or spiritual formation, including a thirty-day retreat. During the next three years, he studied theology, but he also preached and even taught school.

Martinez was ordained in 1558, at age twenty-four, and went with a Spanish military expedition to North Africa as a chaplain. He was left to work for four months at a hospital in Oran while the expedition went on to meet disaster in the countryside. He and two Jesuit companions helped to care for six hundred patients, and the three of them fell sick.

When Martinez recovered and returned to Spain, he did pastoral work and preached, but he felt his theological knowledge was deficient. Superiors gave him two years to study theology at the University of Salamanca, where he read the fathers of the church and the doctrines of the Protestant theologians. Then he wrote to the Jesuit general in Rome and asked to go to Germany as a missionary. His request was forwarded to his provincial superior, who sent him to the new Jesuit community in Monterrey, where he was named superior after a few years.

In 1566, Martinez was overjoyed to be chosen as leader of the first group of Jesuit missionaries to Spanish America. He and his companions, Father John Rogel and Brother Francis Villarreal, sailed with the fleet on June 25. Leaving the Canary Islands on July 13, they crossed the Atlantic in less than a month. Their ship separated from the fleet near Puerto Rico on August 11, bound for the Spanish colony of Port Royal (then called Santa Elena) on Parris Island in South Carolina. They knew the approximate latitude of the colony and had a written description of the coast, but no one on board had been to the area.

They reached the continent on August 28, during the hurricane season. They had been exploring for four days when a hurricane or a tropical storm drove them out to sea, where they lost one of their lifeboats. On returning to land, they were again driven out to sea, and this time it took them four days to return. On September 14, short on water despite the storms, they were at Cumberland Island in southern

Georgia. They launched a boat to fetch water and to see if they could obtain information from the Native Americans about the location of any Spaniards.

Ten of them went in the boat—seven Flemish sailors and three Spaniards, including Peter Martinez—while the other two Jesuits remained with the ship. Those on board waited a day and then fired a cannon to recall the boat, which did not return. In the middle of the night there was another storm, and the sailors headed for open water. The ship may have been damaged in the storms because the sailors had trouble handling it in contrary winds. They entered a lagoon at Cape Canaveral and had a difficult time maneuvering the ship back out. At one point, the ship was anchored for four days while strong winds threatened to drive it onto the shore. The group was actually south of St. Augustine, which had been founded the previous year.[2] If the sailors had heard of the place, they did not know where it was.

Meanwhile, the ten in the boat returned to the rendezvous point and waited for more than a week for the ship's return. They then decided to look for food and to seek directions from the Indians. If they had no been lost, their situation would not have been that bad. They were fifty-eight miles from St. Augustine, there was an inland waterway all the way down, and there were ten of them to row the boat. What they

Sites of First Jesuit Contacts with Spanish America in 1566

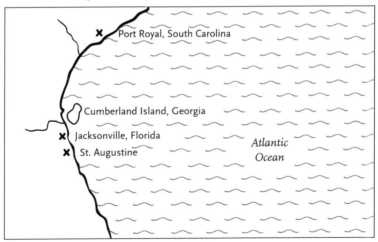

Fig. 1

had against them were unfamiliarity with the area, lack of food, and the possibility of hostile Indians.

Three rivers run between Cumberland Island and St. Augustine: St. Mary's, Nassau, and St. John's. The ten men rowed a good distance up a river (probably St. Mary's at the southern tip of Cumberland Island) and saw no living thing. When they went looking for food the next morning, they came across five vacant huts hidden in pine trees. They took half an alligator and left a jacket and a glass necklace in exchange. The next day, Indians came to the riverbank and offered them corn and fish. The two groups communicated in sign language and pantomime, and the Indians said that the Spanish were located past three chiefs to the south.

The party continued its journey. When the ship entered the Nassau River, it got stuck on a sandbar, and the men had a hard time getting free because everyone was weak from lack of food. Continuing south, they came to an Indian village situated on the shore, and they gave it a wide berth. When they came to another village about three miles north of St. John's River in Jacksonville, Florida, they saw some boys fishing, and the sailors paddled toward them.

Although Peter Martinez objected to going uninvited into a large unknown village, the group landed, and three of the sailors went to obtain fish from the boys. One of the boys ran to tell the adults, and about fifty armed Indians came to the spot. Martinez said to wait for the three on shore, but when the Indians rushed them, the rest of the sailors started to pull away. Two of them, including Martinez, were dragged into the water and onto shore, where they were clubbed to death, and the three on shore were shot with arrows. The five who were left in the boat were wounded by arrows, and two of them died after they were found by a boat from St. Augustine.

Peter Martinez died on September 28 or 29, 1566; he was about thirty-three years old.[3] When he died, the ship with the other Jesuits, Rogel and Villarreal, was still off the Florida coast. The pilot, who seems to have been the captain, decided to start at Cumberland Island and sail north until they found Port Royal, but the sailors more or less rebelled at this announcement because they had no food but bread and crackers, and they may have been without a boat for fetching fresh water. So the pilot gave in, and they left Florida on September 28. It took them almost a month, until October 24, to reach a port in the present-day Dominican Republic.

Martinez's fellow priest, John Rogel, was four years older than he was. Born in Pamplona and with a licentiate from the University of Alcalá, Rogel had studied medicine for two years before entering the Society of Jesus, and like Martinez, he only had a year or two of theology before ordination. John Rogel later founded the Jesuit community at Oaxaca in the south of New Spain. A devout person with a stutter, he worked the last forty-one years of his life as a priest and doctor in the unhealthy port of Vera Cruz, where he died at age ninety in 1619. The third Jesuit, Brother Francis Villarreal, would later be revered in Mexico as a prayerful and holy person. He died in 1600.

Another disaster followed Martinez's death. Borgia sent a second group of missionaries with John Segura as superior.[4] Father Segura, the same age as John Rogel, had also studied at the University of Alcalá, where he obtained a master's degree. Like Rogel, he had studied medicine, and as a young priest he had been superior of different Jesuit houses in Spain. He left Spain on April 10, 1568, with two other priests, three brothers, five catechists who would all enter the Society, and six Florida Indians who had been visiting Spain. The group landed in Cuba.[5]

From Cuba, they attempted to establish a mission to the indigenous people around St. Augustine, but they could do little because of enmity between the Native Americans and the Spanish. The missionaries were also a burden on the meager resources of the Spanish at St. Augustine.

In order to get away from the soldiers and the problems they caused, John Segura decided in the summer of 1570 to go to the James River area in Virginia with Louis Velasco, a friendly Native American from that region. Velasco had been picked up from the Chesapeake Bay by a passing ship. He was baptized in Mexico City and studied in Spain. Since he wanted to go home, he invited the Jesuits to establish a mission in Virginia, and they set sail in August. Those who would remain in

Area Explored by Second Group of Jesuit Missionaries, 1570

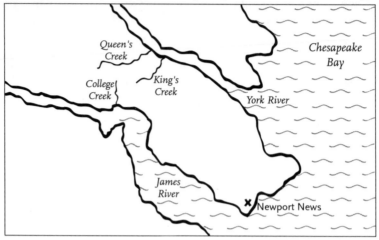

Fig. 2

Virginia included Segura, Velasco, another Jesuit priest, three brothers, a boy from Port Royal in South Carolina, and three catechists who would enter the Society during the next few months.

Delayed by weather, they finally landed at Newport News, at the mouth of the Chesapeake Bay, where Mass was offered in the presence of a thousand or so native people. Sailing up the James River, they disembarked September 10, 1570, at College Creek, which flows south to the James River from present-day Williamsburg. There were no people living near College Creek at that time because they were away searching for food.

After loading their supplies into canoes and onto a boat from the ship, they paddled up College Creek. They then had to carry their supplies across land to either Queen's Creek or King's Creek. Still going north, they paddled to the York River, near a village called Chiskiac, which was about eight miles in a straight line from the mouth of College Creek.

Short of supplies because of the delay in arriving, they had only two barrels of flour left. The native people were also short of food because of a drought that summer in Virginia. Many of the people, who were Algonquians, had left the area in search of game, berries, nuts, and edible roots farther inland. It was imprudent for the missionaries to remain, but it was hard for the group to turn back after making a commitment, and they were anxious to start their missionary work. They sent letters back to Cuba with the ship, including a request that they be sent supplies and seeds for planting as soon as possible.

After the ship left, they started to construct a place to live and a separate place for Mass. For a short time, Velasco helped them get established. He worked with them for two days, and then he helped for five days while living at Chiskiac. After that, he left them and went back to the James River, farther upstream from College Creek. Without his help as a patron and interpreter, the Jesuits were isolated, but they survived for five months.

The people of the area were ruled by the family of Velasco and his brothers. Unlike the rest of the people, the brothers each had more than one wife. Velasco gave up Christianity and went back to this way of life.

The Jesuits survived during the winter as best they could, bartering for food. Twice, they went to Velasco to request his help. In early February, Father Segura, who had shamed Velasco by criticizing his way of life, again sent a priest and two brothers to request his help. They took some homemade mats with them in order to trade for food on the way back.

Velasco decided at this time to do away with the Jesuits. He and his men killed the priest and one of the brothers on February 4, 1571. The other Jesuit brother, wounded, was found and killed the next day. A band then went to Chiskiac and killed the others on February 9, except for the boy from Port Royal, who was given protection by one of the chiefs.[6] Altogether, eight Jesuits were killed.

The Spanish made two attempts to relieve the Jesuits and to find out what had happened. During the second effort in 1572, some of those who had killed the Jesuits were caught and executed. At this time, the boy from Port Royal was allowed by his protector to depart on the Spanish ship.

CHAPTER 2

Mexico City, 1572–1576

In the summer of 1571, King Philip again asked Borgia for missionaries, but this time it was for Mexico City. Borgia responded by choosing Peter Sanchez, a university professor, to be the provincial superior of the new Jesuit Province of New Spain.

Sanchez, forty-four years old, gathered fourteen Jesuit volunteers from different parts of Spain—seven priests, four brothers, and three seminarians who were close to ordination. The seminarians were John Curiel, thirty-one years old; John Sanchez, twenty-three; and Peter Mercado, twenty-six, who had been born in New Spain.

The group sailed from Spain in June of 1572. Going by way of the Canary Islands, they arrived at Vera Cruz on the Gulf of Mexico on September 9, 1572, where it took them nine days to recover from the voyage and to make arrangements for the trip to Mexico City. They had brought little with them and found primitive conditions in Vera Cruz. Each man had a knapsack with a sleeping mat, a blanket, a few books (including the breviary), and some clothes.

They were met at Vera Cruz by two Jesuits who had been in Cuba and whom Provincial Sanchez had instructed by letter to prepare for the new arrivals in Mexico City. There were also three other Jesuits in Cuba from the two earlier expeditions. The provincial first thought to continue the work in Florida and Cuba, but then, within a few years, he transferred the three Jesuits to Mexico City.

The Jesuits at Vera Cruz arrived in New Spain at the end of an era. It had been fifty-one years since the conquest of Tenochtitlán, the capital of the Aztec Empire, by the Spanish and their allies. The era of the conquistadores was over. Spanish institutions had been established, and Franciscans, Dominicans, and Augustinians had evangelized the central valleys.

Since the Jesuits were expelled from New Spain before the "wars of independence" in the Americas, their missionary work took place during a relatively peaceful colonial period. It was homogeneous artistically with the baroque style and was a self-confident and conservative age religiously, shaped by the Council of Trent. But it was only relatively peaceful because the Jesuits arrived during the bloody Chichimec War against the Indians north of Mexico City, and there were serious, local Indian revolts farther north during the Jesuits' time in New Spain.

When the Jesuits arrived at Vera Cruz that September of 1572, it was toward the end of the rainy season. Most of the people they saw were Native Americans (meaning Indian or indigenous), and one of the Indian languages they heard was Nahuatl, the language of the Aztecs and the people around Mexico City. The Nahuatl language, also called Mexican, had an extensive vocabulary and was ideal for expressing poetic and spiritual ideas.

The Jesuits set out for the climb to Mexico City on mules that the government provided, and more than halfway up, they stopped at the new city of Puebla, which the Spanish had founded just south of the Tlaxcalan Nation. The Tlaxcalans (or Tlaxcaltecas), like the Aztecs, spoke Nahuatl, which is one of the Uto-Aztecan languages.

Area of First Jesuit Settlement in Mexico (New Spain) by Third Jesuit Expedition, 1572

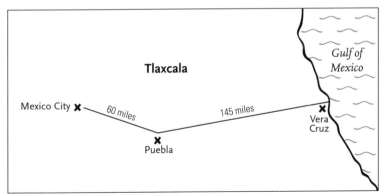

Fig. 3

The Uto-Aztecan languages make up a phylum (a related group of languages) that extends from Vera Cruz on the Gulf of Mexico, across the center of New Spain, up through the northwest of New Spain, and then north to many nations on the eastern side of the Rockies as far as the Shoshone language near the Canadian border in the present-day United States.[1]

The Tlaxcalan Nation had been independent of the Aztecs. The conquistador Hernando Cortés had defeated the Tlaxcalans, who then joined the Spanish in order to overthrow their traditional enemy, the Aztecs.[2] This initial alliance meant that the Tlaxcalans would have a continuing favored relationship with the Spanish. When Spanish immigrants came to New Spain, they stopped at Puebla on their way to Mexico City, and many stayed there. Puebla would remain a very Spanish city although it was racially diverse, with Africans, Indians, and people of mixed race.

Statistics for an earlier year give us a glimpse of the population of Puebla. In 1534, eighty Spanish males lived in the city. Of these, thirty-eight had Spanish wives, twenty had Native American wives, four had wives in Castile, and eighteen were unmarried.[3] In cities farther from Vera Cruz, where there were fewer Spanish women, there was more intermarriage and also concubinage. The government encouraged marriage by giving a land grant or public office only to a married man. Other motives for marrying native women were their many natural endowments and the fact that some of them were landowners.

The Jesuit missionaries left Puebla and continued their climb to the capital. Finally, they caught sight of Lake Texcoco, on which lay the island of Tenochtitlán, the former capital of the Aztecs, which was now Mexico City and the capital of New Spain. Lake Texcoco was about forty-two miles in length from north to south. The width of the lake varied a good bit, from a few miles to about fifteen miles.[4]

The group may have stayed a night in Texcoco, a large city on the eastern shore of the lake that had been the intellectual center of the lake region. Texcoco had formed a triple alliance with the cities of Tenochtitlán and Tacuba. Tacuba (formerly called Tlacopán) was on the western shore of the lake, only about three miles from the island city of

The Cities of the Triple Alliance

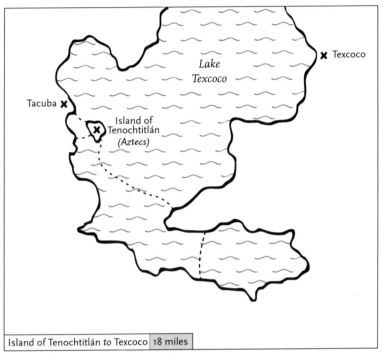

Lake Texcoco

x Texcoco

Tacuba **x**

Island of Tenochtitlán (Aztecs)

| Island of Tenochtitlán *to* Texcoco | 18 miles |

Fig. 4 The dotted lines are causeways.

Tenochtitlán. This alliance, dominated by the Aztecs on Tenochtitlán, had achieved an empire.[5]

Texcoco was also the place from which Cortés had launched his ships for the final assault against Emperor Cuauhtémoc and the Aztecs. The Jesuits would have an early relationship with all three cities of the triple alliance—Texcoco, Tenochtitlán, and Tacuba.

The next day, from a place called Ayocingo on the lakeshore, the Jesuits went by canoe to the island of Tenochtitlán and through the city on a canal to the central square. They arrived in the early evening of September 28, 1572, and that night they found shelter in the Hospital de Jesús Nazareno, three blocks south of the central square. Food was sparse, and extra cots were nonexistent.[6]

At the hospital, the Jesuits were on the spot where Cortés is thought to have first met Emperor Moctezuma in 1519. The Spanish later escaped from Tenochtitlán, where they were under siege, and came back to conquer in 1521. In 1524, Cortés founded this first hospital on the North American continent, and it has been in continual service to the present day. The hospital is an attractive stone building built around open courtyards. Part of the original building was torn down to make way for a street, but part is still used for administrative offices next to the modern hospital building. It was a Catholic hospital until about seventy years ago, when the government took it over. There is a church beside the hospital that was built after the Jesuits' visit.

The following day, the Jesuits went to pay their respects to civil and church officials.

In order to introduce the Mexico City of 1572, let us follow the three seminarians on an imaginary tour. At the hospital, they were at the center of the island, whose area was 5.2 square miles. They walked north to the huge central square, presently called the Zócolo. Across the Zócolo, on the north side, they saw the old cathedral, which was probably being torn down, since construction of the new cathedral began a few months after they arrived. Most of the people they saw were Mexican.

According to the terminology of this early period, *New Spain* refers to the whole country. *Mexico* means the Nahuatl-speaking area centered at the lake. This Nahuatl area was roughly 110 square miles, but from the lake it extended more to the south than to the north. The elevation drops more than half a mile to the south, and tropical crops can be grown there. The indigenous people in this area are the Mexicans (speaking Nahuatl, or Mexican), and the Aztecs on Tenochtitlán were part of the Mexican people.

There were 150,000 people living on the island, reduced from about 200,000 at the time of the conquest. In the Diocese of Mexico City in 1572, there were 10,595 Africans, 9,495 Spanish, and 3,000 of mixed race.[7] The Diocese of Mexico City ran from southwest to northeast. Although it extended from the Pacific Ocean around Acapulco to the Gulf of Mexico, it was narrow and missed many mining towns in the north.[8] In the whole country at this time, there were an estimated 20,500 Africans, 17,700 Spanish, and 5,000 of mixed race.[9]

When Cortés and the Spanish arrived in 1519, there were about 3.3

million Indians in Mexico, or the Nahuatl-speaking area. When the Jesuits arrived in 1572, there were only about 3.3 million Indians left in all of New Spain. The low point for the Indian population was around 1605, when there were between 1 and 2 million in the entire country. A slow recovery of the Indian population took place after that date.

After wandering around the Zócolo and chatting with different people, the three seminarians decided to visit the Franciscans' church and their famous orphanage for Indian and mixed-race children. These buildings were only a few blocks west of the cathedral. The seminarians were welcomed and shown around the huge establishment. In earlier days, up to a thousand orphans at a time had been cared for in this place. There were living quarters and classrooms. The boys and girls learned to read and write, and they also learned a trade, such as carpentry, stone masonry, leather working, embroidery, painting, or carving. Each year, the six brightest boys went on to the Franciscans' Holy Cross College for indigenous and mixed-race students at Tlatelolco, about a mile and a half north of the Zócolo.

Area of Early Jesuit Life and Work in Mexico City

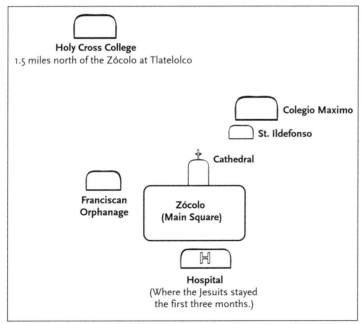

Holy Cross College
1.5 miles north of the Zócolo at Tlatelolco

Colegio Maximo

St. Ildefonso

Cathedral

Franciscan Orphanage

Zócolo (Main Square)

Hospital
(Where the Jesuits stayed the first three months.)

Fig. 5

Peter de Gante, the Franciscan brother who founded the orphanage, was one of the most successful North American Catholic missionaries. When he discovered that neither Mexican nor Spanish families wanted to adopt orphaned or abandoned children of mixed race, he founded the orphanage.[10] It was one of his many accomplishments, which included the publication of two catechisms in Nahuatl, one with the alphabet and one in the earlier Mexican hieroglyphic writing (pictorial characters).[11]

De Gante lived to an advanced old age. A native of the Flemish city of Ghent and originally a lawyer, he died only a few months before the Jesuits arrived. His death was another sign that the first period of the history of New Spain had come to an end. At the present time, the orphanage buildings no longer exist, but the Franciscan church is still there, having sunk a little into the soft ground over the centuries.

The next day, back at the hospital, the Jesuits were still getting adjusted. John Curiel, John Sanchez, and Peter Mercado obtained permission to visit the Franciscan buildings and the Aztec ruin at Tlatelolco, on the north shore of the island and less than two miles from the hospital. Tlatelolco had originally been an island separate from Tenochtitlán and occupied by a people who were related to the Aztecs. The Aztecs incorporated Tlatelolco within their city and created the biggest market in North America there. They also had two schools at Tlatelolco, one for nobles and one for commoners.

From the stone buildings at Tlatelolco, Emperor Cuauhtémoc had directed the defense of the city against the Spanish. Tlatelolco was also the place where he made his last stand and finally surrendered. Only the foundations of the Aztec Center are still in place. It appears that the stone blocks from the center were used to construct the Franciscan buildings of Holy Cross College and St. James Church.

Holy Cross College for the indigenous was founded in 1536. A college was called a *colegio* and was really an academic high school and junior college. The students took only a few subjects, but they studied those subjects intensively. It was possible for a student to receive a bachelor's degree at about the age of nineteen by passing exams at the University of Mexico, which had a monopoly on the granting of degrees within a two-hundred-mile radius of Mexico City.

The University of Mexico, founded in 1551, was more like a professional school than a modern university. If a student went on to the university, it was for graduate study in law, philosophy, theology, medicine, mining, architecture, or indigenous languages. This is still more or less the system in modern Europe.

The Franciscans had a difficult time financing Holy Cross College because many people believed that the Indians should not be educated to the same level as whites. The school closed a few times and then reopened, but it did last almost three-hundred years, surviving as a grammar school rather than as an institution of higher learning.

St. James Church, whose interior is plain but beautiful, still serves a Franciscan parish. The church was the place where Blessed Juan Diego studied the Catholic faith. He was the Native American to whom the Virgin of Guadalupe appeared on a hill called Tepeyac, a mile or so north of Tlatelolco, in 1531.[12]

When the three seminarians returned to the hospital, they learned that John Sanchez and Peter Mercado would do their last year of theology at the Dominican theologate, three blocks north of the cathedral. Since John Curiel had finished theology, he would do tertianship, which is a third year of novitiate. It includes a second thirty-day retreat and the study of the Jesuit Constitutions, as well as pastoral and retreat work.

After a while, almost all of the Jesuits became sick and vomited a lot. One priest died; the rest were moved to a hospital outside the city, where it took them several weeks to recover.

In early December, they were back at the city hospital. At this time, Alonso de Villaseca, an entrepreneur, investor, and the richest man in New Spain, offered them a big lot just a few blocks north and east of the cathedral. The provincial accepted the gift, and the Jesuits built a large hut and chapel on the site, probably of adobe. They were able to move in at the end of December. They now had their own place, and this spot would be the center and heart of the province for nearly two hundred years.

Early in 1573, John Curiel went 185 miles west to the city of Pátzcuaro, Michoacán, where there was a bishop to ordain him. The people in Michoacán were the Tarascans (also called the Purépechas).

In Pátzcuaro, there were thirty thousand Tarascans and a few hundred Spanish. The Tarascan language is completely different from the Uto-Aztecan languages and is not related to any other language in North America. In this respect, it is like the Basque language in Spain.

Although the Tarascans had kept their independence during Aztec times, a cruel conquistador, Nuño de Guzmán, had conquered the area. The Jesuits would have a long relationship with the Tarascans.

John Curiel was well received in Pátzcuaro. The bishop had him preaching in the cathedral even before ordination, and he taught in a school there. He was the first Jesuit ordained in North America, and after a few months he returned to Mexico. The other two theologians were ordained later in the year by a bishop who was traveling through Mexico City.

In January of 1573, the cacique (native governor) of the city of Tacuba offered to build a church for the Jesuits. The provincial accepted the offer, and three thousand workers spent three months constructing the church on the southeast corner of the Jesuits' big lot. The large church must have been made of wood and adobe because it was built so fast. It was a square building with three naves and a thatched roof. It was dedicated in April of 1573, and the Easter Mass was celebrated there.

Also in April, the provincial appointed a novice master and accepted two applicants for the Society, both born in Spain. One was to be a brother, and the other was an older diocesan priest who knew Mexican.

In May, the provincial reported to the general on the condition of the Indians in Mexico:

> They are poorly dressed and subject to a diet so scanty it is a marvel they continue to live. For beds they have mats and for housing very poor huts. They are treated in a manner that is insulting and cruel. Converted into the servants of the conquerors, there falls upon them all the heavy weight of labor. In spite of everything, it has not been possible to bury either their genius or their talent as painters and artisans.[13]

At this time, the Jesuits started to give the Spiritual Exercises of St. Ignatius to diocesan priests and public officials, and John Sanchez went with Hernán Concha (Padre Hernán Suárez de la Concha) to Guadalajara for religious work. Although Guadalajara was far to the northwest of Mexico, or the core Nahuatl-speaking area, the majority of the Indians in the city were Mexicans.

Sanchez and Concha then went north to the mining town of Zacatecas, where the Indians were from many different places. When they returned, they recommended to the provincial that they establish a residence in Zacatecas, but the provincial decided against it.

In July, the provincial accepted four more applicants into the novitiate. Two were born in Spain, one to be a brother and the other to study for the priesthood. The other two were born in New Spain. One of these was a young man who knew Nahuatl and came from Taxco, a rich mining town south of Mexico City, and the other was a diocesan priest named John Tobar, thirty-one years old. Tobar was a valuable acquisition for the Society. Born and reared in Texcoco, he was the best Jesuit preacher in the Mexican language during his lifetime, and he later learned Otomí as well.

The Otomí people lived just north of the lake. Their language is not Uto-Aztecan but is related to the languages in the south around the city of Oaxaca. It seems very likely that the Otomíes were the original inhabitants of the region before the Uto-Aztecan people came into the lake area from the northwest around A.D. 800.

In August, the provincial accepted Anthony Rincón, fifteen years old, as a novice. A Mexican Indian from a noble family in Texcoco, he was educated and knew Spanish.

In the autumn of 1573, since the province had four novices, two of them priests, who knew Nahuatl, a first attempt was made to preach in Mexican. The novices prepared hymns and instructions in Nahuatl. They went out with musical instruments and soon had children joining in the Nahuatl songs and hymns. They went singing through the streets, and many people were drawn to the procession. Then they stopped in a public square, where, standing on a small table, a novice preached in Nahuatl. They went on and made other stops, arriving back at the church with sometimes as many as five thousand people. They had to move outdoors because of the crowds. A Jesuit then gave an instruction in Nahuatl about the faith, or two Jesuits had a dramatic catechetical dialogue.

To help with the work, John Tobar wrote a catechism and some dialogues in Nahuatl. The bishop liked these and had them printed before the end of the year, as he had a printing press that had been brought over in 1535. There were also several private printing businesses in the city. The Jesuits would obtain a press from Europe in 1577, mostly to produce textbooks, and the Franciscans had one at Holy Cross College by 1597. In any case, this first book published by a Jesuit in North America was in the Nahuatl language. Earlier, John Tobar had written a Spanish history of the cities of Tenochtitlán, Tacuba, and Acolhuacán.

It should be noted that Tobar's book in Nahuatl was not the first book published in a native language. By this time, about 110 books had been published in ten Native American languages. They were almost all grammars or religious books, published by members of religious orders like the Franciscans (80 books), the Dominicans, and the Augustinians.[14]

Provincial Peter Sanchez had only had experience with the educational apostolate in Spain. Although the Jesuits had been sent to work with the Indians, the provincial found that the other religious orders were dedicated to this work and that there were few diocesan priests to minister to the Spanish. Also, the other religious orders had more or less divided up the country, and they did not want a new religious order in their areas. So it seemed to the provincial that schools were needed to foster priestly vocations for the dioceses and the religious orders. However, the Jesuit general had told the provincial that he should wait two years before starting any schools.

The Colegio Maximo in Mexico City

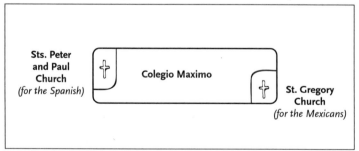

Fig. 6 Construction of the Colegio Maximo began in 1575. The school had opened in rented buildings the previous year with 300 students.

The summer of 1573 was a momentous time for the Jesuits. The entrepreneur who had given the lot offered a big donation to the provincial to begin construction there of what would be the College of Sts. Peter and Paul. The Jesuits usually called the college the Colegio Maximo. The benefactor eventually gave 230,000 pesos, and over half was to build and endow the college.

During the summer, the Jesuits drew up architectural plans for the college, and they decided that there would be two churches attached to it—St. Gregory Church for the Mexicans and Sts. Peter and Paul for the Spanish. They built the two churches so that people could hear the Word of God in a language they understood.

In the beginning, all the Jesuits lived at the college, including the teachers, the parish priests, the provincial and his staff, and the novices and seminarians. At an early date, four boarding residences for students, called seminaries, were founded near the Colegio Maximo, three in which Spanish was spoken and one for Nahuatl speakers. The boarders attended classes at the college, and they had a few classes in the seminaries, for example, in holy Scripture. One or two Jesuits lived in each residence for the sake of supervision and tutoring, and the residences had libraries. Twenty to fifty boarders lived in each residence at different times, and these students tended to do very well at the college.

The indigenous seminary, like the indigenous church, was called St. Gregory. It is difficult to know how many Indians at St. Gregory actually went through the Colegio Maximo. At one point, there were young Mexican orphans, rather than students of the college, living and studying at St. Gregory seminary, and indigenous people were charitably paying for their room and board. Also, many of the students at St. Gregory were the sons of Indian rulers of pueblos outside Mexico City. They studied at St. Gregory rather than at the Colegio Maximo, doing reading, writing, and arithmetic as well as catechism, music, and civics.

In the beginning, and for many decades, an indigenous upper class was the landowning class, but as time went by, this class must have fused with the Spanish or mestizo populations. The indigenous population further decreased because of European and African diseases. What was certainly true, as the centuries went by, was that the mestizo population greatly increased and the indigenous became a poor, rural people.

The Jesuits, by their own rule, did not charge for spiritual or educational work, although they could accept stipends for Masses. So there was no tuition at the Colegio Maximo, which was endowed. The Jesuits did charge for room and board at the seminaries, where there were only a few scholarships.

A boy would start at the Colegio Maximo after grammar school. In classes of twenty or thirty, the boys were drilled in Latin grammar and Spanish for three years. The students were grouped according to ability, and the Jesuits moved them along. After the grammar training, there followed a year each of Latin poetry and Latin oratory. These were followed by courses in philosophy and theology, taught by lectures in Latin to larger classes. There were study groups in the sciences. The students staged Latin and Spanish plays, some of which were pageants with huge casts, using verse, prose, music, and dance. There were also public academic demonstrations. By the age of nineteen or so, a student would be ready for his B.A. examination at the University of Mexico. During the first decades, there were seven hundred to eight hundred students at the Colegio Maximo, but by 1680 there were fifteen hundred.

A second Jesuit college in Mexico City should be mentioned. The Jesuits eventually brought the four seminaries together into a big building between the cathedral and the Colegio Maximo, and the place was called St. Ildefonso. The students still attended classes at the Colegio Maximo, and they were free to attend classes at the University of Mexico near the cathedral. There were also more classes at St. Ildefonso for all the students in the seminaries. St. Ildefonso was not really a second Jesuit college in the city, but it did have a distinct legal identity as a college.

The St. Ildefonso building still exists and is used as an art museum by the present Mexican government. The church of Sts. Peter and Paul also still exists and is presently a Presbyterian church. The Indian church, which replaced the earlier adobe building, is now called Loreto and still stands. The other buildings of the Colegio Maximo were demolished sometime after 1900.

The provincial decided that the Colegio Maximo would open in rented buildings in the fall of 1574, even though the construction of the college would only begin the following year. The college opened with three hundred students for Latin grammar, and the provincial assigned the recently ordained John Sanchez to take one of the classes.

Sanchez, whose interests were mathematical and scientific, later wrote to the general and requested a change of assignment, and the general asked the provincial to make the change. John Sanchez later made maps of New Spain going as far south as Panama on the Pacific side, and in 1603 he helped with an unsuccessful engineering attempt to drain Lake Texcoco, which sometimes flooded Mexico City.

At about the end of 1573, the provincial received a formal request from officials in Pátzcuaro that he send Father Curiel back to take over their school. The officials had a building with a few high school students, as well as a better-attended grammar school; these schools were called the Seminary of St. Nicholas. The officials promised eight hundred pesos a year toward the support of the school, which was like eight hundred dollars at a time when an unskilled laborer made about half a dollar a day. It was not a great deal of money. The officials also offered the former and older cathedral to the Jesuits as their church.

At that time, the bishop and a very few diocesan priests lived in Pátzcuaro. At the new cathedral, there was just one old priest who died soon after the Jesuits arrived. However, Franciscans in the area worked with the Tarascans.

The provincial made a trip to Pátzcuaro to look over the situation, and he decided to accept the offer of the church and the school. He established a Jesuit community in Pátzcuaro around November of 1574, with John Curiel as superior. There were a few students to study Latin, and for these the provincial sent a scholastic who had just arrived with a small second contingent from Spain. (The Jesuits use the word *scholastic* for a seminarian, including one who is teaching full time.) He sent Brother Peter Ruiz, age thirty, one of the Jesuits from Havana, to teach in the grammar school. And there were probably a few more priests and brothers to do pastoral and manual work.

The priests preached often in the cathedral and in their own church. They also did pastoral work in the huge hospital that had been built by the first bishop of Pátzcuaro, Vasco de Quiroga. The Jesuits in Pátzcuaro also studied the Tarascan language, and Brother Peter Ruiz was the quickest to learn it.

Brother Peter Ruiz started with thirty grammar school students, although within a few years there would be three hundred students there. This arrangement was typical of the Jesuit schools in New Spain. The Jesuit brothers administered the grammar schools (*escuelas de leer, escribir, y contar*) and were the teachers. Whenever a permanent Jesuit residence was established, a grammar school opened. The children started at about six years of age. The grammar schools were for everyone, rich or poor, and for children of different races. The priests and scholastics taught in the high schools or sometimes in the grammar schools.

Among the Spanish and mestizo students at Pátzcuaro, there were Spanish-speaking Tarascans because the grammar school of St. Nicholas had been operating for thirty-two years. There would be many more Indian students at Pátzcuaro than in the other Jesuit colleges. However, the school in Pátzcuaro was more of a high school than a college. Philosophy courses were added a few times, but there were not enough students. Before the end for the Jesuits in 1767, the school received large endowments. It was moving toward real college status.[15]

After the Jesuits had gotten started in Pátzcuaro, a young indigenous named Peter Caltzontzín asked to be admitted to the Society. Father Curiel hesitated at first, but when Caltzontzín insisted, Curiel decided to accept him, probably as a postulant (a pre-novice, or someone who is trying out the religious life in the community). It was up to the provincial to accept novices for the Society, and the novitiate was in Mexico City.

Peter Caltzontzín had a good basic education, was literate in Spanish, and knew some Latin, but he needed more preparation before he could do the Jesuits' course of studies. Peter's grandfather had been king, and Peter himself would have been the ninth king of the Tarascans of Michoacán. He helped with the teaching, and he also gave classes in Tarascan to the Jesuits.

Meanwhile, back in Mexico, the provincial decided to open a Jesuit house in Oaxaca, in the south of New Spain, in response to a request by the officials of that city. One of the Jesuits he sent to Oaxaca was Father John Rogel, the companion of Peter Martinez, who had died in Florida.

The languages of that region were very different from the Uto-Aztecan languages, but they were related to the language of the Otomíes. There was a neighborhood of Mexicans in the city of Oaxaca, which is near the impressive stone ruins of two big ancient cities, Monte Albán and Mitla. During the next fifteen years, two Nahuatl-speaking Jesuits ministered to the Mexicans. Only after this time did the Jesuits start to study Zapotecan and the other local language.

The provincial decided on the following policy for Oaxaca and future foundations: The Jesuits would establish a residence. They would do pastoral work and study the local languages. However, they would not attempt to start a college until they had financial commitments, including an endowment, from the local people.

In October of 1574, the provincial accepted Hernán Gómez, thirty-two years old, into the novitiate. Gómez had been born in Africa, but he may have been reared in New Spain because he knew both Otomí and Nahuatl. A diocesan priest who had been pastor of an Otomí pueblo, he would be the main teacher of Otomí to the Jesuits. With the aid of Spanish-speaking Otomíes, he later produced an Otomí grammar and vocabulary book that was never published.

During the first school year in Pátzcuaro, 1574–1575, Brother Peter Ruiz wrote to the provincial requesting permission to study for the priesthood, and the provincial agreed. Peter Ruiz would later be a very successful priest, preacher, and catechist among the Tarascans. He had fine talent, but his health was not strong. He was sick for a few years before he died in 1603 at age sixty-one.

In the summer of 1575, Peter Ruiz bid fond farewell to his students and the people of Pátzcuaro (the school year ran from mid-October to mid-August). He set out on his journey to Mexico in a cheerful frame of mind, little realizing that a typhus epidemic was about to break out. By October of 1575, the epidemic was raging in Pátzcuaro, and classes had to be suspended as the Jesuits and others responded to the emergency.

At this time (for the second school year), there were seven Jesuits in Pátzcuaro: John Curiel, Peter Caltzontzín, Peter Mercado (ordained with John Sanchez and teaching Latin in the high school), an old priest accepted a few years earlier into the Society who was doing pastoral work, a scholastic who was teaching the grammar students, and two brothers who were doing manual work.

The sick were brought to the hospital, where the Jesuits and others struggled to care for them. Some good medicines were available, but not for this disease. Nursing consisted of bringing water and food to the sick. The patients and the hospital had to be kept clean, and the dead had to be buried. Any one of these tasks would have been overwhelming.

The State of Michoacán was not as hard hit by the epidemic as were other parts of New Spain because the first bishop had set up an organized nursing system. Even the smallest pueblo had a building next to the church to serve as a hospital. The sick came there, and designated families in each pueblo worked for a week at a time, keeping things clean and caring for and feeding the sick, no doubt helped by the families of the patients. In each place, there was a small herd (probably goats and sheep) to provide food for the hospital. Even if no one was ill, the designated families went there during their week to clean and presumably to wash the blankets and other things. Once a year they burned the mats and clothes and replaced them with new items. Poor families and travelers also sometimes stayed in the hospitals.

It was an infectious disease that struck in 1575. We might think that the hospitals became centers for the spread of the disease, but such was not the case. With food, water, and basic nursing care, an unknown percentage of the infected recovered, and Michoacán was not devastated like other parts of New Spain.

After a few months, in January of 1576, Peter Caltzontzín contracted typhus and died. Two months later, John Curiel died of exhaustion and from some other disease.

John Curiel was a black man from a poor family near Burgos in Spain. More or less begging his way, Curiel did the Arts Course with distinction at the University of Alcalá. After he earned a bachelor's degree in philosophy, he entered the Society. He was sick for a few years in the novitiate, but the novice master hesitated to dismiss him because of his fine qualities. Curiel recovered his health and took vows after four years instead of the usual two. He taught in Spain and then studied theology before being chosen for the mission in New Spain.

In response to the epidemic in Mexico City, the viceroy promoted prayers and penitential processions. He also ordered autopsies, but the doctors could find no cause for the disease. The symptoms were high fever, stomach pain, and bleeding from the nose. People died from the disease in five or six days.

The viceroy then asked the Jesuits to organize relief and provided them with a great quantity of food along with small boxes for its distribution. The food was cooked at the Jesuits' place, and different Jesuits were assigned to different neighborhoods. Priests from other religious orders came to help, especially with the last rites, because only the few Jesuits from New Spain knew Nahuatl.

Father Hernán Concha (the one who had gone to Guadalajara and Zacatecas with John Sanchez) found a large building in the Tlatelolco neighborhood to serve as a hospital. He went through the city on horseback to beg alms from the merchants, who gave generously. With only basic nursing care, this hospital, like the ones in Michoacán, helped many people to recover. There were also other hospitals in Mexico City. The Indians who lived in the houses of the Spanish also received care and recovered.

This information is from the historical manuscript of the first ten years of the province, written by John Sanchez in about 1609. He wrote that two-thirds of the indigenous people in New Spain died in the epidemic. It was one of the worst that the people suffered.

Speculation arose about the causes of the disease. Some believed that a conjunction of Mars and Saturn had caused it. Some thought that God was punishing the Indians for their former idolatry and blood sacrifices. Sanchez thought that it could be both of these reasons as well as a punishment of the Spanish. He wrote that they were being deprived of workers whom they had exploited. Sanchez did not seem to realize that the diseases were coming from the Old World.

The viceroy, giving the Jesuits a lot of supplies and money, then sent them to the pueblos outside Mexico City, where they did what they could. Sometimes the disease struck a whole family or even a whole village. Infants died of dehydration or starvation because there was no one to care for them. Sanchez wrote that the disease never completely disappeared. In later years, it would occasionally reappear within a family or pueblo.[16]

Sanchez praised Hernán Concha as the "Father of the Poor." He said that Concha died in 1607 in Mexico City when he was about eighty. John Sanchez himself lived to be the last survivor of the original group. He died on the last day of 1619 in Oaxaca, seventy years old, after spending forty-seven years in New Spain and after being sick for a year and a half. His Jesuit obituary says, "He had no equal in Mathematics. He joined virtue to learning. Implacable enemy of slander. Imperturbably calm spirit. He made use of time. He gave a year and a half to prayer before he died."

Forty Jesuits, called martyrs of charity, are known to have died as a result of nursing the sick during the colonial period. On two occasions, whole Jesuit communities were wiped out. The following is a summary of Jesuits known to have died as a result of nursing the sick in epidemics:

- In 1576, in Pátzcuaro, Peter Caltzontzín and John Curiel died.
- In 1630, in Mexico, one Jesuit died.
- In 1635, in Tepotzotlán, two Jesuits died.
- In 1643, in Mexico, one Jesuit died.
- In 1648, a huge quantity of dead fish washed up along the southeast coast of New Spain. A contagion started in Campeche, apparently from the dead fish, then moved south to include Mérida, Yucatán. The Jesuits in Mérida were able to help the sick for some time because not one of the ten got sick. But then all ten got sick, and eight died.
- In 1651, a ship came to Vera Cruz with African slaves and the yellow fever. Two Jesuits died. Other Jesuits probably died over the years in Vera Cruz after nursing the sick, but there are records only for this case and for the yellow-fever epidemic of 1699. Children, by the way, tended to recover from yellow fever

and then to be immune, whereas adults were more at risk of dying. So people from Africa may have had some immunity to this disease. They also had some immunity to malaria.

- In 1676, in Mexico, one Jesuit died.
- In 1699, in Vera Cruz, yellow fever wiped out another Jesuit community. The Jesuits turned the college into a hospital and did all they could. Seven died.
- In 1737, ten Jesuits died after nursing the sick throughout New Spain in the cities of Mexico, Puebla, León, and Querétaro. In this epidemic, forty thousand people died in Mexico; fifty thousand in Puebla; unknown numbers in León; and twenty thousand in Querétaro.
- In 1759, in Mexico, three Jesuits died.
- In 1762, in León, two Jesuits died. This epidemic started with smallpox, and a disease similar to the one of 1737 followed. In this epidemic, ten thousand died in Mexico, mostly children and teenagers.
- There is also one Jesuit who is known to have died in the northern missions after nursing the sick.

To conclude this chapter, here are some "Jesuit firsts" for North America.

- John Tobar was the first Jesuit to publish a book, and it was in the Nahuatl language.
- John Curiel was the first Jesuit to be ordained a priest in New Spain.
- Peter Caltzontzín was the first martyr of charity.

CHAPTER 3

Tepotzotlán, 1576–1584

The typhus epidemic was worst during its first year, in the winter of 1575–1576. It lingered for a few years, and there was no expansion of Jesuit institutions during these years even though new personnel were coming from Spain.

In December of 1576, Alonso de Villaseca, the benefactor of the Colegio Maximo, asked Provincial Peter Sanchez to come to his residence in the country. Villaseca had given two thousand pesos a year during the past few years. Now he gave forty thousand pesos, and he advised the provincial to invest in rural property for the support of the school. The provincial purchased the Hacienda of Santa Lucía, on the market for seventeen thousand pesos. It included 16,800 sheep, 1,400 goats, 125 mares, and eight African slaves. Legally, the hacienda was the property of the Colegio Maximo.

Some Jesuits objected to the ownership of slaves. Nonetheless, eventually the Jesuit general in Rome approved the transaction after a long delay caused by slow communications, the death of one general, and the election of a new one. Within ten years, the property was earning over five thousand pesos a year for the college. Later, a cloth-weaving business was established on the property, and in the 1700s, a liquor called pulque was manufactured there.[1]

There were seventy-five Jesuits in New Spain in 1577, forty-five coming as Jesuits from Spain and the other thirty, many born in Spain, entering the Society in New Spain. They included thirty brothers, twenty-six priests, eleven novices, and eight scholastics.

Also in 1577, the first Province Congregation, hoping to foster native vocations to the priesthood, decreed that the Jesuit colleges were for both the Spanish and the indigenous. The Congregation also recommended talking to the viceroy about sending Jesuit missionaries from New Spain to the Philippines. However, the main purpose of the Congregation was to select a delegate to be sent to Rome; he would report to the general about the province, its work, and its problems. The delegate would also attend a Procurators Congregation, which was an advisory meeting, not a legislative one. A procurator, or delegate, was sent to Rome every three years, and this first one was away for twenty months.

In 1578, Jesuit houses were established in Vera Cruz, in Puebla, and in Morelia, Michoacán. The two Jesuits who were sent to Vera Cruz in 1578 included the doctor John Rogel. They were well received by the inhabitants, who collected sixteen thousand pesos to build them a house and a wooden church.

The port was inhabited by Spaniards, Africans, and Native Americans. A third priest who was fluent in Mexican was sent, and John Rogel worked mostly with the black people, free and slave. Rogel spent eight months of the year at San Ulúa, near Vera Cruz, where the government built a hospital at the request of the Jesuits. The ships

Jesuit Residences Established across the Center of New Spain from 1572 to 1580

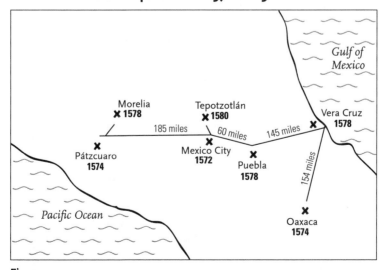

Fig. 7

arrived in autumn and stayed over the winter at San Ulúa. If there was disease on a ship, the newcomers were quarantined there.

The Jesuits who were sent to establish a residence in Puebla in 1578 soon included Anthony Rincón, the Native American from Texcoco. A scholastic, about twenty-one years old and not yet ordained, he taught the first Latin class at the end of 1579 in the new Jesuit college, which in time became quite large and important. Rincón was later in charge of the seminary, or boarding residence, when it first opened, and a chapel was built near the college, where he instructed the indigenous in the Catholic religion. He also preached and gave missions throughout Tlaxcala.

Rincón published a Nahuatl grammar in 1595, *La gramática o arte de la lengua Mexicana,* which was reprinted in modern Mexico in 1885 in 114 pages.[2] He also wrote a Nahuatl catechism. It was not published, but later Jesuit missionaries in the north translated it into other Uto-Aztecan languages. Anthony Rincón died in November of 1601, forty-three years old.

The Jesuits were forever writing, copying, and trying to memorize manuscripts about the indigenous languages. These manuscripts included grammars, vocabularies, the catechism, prayers, homilies, and sometimes the lives of the saints. During the colonial period, the Jesuits published about eleven grammars of different indigenous languages. Except for an Otomí grammar, they were all of various Uto-Aztecan languages. The Jesuits tended to promote the knowledge of Nahuatl (the lingua franca throughout New Spain before the Spanish arrived) because it was the first native language that most of them studied.

In 1578, the Spanish were building a new capital northeast of Pátzcuaro for the Province, or present-day State, of Michoacán. This city—called Guayangereo before the Spanish came, then Valladolid by the Spanish—is now called Morelia. When the Spanish attempted to move the bishop's residence and the Jesuit college from Pátzcuaro to Morelia, the Tarascans strongly objected. So the Jesuits decided they would have a school in each city. The one in Pátzcuaro became almost exclusively for the Tarascans.

The two schools were slow to prosper. Each had about eight Jesuits as faculty over the decades. Like other Jesuit colleges in New Spain, the schools were often burdened with debt. In 1653, for example, the school in Pátzcuaro owed ten thousand pesos.

For about seventy years, Pátzcuaro remained very important to the Society. The Jesuit residence was a base for pastoral work throughout Michoacán, and Jesuits went there to study the Tarascan language. After 1650, less pastoral work was availabe for the Jesuits in Michoacán because there were more diocesan priests. More of the native people were probably speaking Spanish, and the mission work to the north was absorbing Jesuit personnel.

Back in Mexico in 1578, the provincial asked Father Hernán Gómez to teach Otomí to a group of Jesuits. One of the students was John Tobar, who was fluent in Nahuatl. The students went to an Otomí pueblo west of Mexico City for a total-immersion experience, and they made fair progress with this very difficult language. Otomí is a guttural language, and an Otomí word can have different meanings according to its tone.

After a while, the students went from the pueblo to try to teach catechism and to preach in other Otomí pueblos. However, living conditions were very primitive, and when the bishop offered the parish of Tepotzotlán in 1580, the provincial accepted it and made it a center for the study of both Otomí and Nahuatl. Tepotzotlán was toward the northern end of the lake on the west shore, about twenty-eight miles from the island of Mexico City. The people at Tepotzotlán and in five dependent pueblos (within six miles) were mostly Otomíes.

Before the typhus epidemic of 1575–1576, there had been about 2,300 people at Tepotzotlán and about 5,500 in the five dependent pueblos. Some of these Indians were nobles or landowners, and others were workers or tenant farmers. Except for the Jesuits, very few Spanish lived in the area, and this would continue to be true.

Some Indians in the area engaged in lewd conduct associated with drinking. The drink was called wine, but it was made from corn or wheat. The people responded well to the Jesuits' preaching. They cut down or eliminated the drinking, and the lewd conduct disappeared. The people were devout, and three hundred received communion on principal feast days.

Area of Jesuit Expansion into the Country Northeast of Mexico City following the Typhus Epidemic of 1575–1576

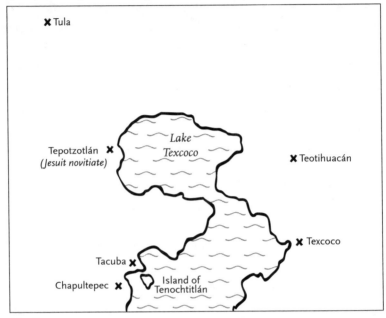

Fig. 8

Tepotzotlán is not far from the ruins of two important ancient cities, Teotihuacán and Tula. The ruins of Teotihuacán are about twenty-five miles east of Tepotzotlán on the other side of the lake. It was the first great city in the central part of the country, and it dominated the area from the time of Christ until about A.D. 750. It is not known which people ruled from Teotihuacán.

About A.D. 800, the Mexicans, or their ancestors, came into the central area from the north. Some of these people, the Toltecs, built the city of Tula, twenty-five miles north of Tepotzotlán, about A.D. 950. The Toltecs ruled from Tula for two hundred years, until the city was destroyed about 1150. It may have been the Otomíes who overthrew Tula, because the Otomíes lived in that area and all the way down to the lake when the Spanish arrived in 1519.

When their city was destroyed, the Toltecs moved south, and many of them settled at a place called Chapultepec on the western shore of Lake Texcoco, only a few miles from the island of Mexico City. A causeway connected Chapultepec to the island, and an aqueduct had been built before the Spanish arrived. At the present time, Chapultepec is a park, and the world-famous Museum of Anthropology is located there.

After the fall of Tula, a new people, the Aztecs, migrated into the lake region from somewhere in the north. A poor people who spoke an Uto-Aztecan language, they became part of the Mexican people. In 1325, the Aztecs settled on the island of Tenochtitlán, and in 1428, as part of the triple alliance, they became dominant in the region.

Hernán Gómez and his Jesuit students of Otomí went to Tepotzotlán in 1580, where Gómez had been pastor before he entered the Society. In 1582, the bishop took back the parish but gave the Jesuits a house in Tepotzotlán. In that same year, the Indian governor, or cacique,[3] of Tepotzotlán, Martin Maldonado, offered part of his land and some houses on the plaza if the Jesuits would start a school for Native Americans. The Jesuits agreed to the proposal, and the school came to be named St. Martin's.

When it all came to an end for the Jesuits in 1767, there were twenty-three Jesuit colleges—five to the south in Oaxaca, Chiapas, Campeche, Mérida, and Guatemala; two in Cuba; five across the center; and the remaining eleven to the north and northwest, where the Jesuit mission work took place. Besides these colleges, other schools were sometimes called colleges, such as the school at Tepotzotlán, the seminaries, and the principal school of a mission area.

Three Jesuits from New Spain were sent to the Philippine Islands in 1581. One of them was Father Anthony Sedeño, who had arrived in Cuba with John Segura in 1568. He was one of the first Jesuits in Mexico City, because he and a Jesuit brother had been sent ahead to make preparations for the first group to go there under Provincial Peter Sanchez. Now, in 1581, Sedeño was one of the first three Jesuits in the Philippine Islands.[4]

In the Philippines, Sedeño lived in severe poverty for four years in a native village, where he learned the principal native language, explained the faith, and helped the people with farming and construction. Later, he taught in a new Jesuit school in Manila. During these early years, some of the Jesuits started studying Chinese and Japanese because of the different populations in the Philippines. In 1604, over a hundred Jesuits lived in the Philippines, and they were formed into a new province, independent of the Jesuits in New Spain.

In 1583, back at Pátzcuaro in New Spain, lightning struck and set fire to the Jesuit residence and the wood church. The Tarascans saved the church, but the residence was lost. The buildings were repaired and rebuilt. Also in this year, the Spanish king donated ten thousand ducats to the Colegio Maximo, with the promise of a thousand a year for ten years.

The new school opened in 1584 with eighty resident students at Tepotzotlán. The school was unusual in that it was a leadership-training school, unlike the colleges and the later mission schools of the north, which were grammar schools. The intent was to educate the leaders of the people with the hope that they would govern well and also assist the missionaries in evangelizing the country. The students who came probably varied in age. Some stayed for only a semester or two, but others studied for several years.

The children of Tepotzotlán attended the school along with the sons of caciques outside of Tepotzotlán. Besides basic instruction in Spanish, mathematics, history, and religion, the students did a year of Latin and were also, it seems, instructed in reading and writing Mexican. They put on plays in Spanish, Nahuatl, and Otomí. There was also an emphasis on practical civics and music.

Music was highly valued by the Indians, who had a band in every pueblo. Each student at Topotzotlán learned a musical instrument— the drum, the trumpet, or a woodwind instrument. The choir was famous and traveled around the lake region. Many graduates were hired as music directors for the churches and cathedrals, and others were elected governors of indigenous towns. A few went on to the Colegio Maximo for further study. It was a fine education at a time when many Spanish were probably illiterate. However, relatively few of the Indians were being educated.

The provincial wrote to the general to request teachers for sculpture and painting at Tepotzotlán. He also requested a printing press because books were so expensive to have printed and the Indians at Topotzotlán could easily learn to handle a press. By this time, the unpublished manuscripts at Tepotzotlán included the Otomí grammar and vocabulary of Hernán Gómez, as well as lives of the saints in both Otomí and Nahuatl by John Tobar.[5]

Two Otomí students from Tepotzotlán became diocesan priests. At an early church synod in Mexico City, it was decided that Indians, mestizos, and Africans would only be ordained with great care and circumspection. The Franciscans decided in 1570 not to ordain the indigenous. The Jesuits talked as though they themselves were not discriminatory. For example, they complained that the bishops were too reluctant to accept good native candidates for the priesthood, but only one indigenous man, Anthony Rincón, is known to have become a Jesuit priest.

As the school opened in Tepotzotlán in September of 1584, twenty-three new missionaries landed at Vera Cruz, and among them was the very young Gonzalo de Tapia, who would begin the Jesuit missions in the north. That same year, the provincial (now the third one) wrote to the Jesuit general that only eighteen of more than one hundred Jesuits were proficient in a native language. Ten knew Mexican, four knew Otomí, and four knew Tarascan. The provincial decided to require a class each day in Mexican for the seminarians, and he sent other Jesuits to Tepotzotlán and Pátzcuaro to study the Otomí and Tarascan languages.

The novitiate was moved from Mexico City to Tepotzotlán in 1585. Except for a fifteen-year period when it moved to Puebla, the novitiate was at Tepotzotlán all through the colonial period. The novitiate was a two-year period of spiritual formation, including the thirty-day retreat of St. Ignatius of Loyola. A novice could enter the Society of Jesus after he had finished five years at a college, including three years of Latin grammar, a year of Latin poetry, and a year of Latin rhetoric.

After the two years of novitiate, there was another year at Tepotzotlán called the juniorate. During this year, the seminarians studied Latin, Spanish, and the Mexican languages. The Jesuits had ten to fifteen vocations a year in New Spain during the colonial period. An indigenous town, especially at that time, seems an ideal place for the novitiate, yet some Jesuits said that the novices were too much removed from the poverty and problems of the city.

An epidemic swept through Tepotzotlán in 1607, and the population greatly declined. At the same time, Indians were moving to Tepotzotlán from other places, and eventually Nahuatl replaced Otomí as the spoken language at Tepotzotlán.

During the next century, a hostel was built at Tepotzotlán along with an aqueduct to bring water to the site. St. Xavier's Church was dedicated in 1682, having been built with money given by the parents of a Jesuit. It is one of the most beautiful baroque churches in modern Mexico.[6]

Also during the seventeenth century, there lived a famous Indian lay teacher, Don Lorenzo, who had a master's degree in sacred Scripture from the University of Mexico. A celibate, he consumed neither alcohol nor chocolate and was admired for his spiritual and ascetic life. He taught for forty years at St. Martin's and at St. Ildefonso. He showed the students how to perform the dance of Moctezuma, a slow and dignified dance that the Aztecs had performed for the emperor. Wearing traditional dress, the students performed the dance on the feast of Christ the King. Before he died, Don Lorenzo took the Jesuit vows of poverty, chastity, and obedience—an offering of himself to God.

There was a lot of activity at Tepotzotlán, and it became something like a shrine. People went there to attend the religious services, to hear the choir, and to spend a day in the country. In later times, some old Jesuits from the northern missions would retire there. The buildings are now a national monument and a tourist attraction.

CHAPTER 4

Gonzalo de Tapia, S.J., 1584–1594

Gonzalo de Tapia was born in 1561 in Quintana de los Raneros, Spain. By the time he was ten years old, his two older brothers had been killed in foreign wars, and he was the sole male heir. His parents took him to the Jesuit boarding school in León, thirty miles from their home in northwest Spain, where he studied for five years, with three years of Latin grammar and two years of Latin poetry and rhetoric.[1]

When Tapia was fifteen years old, he entered the Society of Jesus. He gave up position and a great deal of wealth in order to follow our Lord as a religious. He completed the two years of novitiate, followed by six years of philosophy and theology. He finished theology in the spring of 1584, when he was twenty-three years old, but by church law he had to be a year older in order to be ordained.

When he asked to go as a missionary to New Spain, he was chosen. He departed with twenty-two other Jesuits, and they arrived at Mexico City in the autumn of 1584. Since one of the professors at the Colegio Maximo had fallen sick, the provincial assigned Tapia to teach the first-year philosophy course. It was his first experience of teaching, and he must have done well because the provincial asked him if he wanted to study for the doctorate in theology. Tapia replied that he could have done that in Spain and that he desired instead to be a missionary.

Tapia was shorter than average, with a dark complexion and a full, black beard. He was shortsighted, brilliant in languages, witty, and amiable. In the autumn of 1585, the provincial sent the newly ordained Father Tapia to do mission work in Pátzcuaro, Michoacán. This was the year that St. Gregory's seminary for Native Americans, attached to the Colegio Maximo, opened in Mexico City.

The Jesuits were surprised at how quickly Tapia learned the Tarascan language. During that year, he did pastoral work in Pátzcuaro and in the towns of Michoacán. The next year, 1586, Tapia did tertianship in Morelia. This was also the year that the Jesuits established a residence in Guadalajara.

Having finished tertianship, Tapia was back at Pátzcuaro in the autumn of 1587, and he was restless. Michoacán was settled and peaceful, but to the north there was a mining boom as well as war and chaos. Tapia had been in the country for three years, and the Jesuits had been there for fifteen, but no missionary move had been made to the north. The Jesuit general and the Spanish king had sent the Jesuits to New Spain primarily to preach the faith to non-Christian people, but the provincial in Mexico City at that time thought that Jesuit manpower was not yet sufficient for further expansion.

The Indian nations to the north had been independent of the Aztecs and were collectively called the Chichimecos, a Nahuatl word meaning "uncivilized." These Chichimec nations were a mixture of Otomíes and Uto-Aztecans, with the Otomíes being closer to the lake. The Otomíes were between the Mexicans and the other Uto-Aztecans to the north with regard to political organization, culture, and agricultural development.

The Otomí people were concentrated in the smaller states of Guanajuato and Querétaro, northwest of Mexico City and extending

Jesuit Expansion to Northwest of Mexico City under Gonzalo de Tapia, 1588–1594

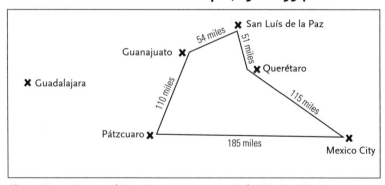

Fig. 9 Guanajuato and Querétero are state capitals. Mexico City is a state capital as well as the capital of the country.

down to Tepotzotlán. In lesser concentrations, they extended east and west across the center of New Spain. To the east, the Otomíes lived around the Tlaxcalans, north of Puebla, and they had served as soldiers in the Tlaxcalan army. To the west, they must have lived in Michoacán, because Jesuits went to Pátzcuaro to study both Tarascan and Otomí. In fact, Tapia worked on the Otomí language for over a year in Pátzcuaro, and there is mention of groups of Otomíes living in Colima, a small state on the Pacific Ocean almost directly west of Mexico City.

After the conquest of the Aztecs in 1521, the Spanish and the civilized Indians began a slow movement to the north, motivated by a desire for gold and silver. Then, when rich silver deposits were found at Zacatecas in 1546, the movement north greatly accelerated. The Chichimec peoples resisted this invasion. They started to attack wagon trains and smaller settlements, and a forty-year war developed, called the Chichimec War, which lasted from 1550 to 1590.[2]

The newcomers built blockhouses, or forts, in order to protect the road from Mexico City to Zacatecas. This road was more than three hundred miles long, and another long supply road ran from Guadalajara to Zacatecas. The blockhouses were also hotels with corrals for mules. Merchants took supplies to Zacatecas and other newly opened mining sites and carried silver and gold back to Mexico City and Guadalajara.

In the beginning, there were outcroppings of precious metals, and the Indians from the center of New Spain participated in the economic activity as mine owners, merchants, and hotel owners. Also, many Tarascans, Mexicans, Tlaxcalans, and Otomíes fought with the Spanish against the Chichimecos. Some of the Otomíes were commissioned as captains in the Spanish army, and they led their people against the Chichimecos. One of the Otomí captains was actually named James de Tapia. Governor of Querétaro, he discovered many mining sites and ended up a wealthy land and mine owner. There were also silver mines at the towns of Guanajuato and Querétaro.

The soldiers were poorly paid, almost volunteers. They sold any prisoners they took as slaves and made raids to obtain more slaves for the mines. As time went on, the violence increased as the Chichimecos acquired horses, and the Spanish eventually established more than thirty forts.

A new viceroy, Marqués de Villamanrique, wanted to end both the slavery and the costly war. After lengthy consultation with his advisers in 1585, he decided on a new policy. He reduced the number of soldiers, prohibited the entry of any more whites to the area, and promised continual big allotments of food and clothing to the native people. He encouraged civilized Indians, especially Tlaxcalans, to settle in the north, and he looked for missionaries to evangelize and discuss peace with the native people.

Gonzalo de Tapia was asked to evangelize and discuss peace with the Otomíes, many of whom were on the side of the Chichimecos. So about the end of December 1588, Tapia entered the State of Guanajuato from the south. He found a place to concentrate on the language and then moved around as a guest of the people. He would visit, talk, and explain the Christian faith in two hundred villages during the next two years. Great numbers of people became Christians in response to this priest who spoke to them in their own language.

To help him with the work and to give him a means of escape in case of danger, someone sent Tapia a horse, but he gave it away. He remained alone and dependent on the people, but a giant of an Indian took Tapia under his protection, traveling with him and introducing him to the people in the different villages.

After the first seven months, Tapia asked for a Jesuit companion, and the provincial sent one who knew Otomí. Tapia now started talking to the people about forming larger villages and planting crops. When the site of San Luís de la Paz was picked as one place to gather, people started to move there. A mixture of Otomíes, mulattoes, and Chichimecos began the construction of a temporary chapel. Tapia's accomplishments in bringing peace to the States of Guanajuato and Querétaro during the two years he spent there were amazing. He was very young, but he had the talent—the right personality, language ability, and religious zeal.

Toward the end of 1589, the two Jesuits were called to Mexico to discuss the situation with superiors. At the beginning of 1590, a Jesuit visitor, Father James Avellaneda, arrived from the Jesuit general.[3] He spent a year visiting the Jesuit houses and talking to every Jesuit. He had authority from the general for a limited time over the provincial and the whole Jesuit Province of New Spain, having been commissioned by the general to correct any faults and to get the mission started to the non-Christian people of the north. One fault that he found was a neglect of tertianship in favor of work. He also urged local Jesuit superiors, who were mostly in their thirties, to be less demanding and harsh toward their Jesuit subjects.

In this same year in Mexico City, there was a nine-year-old boy named Peter Velasco, a future Jesuit missionary. His grandfather, Luís de Velasco I—known as the Liberator because he had freed the Indian slaves—had been viceroy of New Spain, and now his uncle, Luís de Velasco II, was appointed viceroy. Viceroy Velasco maintained the policies of his predecessor toward the Chichimecos, including the large allotments of food and supplies that continued for twenty-five or thirty years. The Spanish were buying peace, and although the price was high, it was less than the cost of war.

Area Opened to the North by Tapia and Companions during the 1590s

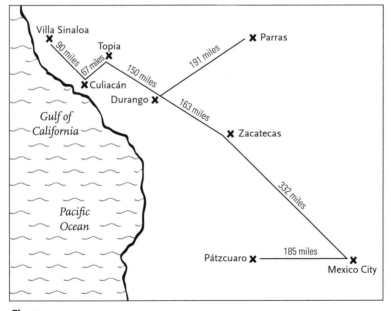

Fig. 10

Tapia was called to the capital to talk to the visitor, Father Avellaneda, toward the end of 1590. Tapia wanted to open up all of the north to the faith. Avellaneda approved the idea, and he sent Tapia north to Zacatecas to await developments. When Tapia arrived in Zacatecas, a city 8,050 feet above sea level, he found four Jesuits, who had just established a residence. One was Jerome Ramirez, whose fine missionary work will be described later.

The city had been home to the Zacateca people (Uto-Aztecan) and was now one of the richest silver-mining sites in the world, with lesser amounts of gold, copper, and tin. The Spanish clashed with the indigenous miners, over six hundred adult Tarascan males, mostly from Michoacán as well as others from Mexico. There were also miners from other nations, such as the Otomíes, Zacatecas, and Tlaxcalans, and each group lived separately from the others. When the liquor flowed, fights broke out between the ethnic groups, brawls with rocks and knives in which people were wounded and killed. The preaching of the Jesuits in Nahuatl, Otomí, and Tarascan (spoken by Ramirez) helped reduce the violence.

Four hundred adult Spanish males resided in Zacatecas in 1591. The majority were merchants, and the others were miners and public officials. Outside the city, the Spanish lived on ranches and farms or with their Indian servants at nearby pueblos, which were probably mining sites. This was the largest Spanish population outside of Mexico.[4] It seems a small Spanish population for such a rich mining site, but development had been held up by the forty-year Chichimec War, the scarcity of mercury for refining the silver ore, and the fact that other mining sites were attracting prospectors.

The Franciscans also had an important missionary training center in Zacatecas. Although this book is about the Jesuits, it should be noted that the Franciscans were the principal evangelizers of New Spain, and they also had many more martyrs than the Jesuits. They were first in every place, and they tended to be braver or less prudent in exposing themselves to danger.

Tapia spent the first few months of 1591 teaching reading and writing in a native school in Zacatecas. In May, the provincial sent

Father Martin Pérez as a companion and authorized the two of them to move north to Durango, then called Guadiana, where there was silver and iron ore. A Jesuit parish and a school would open there within four years. The governor of northwest New Spain had his headquarters in Durango, and a bishop for the vast northern region would be appointed in 1623.

Meanwhile, things were moving along at San Luís de la Paz. Viceroy Velasco promised an allotment of food to any Native Americans who settled there. Some Otomí Christians from farther south moved up and received land. In 1594, the provincial sent two Jesuits to care for the parish and to start a school. Four Otomí students from St. Martin's in Tepotzotlán went with these Jesuits to help start the school.

It was a good arrangement because the Otomíes lived between Tepotzotlán and San Luís de la Paz. Some attended the school at Tepotzotlán, and now the new school was located at the northern end. San Luís de la Paz also became a base from which the Jesuits did pastoral work in surrounding towns and villages. It is interesting that Tapia did not think of staying in Guanajuato or Querétaro. He was looking for new fields to conquer for Christ. However, the provincial was able to follow up Tapia's work in these two small states with Jesuit personnel and permanent institutions.

Tapia and Pérez went up to Durango to consult with the governor in May of 1591. Tapia was thinking of New Mexico. When the Franciscans were chosen to go with the Spanish to New Mexico (leaving in 1597), the governor recommended the Sinaloa area along the Gulf of California to Tapia, so that is where the Jesuit missionary work began.

Viceroy Luís de Velasco II promised 250 pesos a year to each of the Jesuits in order to help with the work. Later, the government gave 300 pesos a year to each missionary, but the missionary had to work in a place in which the government was interested. For example, since the government had little interest in Baja California, the extensive work there was supported by private donations to a charitable fund in Mexico City.

This sum of 250 or 300 pesos was not enough to support a missionary for a year; at that time a laborer, a poor person, made about half a peso (or half a dollar) a day. However, the stipend was a big help. It was used to buy sugar and chocolate as well as church supplies, such as candles, altar wine, and vestments, and this way the Jesuits were able to ask for less from the new Christians. The Jesuits and the new Christians would support themselves with gardens, farms, and some goats and chickens. Cattle herds were developed where possible.

Within the month, Tapia and Pérez left Durango with mules and supplies. Tapia was thirty years old and the superior, and Martin Pérez was thirty-four. Pérez had been born at San Martín, a mining town between Zacatecas and Durango. He studied at the Colegio Maximo and entered the Society when he was twenty-one. After two years of novitiate, he was in charge of a seminary in Mexico City for two years. He was minister (the administrator under the local superior) at Puebla for some years. Then he went back to his studies, did theology, and was ordained. He would spend thirty-five years as a missionary along the Sinaloa River, often as superior.

When he was sixty years old, Martin Pérez became ill and was bled excessively. As a result, he became feeble and was unable to lift himself out of a chair without help. He lived in this condition for the next ten years. However, his mental capacity was not affected. He was superior during this time and wrote a history of the mission that would be much appreciated by later historians. He died at age seventy.

So Tapia and Pérez started out for their new mission. The fastest way to Villa Sinaloa from Durango, a trip of some 250 miles in a straight line, was over the Sierra through a mining town called Topia. However, since there were tribal wars at that time in the Sierra, the two Jesuits and their guide went southwest through the very mountainous state of Nayarit, which added about two hundred miles to the trip. The way was arduous, through valleys and over high mountains, and even today the area is remote and dangerous.

The group met a few Spanish who were prospecting or home-steading. Then, for a seven-day period, they passed through clouds of mosquitoes that tormented the mules and the travelers. During these seven days, the men saw no other living things except birds. Then they met a large group of native people who were not farming and who spent all their time hunting for food. These people generously shared the food they had. The people of this area (estimated at twenty thousand) had already requested a missionary. The travelers then followed a river down to sea level near the Pacific Ocean.

The entire central area of New Spain is over a mile high. To the east, the land slopes down to the Gulf of Mexico. To the west, the land more or less drops off. It is difficult even to follow a river down to sea level. The rivers that drain the Sierra to the west flow through deep canyons.

The two Jesuits reached sea level on May 30, 1591. They were south of the State of Sinaloa, and the heat was often intense. They had to be careful not to exhaust their mules in this area because the extreme heat could kill them. At times, a mule became so exhausted that it had to be bled.

The south of Sinaloa was underpopulated. After the conquest of Mexico in 1521, a marauder, Nuño de Guzmán (mentioned earlier), went through Michoacán and ended up in the south of Sinaloa, where he pillaged and took a great number of Indians as slaves. He was eventually tried for his crimes and exiled to Spain, and the area slowly regained its population with the help of Indian immigrants from Mexico.

Tapia and Pérez spent all of June traveling north through Sinaloa, meeting people, making friends, and doing pastoral work. The trip was encouraging because everyone welcomed them with pleasure. The Jesuits were benefiting from the earlier work of Franciscans in the area.

The biggest town they visited was Culiacán, a mining site with an organized government. Tarascans lived there, as well as some Spanish and a priest. At Culiacán the Jesuits met a ten-year-old boy named Hernando de Tovar, who would one day be a Jesuit missionary and who would die in the Tepehuán revolt of 1616. They also met an older indigenous woman named María, who was native to the area and who knew Mexican. She offered to interpret for them and to help them learn the local languages, and she and her son went north with the Jesuits toward the Mocorito River.

When they were one day south of the Mocorito River, Tapia and Pérez pitched camp. In the middle of the night, a cacique and some children woke them up, the cacique having brought the children to be baptized. The Jesuits made their guests as comfortable as they could until morning, when one of the priests offered Mass on a field within a circle of children, and baptized the children afterwards. It was the custom to baptize children if there was a good chance they would receive instruction.

They went north a little farther to a native village, where Tapia addressed the people through an interpreter. He said, "We come to you alone, few in number, and unarmed. We come only to give you the knowledge of the creator of heaven and earth, for without this knowledge and faith you will be unhappy forever." The people seemed to appreciate his words.

While the Jesuits were traveling through Sinaloa during June of 1591, Viceroy Luís de Velasco II was negotiating with the Tlaxcalans to found six towns in the north with 401 families. The Tlaxcalans negotiated certain rights, privileges, and tax exemptions before agreeing, and the Jesuits came to have a relationship with the people in two of the six towns: San Esteban de Nueva Tlaxcala, established by eighty settlers near Saltillo in the far northeast, and San Andrés in the western Sierra. People from these locations would later help establish the Jesuit missions at Villa Sinaloa and Parras.

There are no other known official settlements from Tlaxcala to the north, but individual Tlaxcalans moved north to mining sites and probably to the six towns. Later Tlaxcalan settlements to the north, including into New Mexico and Texas, originated from the six towns rather than Tlaxcala.

Tapia and Pérez continued north past the Mocorito River to the Sinaloa River, then called the Petatlán River. On July 6, 1591, they reached their destination, Villa Sinaloa, then called San Filipe, on the Sinaloa River. Five Spanish men lived there in destitution, the remnant of an attempted settlement farther north, and no Spaniards lived beyond the river. One of the Spanish at Villa Sinaloa had been designated captain, or mayor, by the governor of Durango.

The two Jesuits arrived just as the rains started. During the rainy season, the temperature is often over 100 degrees, going as high as 125 degrees, and the heat produces thunderstorms with rain that falls unevenly. Villa Sinaloa receives an average of twenty-four inches a year, with twenty of the twenty-four inches falling during July, August, and

September.[5] Another two inches fall during October, November, and December. Then there is almost no rain during the other six months. However, there is rain all year in the Sierra, so the Sinaloa River always has flowing water, unlike other rivers along the coast, which often dry up or turn into a series of water holes.

The whole area was very hot and desertlike, but it was able to support a big population because of several rivers flowing west from the Sierra to the Gulf of California. In the rainy season, the rivers overflowed (before there were dams) in strips up to five or sometimes ten miles wide, fertilizing and irrigating the land. Because of the alluvial deposits, the same land could be farmed year after year, and it was not necessary to keep moving with the slash-and-burn method used in other junglelike areas. Also, the floodwaters sank into the ground, and the people did not have to dig ditches to irrigate the land. They did, however, work hard to weed the crops lest they be choked by fast-growing vegetation. It was possible to obtain two, or even three, harvests a year, and it was the custom both to plant and to harvest after a full moon.

Many different languages were spoken in the State of Sinaloa and in southern Sonora. Almost all of the languages were Uto-Aztecan. They formed a subset of the Uto-Aztecan languages and are called the Cáhita languages, which are close to Nahuatl, or Mexican. In fact, the Mexicans and the other Uto-Aztecan people in the center of the country are thought to have come from this general area. They seem to have gone down the gulf coast and to have crossed through Nayarit and Michoacán into the center of the country and then across to the Vera Cruz area. Also, both the Toltecs and the Aztecs said that they came from the north, and Sinaloa is much farther to the north than it is to the west.

Although the Cáhita languages are close to Nahuatl, Tapia had to work for a month and Pérez for three months before they started to understand and be understood. It was a help to them that the vocabularies of the Cáhita languages were much smaller than the Nahuatl vocabulary. The local Cáhita languages in this area are difficult to sort out. The Jesuits speak of four, or even six, languages on the Sinaloa River. For the Jesuits, they may have been distinct languages, but for native speakers, they were probably more like dialects.

Ten miles downriver from Villa Sinaloa was a Pima village called Bamoa. At an earlier time, these Pimas had come down from the State of Sonora with some Spaniards. This group of Pimas was very friendly to the Spaniards and interested in the Christian religion. But the Pima language, although Uto-Aztecan, is different from the Cáhita languages.

There was also a Tepehuán village in the area. The Tepehuán people lived mostly in the Sierra and on the other side of the Sierra, north of Durango. The Tepehuán language is related to the Pima language and not to the Cáhita languages, yet most people in the area seemed to understand Tepehuán as a local lingua franca.

Forests in the river valleys extended back several miles from the rivers. Thick, tall, junglelike vegetation grew along the banks, where the people fished and hunted. Fish and shellfish were more abundant toward the gulf, and the people often preserved fish, but not meat, by drying and salting it. None of the people lived between the rivers, where the land was arid and covered with low bushes.

When the people hunted, they had two different methods. By one method, a group of four or five, specializing in one animal, hunted rabbits, deer, or peccaries (similar to pigs). By the other method, hunters used a circle of fire to drive animals toward men with bows and arrows. They also hunted jaguars and mountain lions (cougars or pumas), which lived further into the hills, for their skins. In the winter, they hunted geese and ducks.

The people cultivated tobacco, a poor-quality cotton, corn, beans, other legumes, and gourds. The hard skins of the gourds were used as containers, and strips of these vegetables were preserved by drying. The people also made use of roots and some wild seeds. Melons were their only cultivated fruit, but good wild fruit was available in season on the pipe-organ cactus and other trees. They did not cultivate tomatoes and chilies, which were native to the Americas. With corn and other products they made alcoholic drinks.

Even with this plentiful supply of food, however, famine was not unknown, and the problem was the water supply. Floods could be destructive, and on rare occasions they wiped out almost everything. Some people had tree houses in which they could wait out a flood, and they even built small fires up there. But much greater than the problem of floods was the problem of too little water. Droughts were very frequent.

Houses were made of wood and clay with thatched roofs. A hole in the middle of the roof let in sunlight. Each house had a porch with a thatched roof at the front entrance on which they stored corn and other food. The people slept on mats on the porch except for four months over the winter when they slept inside.

The adult males were two or three inches taller than the Spanish. They and the women wore ornaments in pierced ears. The women had long, loose hair, and wore garments of cotton, grass, or animal skin from the waist or shoulders. The men had long, braided hair and wore little for most of the year. A few men had more than one wife, but a man had to plant a field for each wife, and the wives harvested the fields. Adultery was rare, and it was shameful for a girl not to be a virgin at marriage. Divorce was hard for a woman if she did not remarry.

The Sinaloa Area, Explored and Established by Gonzalo de Tapia and Martin Pérez in 1591

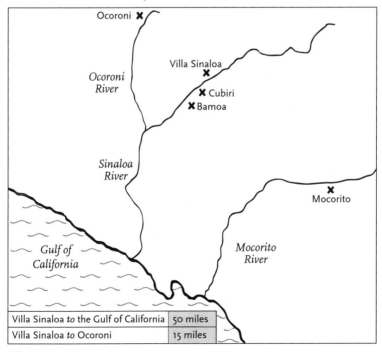

Fig. 11

The principal athletic contest was a team race, village against village, which also involved gambling. The race was over two or three miles; along the way each team would kick a piece of wood to the distant goal.

Stealing was rare, and each nation lived rather peacefully within itself, but violence was frequent between the different nations, consisting of raids rather than warfare. When there was warfare, a leader was chosen, as there was ordinarily little political organization. They fought with the bow and arrow, the club, and the javelin. They buried the dead, and sometimes they cremated them.

That first evening, July 6, 1591, Gonzalo de Tapia and Martin Pérez met together. Placing themselves in the presence of God, they dedicated their lives to the spiritual conquest of the area. They would not retreat from this commitment until they had accomplished the task or ended their lives. They placed the mission under the patronage of Our Lady of the Angels of Sinaloa and discussed the whole situation. The Spaniards had promised to provide what food they could so that the two Jesuits would be free to work, and had said they would build a church. The Indians had built them a hut and given them sleeping mats. Villa Sinaloa would be their base for the time being, and María, the Indian from Culiacán, would be their language teacher and interpreter.

They then studied the sketch of the rivers and villages that the Spaniards had given them. Martin Pérez would work downstream from the villa to the gulf, and Gonzalo de Tapia would work upstream and on the Ocoroni River.

Starting with a good grasp of Nahuatl, they then studied the local language for some weeks with Maria's help, and Tapia wrote a short grammar. The two men also wrote a short catechetical instruction. Then they set out from the villa to visit the villages and introduce themselves, to get to know the people, to explain the faith, and to invite people to be baptized.

During the first winter of 1591–1592, Tapia and Pérez were very busy teaching the prayers and the catechism and building crude chapels. Two letters written by Martin Pérez to the provincial at the end of 1591 give an account of the situation.

> We are learning the first two languages very rapidly. After three months we could easily understand the Indians when they spoke to us. We started to

instruct them in the catechism. We exhorted them to keep the commandments and to have no fear of us. On their part they are pleased to receive the doctrine in their own language. Twice a day I am teaching the prayers and catechism, which they learn quickly and exactly, to children and adults, and continue to work on the languages.

The people are very affable and great workers, and we had to persuade them not to work on Sundays. They eat little meat even though there are many deer and rabbits. The Spaniards sometimes kill wild cattle, which were brought here at an earlier time, and give us strips of dried beef, which the Indians dislike. There are also some European chickens. The Indians dry and preserve some vegetables, especially the gourds. With their excess food and cotton cloth they gamble, using these things as prizes when one village meets another in an athletic contest.

The Indians are very healthy, and until now I have seen only one sick Indian. Blind or crippled people are very rare. The Indians are also great swimmers, and one time they pulled me from the river. On Sunday I go to say Mass with the Spanish who are about a mile from here. I cross the river which is deep in the middle, sometimes on horseback and sometimes, when it is full, on a raft. Once, the water swelled and the Indians pulled me out. They live by the river and swim from infancy. The children bathe for two or three hours during the hottest part of the day, especially when the river is full.

We have baptized 1,100 adults and children, and married 60 couples. We found 400 Christians who had been baptized by the Franciscans. The people are chaste although there are some, usually the principal men, who have two wives. They consider their first wife to be their true wife, and are easily persuaded to give up any others. Homosexuality is very rare.

Recently I visited the people along the river. Within 13 miles I found at least 4,000 warriors besides the women and children. Some of these people keep company with the devil and commit terrible sins. They took their children to the mountains in order to avoid baptism. However, there are so many who request baptism that we cannot instruct them unless some help comes to us. I often wish for some time to myself, but the crowds are so insistent that they give me no rest. They ask personal questions and talk about themselves.

They are bright and docile although they have had no teacher whose instruction could develop their natural powers. They live in groups of villages. Their houses are closely joined to each other. These are built of clay and timber with mats decorating the interior. The roof is a covering of reeds.

In the beginning the natives were reserved. Then the report spread that some men had come who appeared to be Yoris, which is their word for Spaniards or demons, but they did not carry the musket, nor demand maiz and meat. They were alone without an escort.

Their only business was to speak of Virigeva which is their word for God.

They believe in a God who is the author of all, who is on high, and who has power (providencia) over what is below. But this is independent of our actions, and so, although they fear and respect him, they do not invoke him, try to please him, nor ask anything of him. They have no rites or religious ceremonies.

There are now 13 churches on the three rivers [including the Ocoroni tributary to the Sinaloa and the Mocorito River to the south]. We have no vestments nor church furnishings except what we carry about. The only altar belongs to the Spaniards. We did set up one rough altar with a cross and some paper images which we brought from Culiacán. We look to your reverence for other furnishings. The people are delighted with these ornaments.[6]

With all the work they were doing, it should be noted that the two Jesuits were also supposed to spend about two and a half hours each day in prayer, to nourish their own spiritual lives and to make their work fruitful. The prayer included celebrating the Mass, spending an hour in meditation, and saying the breviary (a large prayer book based mostly on Psalms and the New Testament). The spiritual life of the people would be nourished by the Mass, the rosary, novenas, and confraternities.

During the Jesuits' first years in Sinaloa, all the churches were large huts with thatched roofs, supported by wooden poles and probably without walls. The people didn't have the time or resources for a better building material like adobe. Adobe blocks are sun-dried clay blocks mixed with straw and about the size of cinder blocks. They are serviceable and last a long time.

Visitor James Avellaneda sent a report to King Philip II in 1592. As mentioned earlier, he had visited every house and spoken to every Jesuit. After his visitation, having authority from the Jesuit general, he named the next provincial, choosing a Jesuit from the first group, which pleased everyone. Here are excerpts from his report to the king.

The General has decided that no Jesuit will be ordained a priest unless he knows a native language. . . . In every house there are two or three priests who are attending to the spiritual needs of the native people in their own language. During the past Lent there were more than four thousand people at a time coming to the Mexican church next to the college in Mexico City. The pulpit had to be taken outside.

There is a confraternity of Mexican people in Mexico which comes together for prayer, instruction, and the reception of the sacraments. These people visit the prisons and the sick. They give food, clothing, and money to the poor with graciousness from their own resources.

One way to help the Indians is to rear them from childhood as Christians, teaching the Christian doctrine, teaching those to read and write who are most capable, and by fostering devout and Christian customs for all.

Indians and Spanish are attending the schools in Puebla, Mexico, and Pátzcuaro without distinction. However, since it is not possible nor convenient to educate everyone, the Jesuits in Tepotzotlán and Mexico City are choosing the sons of the leaders and principal people, those who have the most capacity to learn. Later they will be able to govern their people and to be an example to all.

Since it would be good for the faith of the native people if there were native priests, it should be seen to that some study Latin. This is being done with four students at the Colegio Maximo, for whom there is good expectation, in order to see if it turns out as it is so much desired.[7]

Avellaneda mentioned a Mexican confraternity. The confraternities were an important Jesuit work all through the colonial period. For example, the confraternity at the Colegio Maximo, made up of students and alumni, was a prayer group that engaged in charitable work. It met on Saturday afternoons to honor the Virgin with chanted prayers, songs, and music. The members were obliged to confess and communicate once a month. They met on occasion to listen to a sermon, to hear a reading from a spiritual book, or to dialogue about the virtues. The charitable work was directed mostly to hospitals and prisons, which were visited once a week and were quite primitive in comparison to our modern counterparts. If the members of the confraternity carried blankets or oranges to these places, it could have been more than just a kind act, as the items may have been sorely needed. At Christmas and Easter, they gathered the poor, who went begging from door to door, into the college for an abundance of food and clothing.

The Indian confraternity at St. Gregory's met on Saturdays for the Mass of Our Lady with songs in Nahuatl. The students were the sons of caciques, and they shared their resources with the poor. On Thursday afternoons, they accompanied the Jesuits with Nahuatl hymns, going through the streets to the markets where the Jesuits preached in Nahuatl. By 1599, there were 150 confraternities in the country, and one in Oaxaca had a hundred members.

During this time, a problem developed in the province: priests started to leave the order. During the first twelve years, no priest had left or been dismissed except for a diocesan priest who had entered and left the novitiate. But during the next twenty years (November of 1584 to February of 1605), nineteen priests left or were dismissed, including two in the Philippines. About twelve of the nineteen had been born in New Spain. These priests were the most recently ordained, and many were very good in Nahuatl.[8]

This is a high number in a small province. In 1599, after most of the nineteen had left, there were 272 Jesuits in New Spain, with another 42 in the Philippines. Of the 272, there were 97 priests, 92 brothers, 57 scholastics, and 26 novices. One of the reasons for the departures was probably that the candidates were being accepted at too young an age for a course of studies that was rather short. They were also being ordained very young.

Another reason was tension between those born in Europe and those born in New Spain. Father Anthony Mendoza, provincial from 1584 to 1590, caused discontent by favoring the Europeans over the Americans, and he favored work with the Spanish over work with the Indians. He was also too quick to dismiss Jesuits.

The general reacted to the crisis by advising the provincial to be more careful in admitting novices who had been born in New Spain, and to be even more careful in admitting mestizos and Indians. Also, an applicant born in New Spain had to wait a year after applying before he could be admitted to the novitiate, and he had to be at least twenty years old, although the provincial could suspend these requirements if he had good reasons. At an early date, the general started to alternate the office of provincial between the Europeans and the Americans in order to reduce tension between the two groups.

It was also decided that a Jesuit could become a professed father if he was proficient in a native language, even if his knowledge of theology was average. A professed Jesuit is a priest who takes a special fourth vow to go and work anywhere that the pope wishes; it implies fidelity to the pope. Also, a few positions—like that of provincial and novice master—are reserved for the professed. This decision gave an additional motive for learning a native language, and it also ensured that more of those born in New Spain would become professed fathers. All of these steps, along with the customary strong emphasis on obedience, enabled the province to avoid the public conflicts that occurred between Europeans and Americans in other religious orders.

The general was also concerned that there not be two classes within the province, an upper class working with the Spanish and a lower class working with the Indians. He decreed that everyone had to learn a native language in order to be ordained and that after ordination everyone had to work three years with the Indians. However, the provincial could also suspend these requirements. It was later decided that veteran missionaries would occasionally be reassigned to teach in the colleges. The general also wanted a detailed list every third year of those who knew a native language. The first list, in 1592, recorded thirty-seven Jesuits who knew one or more of the Indian languages.

Each general seems to have done a good job of managing the province. The Jesuit order was smaller at that time, and a general would have had more time for details. A general also had a lot of information because individual Jesuits in New Spain felt quite free to write to him directly, as they had the right to do, in order to express their opinions on various subjects.

During the first six months on the Sinaloa River, Tapia made a trip north to the Fuerte River to meet the Suaqui people, who received him with kindness. They were moved by his words and asked to be baptized, but since he had no base on the river, he put off baptizing at that time. The people were responding to the Jesuits with interest and even enthusiasm. They were hearing about the faith in their own language. They were being baptized, and they were providing the Jesuits with shelter and food.

That winter, Tapia and some of the indigenous men cut trees to build a schoolhouse six miles below Villa Sinaloa at a place called Cubiri. The school was probably an open structure, but Tapia needed substantial support for a bigger wooden and thatched roof that would give some protection from the sun and rain. He started to teach reading and writing to some of the children. Tapia also decided to build a headquarters for the mission at Cubiri. He and Pérez wanted to distance themselves to some extent from the Spanish at Villa Sinaloa and to insert themselves more into the native population.

In the midst of all this, Tapia became sick, and Pérez persuaded him to go for a rest to Topia in the Sierra. Arriving at Topia during Lent of 1592, Gonzalo de Tapia met Tarascans who were mining for silver and with whom he could speak. There was a doctor there, as well as an old Jesuit who had come up to Topia from Guadalajara to recover his health. Near Topia was the town of San Andrés, one of the six towns that had been founded by Tlaxcalans the previous year.

Tapia recovered his health and started evangelizing the native people of the area. These people, the Acaxées, were fierce, but they allowed Tapia to circulate freely from one ranchería to another. He talked about religion and about forming settled pueblos. He stayed for several months, and a Christian village was established.

When Tapia returned to Sinaloa, two new Jesuits were at the mission. One stayed a short time; the other was John Velasco, born in Oaxaca (not the viceroy's nephew). The two new Jesuits were shocked when they saw the conditions in which Tapia and Pérez were living: sleeping in shacks, eating handfuls of scorched corn and dried fish, and working day and night. Tapia was annoyed by their lack of enthusiasm, although John Velasco would turn out to be a fine missionary who would spend the rest of his life in the area.

In August of 1592, after one year, Tapia wrote a report to the Jesuit general in Rome. Here is an excerpt:

> The people live in groups on the banks of rivers. They recognize no leader except in time of war, yet they get along very well with those of the same language, although there are very many languages. The land abounds in ordinary food products. They have no religion nor idols. They believe in a creator who lives beyond the mountains, but do nothing to honor him. They believe in a future life, but one of misery for all the dead.
>
> They are vivacious, curious, talkative, and intelligent enough to understand anything. They make no resistance to the Gospel. But obedience to its

precepts is not practiced except among those preordained to eternal life, generally those under 30 years of age. Only some of those over 30 have responded well.

Of the different languages I have learned so far, I can preach in three without an interpreter. This year the number of baptisms, including children and old people, should be near 5,000. A large part of this province is in land grants to the Spaniards. As the people here are brought up with so much freedom, the government cannot be forceful in putting things in order.[9]

Gonzalo de Tapia went on to criticize the Jesuits born in New Spain. He thought that the Jesuits from Spain considered the conversion of the Indians more and that those born in New Spain and raised among Indians were more impatient of hardship. However, he had the highest regard for Martin Pérez, who was born in New Spain.

During 1592, there was an uprising in the Sierra, and sixty-five Tlaxcalans were killed by the Acaxées at San Andrés. In December of that year, many Tarascans came down from Topia in order to see the coastal area and to provide music and a choir for the Christmas Mass.

After Christmas, Tapia decided to journey to Mexico. It would take him away for six months, but he knew that the mission had to be better organized and set on a firmer material foundation. He also needed supplies and more Jesuits. He left with a group of young men from among the people, and on the way he was able to visit friends in Pátzcuaro. The meetings in Mexico with the viceroy and the provincial were very encouraging. He left Mexico with supplies, with a great construction worker named Brother Francis Castro, and with the promise of more priests.

To this point everything had gone well, but now disaster struck. On the return trip, all but one of his young native companions died of smallpox in Morelia. Moreover, when Tapia arrived back at Sinaloa in the late spring of 1593, he found the area devastated by both smallpox and measles. Tapia wrote that two-thirds of the children whom he had baptized had died. Tapia had a year left to live, and opposition was already starting to gather. He had taken those young men to their death in Mexico, and some blamed him for the diseases. Some people turned back to the public dances, which involved heavy drinking and sexual license.

During the next months, much effort was put into the school. At Christmas of 1593, the people had a beautiful social and religious get-together with Spaniards and hundreds of indigenous, not at Sinaloa, but at a bigger church in a village on the Ocoroni. After Christmas, Tapia made another trip to the Fuerte River to prepare the ground for future work. By this time, he was living fifteen miles north of Villa Sinaloa at Ocoroni, which was a large and friendly village.

The leader of the developing opposition was an older *hechicero,* a medicine man or sorcerer, named Necaveva, in the village of Teborapa, a mile or two north of Villa Sinaloa. Necaveva was pushing the dances aggressively and going into the Christian villages to mock the Christians. Tapia asked the mayor of Sinaloa to threaten him with a beating if he did not back off. When the elderly *hechicero* was threatened, he became enraged. He kidnapped some Christians and went to the mountains. When he was found, he was whipped, so he resolved to kill Tapia.

Tapia came down one Sunday from Ocoroni to say Mass in Teborapa. Although he was warned of the danger, he did not want to show fear. He and others stayed the day at the village teaching catechism. That night, on July 11, 1594, he was clubbed to death in his hut.

It was almost three months before news of his death reached the south. On September 30, a letter in Tarascan from the pueblo of Topia arrived at Pátzcuaro, informing the governors, mayors, rulers, and more important people that Indians in Sinaloa had martyred the saintly Father Gonzalo de Tapia, the father of us all, and requesting that the letter be sent to all the pueblos in the Province of Michoacán.

Another Tarascan letter from Culiacán gives some details of the martyrdom.

> To our esteemed lords, resident in Pátzcuaro, Suinan, Naguate, Cheran, Arantlan, and all other pueblos of the Province of Michoacán where our language is spoken. To all of you we give notice, that you may tell the smaller pueblos, that our very reverend Father Gonzalo de Tapia is dead. He had come to Sinaloa to teach the faith of Christ to these people, and they killed him and made him a great martyr. They cut off his head and left arm, and with his right hand alone (thumb and index finger) he made the sign of the cross to signify how he died. He was lying outside the door of the house where they attacked him. He died alone. The other Fathers are at Ocoroni.

So we tell you of his death so that all may recite for him a Pater Noster. We are preparing to have a Mass said. Do not doubt what we say for it is true that he died. So we ask you to tell everyone. We who write this letter are John of Cheran and the principal people in Culiacán. God be with you and our Lady, the Virgin Mary. These things are written about what happened on the eleventh of July, Sunday, the night the father died.[10]

After Tapia's death, there was shock and agitation in the area for five years. Many non-Christian people were disturbed that a great *hechicero* had been struck down with violence. Some asked that he be replaced, and new nations asked for missionaries. Other people left the area in fear of reprisals by the Spanish, and those who had killed Tapia became the leaders of an anti-Spanish faction.

Twenty-four soldiers arrived at Villa Sinaloa in 1595. Tapia had asked for these soldiers as a police force for northern Sinaloa. One of the soldiers was the mestizo James Martinez Hurdaide, who would serve there for thirty-one years. From Zacatecas, his father was Spanish and his mother Aztec, so he probably learned the Uto-Aztecan languages of the area with some ease. In 1599, Hurdaide was named captain, and he would be the highest civil authority in the area for the next twenty-seven years.

It was Hurdaide who restored order in 1598 when the leader of the attack on Tapia was captured. When the leader was condemned to death, he requested baptism, and Martin Pérez instructed and baptized him before he died.

The historian W. Eugene Shiels describes Gonzalo de Tapia.

[He was] an optimist with strong zeal. He was young to be a superior, but the affection of his subjects proves that he treated them with true courtesy and friendship. The great memorial to Tapia is not so much what is written but the mission system that arose on him as its foundation. He worked a short time, but in those three years he set the pace, the method, and the line of attack which was followed and developed for the next 175 years. His untimely death did not take away the effect of his life. For though the first results were depressing, in time his martyrdom came to be esteemed as the most important single fact in the rise of the missions.[11]

Tapia was a Jesuit who showed his love for God, as St. Ignatius recommends, through deeds as well as words.

CHAPTER 5

The Tepehuanes, 1590–1616

The Tepehuán people lived in the western Sierra and on its eastern slope.[1] They also lived north of Durango City on the plain between the western and eastern Sierras. There were about ten thousand Tepehuanes when the Jesuits first met them. About six thousand lived in the Sierra, and about four thousand lived on the plain, extending all the way to Balleza, 210 miles north of Durango.

The two Sierras come from the north and join together around Zacatecas. The plain between the Sierras is eight thousand feet high near Zacatecas, decreasing in altitude as it goes north to the United States border.

Scholars say that the native people in the United States were very numerous along the Atlantic and Pacific coasts but that there were few people on the central plains until they had horses. It must have been the same in New Spain. There were many Indians living in Sinaloa and Sonora along the Gulf of California, but relatively few people on the central plain. Still, before the epidemics, there were, no doubt, more than ten thousand Tepehuanes, because they had been the dominant nation in the north.

As was mentioned earlier, the Tepehuán language is close to the Pima language. The Pima people live west of the Sierra Occidental in the States of Arizona and Sonora. At some time in the past, the Tepehuanes must have crossed over the Sierra and come south toward Durango.

Immediately west of the Tepehuanes were another people called the Tarahumaras. They lived in the Sierra Occidental, and their language was similar to the Cáhita languages of Sinaloa and Sonora. There were an estimated forty-five thousand Tarahumaras, mostly in the Sierra north of Topia, but with some on the plain north of Balleza. Although many Tarahumaras would integrate themselves into the general population over the centuries, today there are still some forty-five thousand Tarahumaras in the Sierra.

The Tepehuanes, who had not fought against the Spanish in the Chichimec War, had more or less accepted the Spanish, and there had been no wars of conquest. The Tepehuanes worked on Spanish ranches, and many became cowboys and fine horsemen. They had wood, or even stone, houses. They farmed and had acquired livestock, and their clothes were made of cotton or wool. As the former dominant group in the area, they were self-assured and competent. They had taken tribute from the Tarahumaras, Acaxées, and other nations. They had captured women from the other nations for their own purposes or to be held for ransom. Like other northern indigenous, they were a few inches taller than the Spanish. They did not steal, lie, or have more than one spouse, except for their caciques.

Their medicine men were numerous and influential. The people tended to be very superstitious, and they appeased or worshiped stone idols. Among the northern nations, idols generally included colored rocks, animal bones, and human bones. The rites with these objects usually included dancing and drinking, with the goal of the ceremonies being recovery from sickness, success in war, or a good harvest. The most common rite among the nations was with human bones, to honor the courage of enemies and to absorb their valor.

The Jesuits had a high opinion of the Tepehuanes. One of them wrote:

> It is sufficient to say that the Tepehuanes have great advantage over the Laguneros [people of the lagoon who were further east near Parras] for receiving the faith because they are naturally more mild and more given to reason. They even enjoy a bit of political organization which those of the lagoon lack. They educate their children with love and care, and it looks as if God were inviting them into the faith.

In contrast to the Tepehuanes, the Tarahumaras had wood houses or lived in caves in the Sierra. Being more nomadic, they lived high in the Sierra during the summer, and in the winter they descended into the tropical canyons. They lived more by hunting than by farming. The Tarahumaras, more than the Tepehuanes, were committed to dances, with excess drinking and some sexual license.

The Spanish immigrants had gone north very early in search of gold and silver—to Zacatecas in 1546, to Durango in 1563, and up to Santa Bárbara in 1567. Some Jesuits had given missions in the north soon after they arrived in New Spain. Then, in 1591, Father Jerome Ramirez and three other Jesuits established a permanent residence in Zacatecas. Three years later, a grammar and Latin school was started, which was endowed as a college in 1617 with a large donation.

In 1594, Father Jerome Ramirez, a thirty-five-year-old who knew both Tarascan and Nahuatl, and Father John Augustine Espinosa, a twenty-six-year-old who knew Nahuatl very well, went northeast a good distance from Zacatecas to visit Cuencamé, where there were Zacateca people. The Zacatecas, not numerous or no longer numerous,

Mining Sites among the Tepehuanes in the 1590s

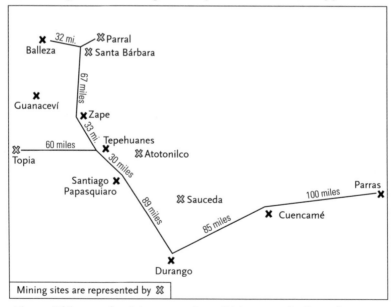

Fig. 12 Of these early mining towns, Santa Bárbara was the first to be established, and Parral the latest.

extended from Durango through Cuencamé to Parras. One of them greeted the two Jesuits with these words:

> We welcome you, fathers, because we know that you have not come self-ishly, seeking gold and silver, as do many other Spanish, but only to see that our souls are taken to heaven. Since this is your motive, we know that you will not look down on us because of our poverty.[2]

At this time, there was one adobe house in the Cuencamé area, built by an Indian from the center of the country, and there were no other buildings of similar or better materials. Around December of 1595, Jerome Ramirez went with a companion farther north from Zacatecas to establish a residence in Durango. This would be the Jesuit headquarters on the northern plain, and the missionary work was about to begin. Jesuits would go northwest to Topia in the Sierra, north to the Tepehuanes and Tarahumaras, and northeast to the Zacatecas and Laguneros near Parras.

At this time, Father John Augustine Espinosa, who had been born in Zacatecas, was either living at Cuencamé or making lengthy visits from Durango. A Jesuit companion of Ramirez worked with the Spanish in Durango, where a school was started. It was very slow to develop, but there was Latin in the school before 1632. The school building was made of cement and adobe, and another impressive building was constructed just before the Jesuits were expelled.

Father Jerome Ramirez made friends with the Tepehuanes who worked in Durango, and they invited him to visit their villages. In Lent of 1596, Ramirez went forty miles north to a mining site called Sauceda.[3] He preached and instructed the Spanish, the Mexicans, and other native people from the center of the country who had come north to work, as well as some of the Tepehuanes. They had attractive processions during Lent, at Easter, and at Pentecost with the accompaniment of good music. Some Tepehuanes were well instructed during these months, and they started to act as catechists in their home villages. One of the converts was an old hechicero, and his conversion liberated him from a stone idol. The stone, about the size of a grapefruit, had spoken to him, and for a long time he had carried it around and cared for it.

Ramirez returned to Durango in the spring of 1596. In the fall, he made another trip of three months to Tepehuán villages a hundred or more miles north of Durango. Before Lent of 1597, he went to visit Sauceda, then spent Lent and Easter at five villages in the vicinity of Atotonilco, where there were also some Spanish farmers. On Good Friday, they had a procession, a scourging, and the carrying of the cross, followed on Sunday by an Easter celebration with Mass, music, and the baptism of the children whom Ramirez had instructed each day of Lent. Then he went back to Sauceda.

From Sauceda, he made an eight-day trip to the west to visit Tepehuán villages. Ramirez was now starting to meet new people who had been well instructed in the faith by other Tepehuanes. Back in Sauceda, he met the hechicero who had become a Catholic the previous year. The old man said to him:

> For some years I have been in contact with the Spanish, but none took any notice of me. You alone respected me and helped me with the waters of baptism. You named me with your own name which is Jerome Ramirez. I have fulfilled all that was commanded of me. I pray to God, and when I am alone in the fields, I cry out to Him asking with all my spirit that he pardon my sins.

In the summer of the same year, Ramirez returned to the vicinity of Atotonilco. Then, moving southwest, he and Christian Tepehuanes founded the pueblo of Santiago Papasquiaro in a beautiful river valley. A governor and officials were elected, and Ramirez appointed a fiscal, who was in charge of church affairs. Then Ramirez went north and helped found Tepehuanes, then called Santa Catalina. Toward the end of the year he was farther north, and the pueblo of Guanaceví was founded.[4]

While Ramirez was working with the Tepehuanes, Espinosa made long trips from Cuencamé to meet new people. Going a hundred miles to the east, he met the People of the Lagoon, or the Laguneros. Scantily clad, the Laguneros did not farm and were relatively primitive.[5]

In response to the friendly reception they received, the Jesuits decided to establish a permanent mission among the Laguneros. On January 23, 1598, Father John Augustine Espinosa went east from Cuencamé with a Spanish captain. They went to meet a group of Tlaxcalans (Nahuatl-speaking people from north of Puebla) who had gone far north to found San Esteban de Nueva Tlaxcala near Saltillo. The captain had asked some of these people to help found the pueblo of Santa María de las Parras (Holy Mary of the Grapevines). They agreed, and everyone met at Parras. (The people at Parras were the Irritila Nation). To Parras also came fifteen baptized Lagunero chiefs with their people.

Almost everyone in the area could understand Nahuatl or Zacateca, although many spoke the languages poorly. Espinosa had a translation into Zacateca of the prayers, the commandments of God and of the church, the method for confessing, and the catechism. He also had hymns that had been translated from Nahuatl into Zacateca.

The people in the area were numerous, and the land was fertile. Twelve thousand people, including some Zacatecans, lived around the lagoon, which was west of Parras. When the lagoon was full, it was twenty-two miles across, and the people took fish and ducks from it. They searched for other food like plants, insects, roots, berries, and nuts.

They found the change to farming difficult because it required more work and discipline. It is surprising that they were not farming, because there had been farming in the country for five thousand years, and they lived close to the agricultural civilizations of central New Spain. Except for these people and those in Baja California, almost all the people whom the Jesuits evangelized in northwest New Spain were farmers.

Sixteen hundred people established Parras. They laid out lots for houses and fields for cultivation, and the government in Mexico helped by sending salt, chilies, corn, and clothing. Some Spanish ranchers donated livestock. People enthusiastically learned about the faith, memorizing the prayers and the doctrine. However, some old men put off baptism until such time as they were in danger of death.

In the beginning, people had to put aside superstitions. For example, they might believe that a certain rock was possessed by a spirit or demon. But they lost their fear when they saw Espinosa pick up the rock and throw it into a fire without being struck down. Many claimed that a demon had appeared to them and threatened them. The Jesuits believed that Satan was at work, especially among the *hechiceros.*

Espinosa taught people how to use crosses and to pray in order to be protected from Satan.

There were other superstitions. A mother might strangle her infant as the result of a dream. When a woman gave birth, the husband went to bed and fasted for five days. Also, some people believed they would die if they saw someone else die, which resulted in sick or old people being abandoned in the forests.

John Augustine Espinosa worked for a year at Parras without Jesuit companions, and at Christmas the people had a grand celebration. They started to roast a young bull on Christmas Eve. The people entered the church, which was lit with torches, to adore the child Jesus and his mother. Then they came outside to the spacious patio, also lit, where they prayed during the night with song and dance.

The words of the songs were in their own language, repetitive and simple, but the music was complex. In song, they repeated different sentences: "Worthy to be praised is God, our Lord." "Let all people praise our Lady, Mother." "We reverence [adoremos] the place where our Lady is, who is mother of our Lord." There were many notes for each word or syllable, and the dance kept time with the music.

When it was still night, Father Espinosa offered the first of three Christmas Masses, with the second at daybreak. In the morning, the people had a feast with the roasted bull and with other pots of beef and corn. A week later, New Year's Day 1599, a governor, town councilmen, and other officials were elected, and Espinosa appointed church officials and catechists.

Despite this success, John Augustine Espinosa sometimes suffered depression at this isolated outpost. At one point he wrote to a Jesuit friend:

> Besides the continual teaching of doctrine and the catechism, I must baptize, confess, marry, and pacify the Indians (naturales) as well as strangers and Spanish when the occasion offers itself. I do it with pleasure, but also with confusion when I see all the ways in which to serve God, Our Lord, and how poorly I am disposed to be the instrument of his Divine Majesty for the salvation of souls.
>
> The Demon opposes me and sometimes crudely. A few days ago, I was so bored, sad, and desolate that I despaired of my life. How much patience

and confidence in God is necessary for these ministries in this land. What loneliness! What journeys! What deserted places! What hunger! What bad tasting and smelly water! What nights in the open air! What heat from the sun! What mosquitoes! What thorns! And what people—childish, garrulous, contradictory! But if all things were flowers, what would remain to be enjoyed in heaven? May the will of the Lord be done in me. In His will I wish to walk and not in my perverse will. May I be in His hands which He placed on the cross for me, and not in my sinful hands. . . .

Every day I hope for death. And in order to receive it, I ask my God for a contrite and humble heart so that the sacrifice of my soul will be accepted, and that He will supply the last sacraments if there is no one to give them to me. I have been without confession for four months.[6]

A companion soon came and then many other Jesuits, for Parras was an important mission. But John Augustine Espinosa died in 1602 at age thirty-four, after four years at Parras.

Jerome Ramirez was made superior of the mission in Durango in 1600, and in that year John Fonte came up to the city. Ramirez had been born in Seville, Spain. His first work as a priest in New Spain had been at Pátzcuaro. After his work in Durango and with the Tepehuanes, he and another Jesuit were sent to Guatemala in 1606 to establish a residence and school. After many years, he came back and taught at St. Ildefonso. He was a prayerful person, good at spiritual direction, and he spent his life as a priest with the Native Americans. When he was sixty years old, he was asked to go to Pátzcuaro to replace a priest who had died. He was in the south of Michoacán, sixty-four years old, when he suddenly became sick. Another priest reached him, and he received the Eucharist before he died. He is buried in Pátzcuaro.

John Fonte (Joan de Fonte), twenty-five years old, came to Durango to help Ramirez in early 1600. Born in Tarrasa, near Barcelona, Spain, Fonte had arrived in New Spain a few months earlier. Recently ordained, he had to do the year of tertianship, but he was given only thirty days because of the great need for priests in the north. He had no knowledge of Nahuatl, but four years later the province catalog says that he was proficient in both Nahuatl and Tepehuán. He would be the founder of the Tarahumara mission and a martyr at the hands of the Tepehuanes in 1616. Fonte wrote the following to the provincial after arriving:

I cannot help repeating, my Father Provincial, how pleased I am to be here and how much this mission conforms to my own heart. I think it was a very good thing to have left my country, my relatives, and the rewards and comforts which the colleges offer and to find myself here where, for Our Lord Jesus Christ, I suffer something. And there await me greater things, which I see from afar, and among them death, which, when it comes, I will accept as that which I have much desired all the time I have lived in the Company. It was one of the motives, even the principal one, which moved me to ask to come to the Indies.

I want to write this to your reverence, my very beloved father, in order that you would know how content and with what satisfaction I am in this mission. To sum it up in a word, I have had not one feeling of regret, that I remember, for having come here. And so, with great consolation, may I never turn my back on the missions in which superiors wish to place me.[7]

John Fonte's first work was in Santiago Papasquiaro. Then, in 1604, he was invited north by the Tarahumaras. He made the trip with a Spanish captain to the area that would later be Balleza. After that he was at Zape with the Tepehuanes. It was about this time that Fonte translated a Nahuatl catechism of Anthony Rincón into Tepehuán.

There were four Jesuits with the Tepehuanes and six with the Laguneros in 1604. There were five Lagunero villages with a total of fifty-five hundred baptized people, but some of these villages were forty-five to ninety miles from Parras. Sometimes people were driven to Parras by famine in the Sierra Oriental, and the Jesuits would invite them to stay. If they returned to the Sierra, they might leave a few boys to study in the school. From Parras, the Jesuits were evangelizing as far north as Saltillo.

John Fonte moved to Papasquiaro in 1606 when he was made superior of the Tepehuán mission. In 1607, he made a second, long trip to the Tarahumaras, to the west of Chihuahua City, to the present-day city of Guerrero (then called Papigochic by the Tarahumaras and Villa de Aguilar by the Spanish). At this time, the Tepehuanes were planning to go to war with the Tarahumaras. When they asked Fonte's advice, he persuaded them to make peace.

A devastating plague swept through the Parras area in 1608. The Jesuits believed that the diseases were the work of Satan, although even in those days they had some ideas about how diseases were spread. For example, in the Paraguay Reductions, the Jesuits tried to quarantine a town where there was an epidemic.

In 1611, Fonte was back in the north to stay. He persuaded some of the Tarahumaras to come down and settle the new village of Balleza with some of the Tepehuanes. He wrote to the provincial that in the beginning there were no houses, churches, or food. He asked for help, and especially for a Jesuit brother, because he found it intolerable to be teaching and building at the same time. He mentioned that the Indians plant seed with a stick, choosing land that is not shaded by pine trees.

Fonte said that the Tarahumaras believed in an afterlife, a better place for those who lead good lives. They had cemeteries, unlike other Indians, who buried the dead anywhere. The Tarahumaras sometimes had many houses within a large cave. If someone died, their house was demolished or burned.

In writing about the Tepehuán area farther to the south, Fonte said that the people were producing a great deal of food and trading some to the Spanish for clothes. He asked the viceroy to distribute two thousand sheep to the Tepehuanes, and he mentioned that the Mexican Indians were a better example of Christianity for the Tepehuanes than were the Spanish.

The Mexicans among the Tepehuanes wanted a statue such as they had had in Mexico. When one was obtained, they formed the Confraternity of Our Lady's Conception, a prayer and charitable group like the ones in Mexico. They went to Mass on feast days of the most holy Virgin and confessed while the more mature communicated. They met every Sunday in a house, like an oratory, where they discussed increasing the membership and other business, and finished by singing the Salve Regina in Nahuatl. Fonte thought their example was more effective than his preaching.

When the Tepehuanes revolted in 1616, five Jesuits were working with them north of Durango City. There were also a fair number of Spanish and Mexicans in the area, and there were some Spanish and Mexicans living with the Tepehuanes in Papasquiaro. The Tepehuán revolt of 1616 is a sad chapter in the history of the Jesuits in North

America. It was one thing to be abused by the government during the expulsion, and quite another to be killed by poorer people whom they were attempting to serve.

The specific reasons for the revolt are not known. The rights of the native people to water and land were protected by the courts, at least in the case of the land they were actually farming or grazing. But the economic activity of the country was mostly in the hands of the Europeans, and the land was also passing into their hands. There were Spanish ranches in the area, and ranches often meant encroachment on water supplies and damage to native farm crops by cattle and horses. There were also mines at Sauceda, Atotonilco, Santa Bárbara, and other places, and the mines often meant forced labor for the indigenous at low and exploitative wages. But the Tepehuanes had gotten along well with the Spanish, and the exploitation of native labor in the north was less harsh than it would be in later times. The rebellion seems to have been a reaction against the changes that were taking place, a reaction shaped and controlled by the Tepehuanes' religious beliefs.

The leader of the uprising was an hechicero named Quatlatas, who went around with a small idol. There were prophecies that the Spanish would be driven from the land and that they would not return. Anyone who was killed in the uprising would be raised from the dead when it was over. The revolt was planned for November 21 at Zape. The plan was to wipe out all Spanish and perhaps the foreign Indians, and then to attack Durango.

The missionaries used to get together once a year to see one another, to report on progress or difficulties, to pray together, and to do some planning. The occasion for the meeting this year was the dedication of a new statue at Zape on November 21. Since the priests at Zape knew that something was wrong, they sent messages to the other Jesuits that they should not come, but only one received the message.

The revolt started early because of a desire for plunder. There was merchandise at Tepehuanes, which the Spanish planned to ship out before November 21.

On November 15, Father Hernando de Tovar and a companion were traveling from Topia in the west to Tepehuanes. Hernando de Tovar, thirty-five, was from Culiacán, Sinaloa. He had been inspired to become a priest after meeting Gonzalo de Tapia and Martin Pérez. An excellent student, he studied at the Colegio Maximo and entered the Society when he was seventeen. After his seminary studies, he worked for seven or eight years with the Laguneros.

The provincial had called him to Mexico in order to see his widowed mother before she entered a convent. On the way back to Parras, the superior in Durango had sent him on an errand to Topia.

After camping overnight by the trail, they were mounted and on their way the next day when they saw a group of Tepehuanes riding quickly toward them.

"Let's go," said the companion. "They are coming to kill us."

But they were on mules and could not escape. Father Tovar replied, "Let us offer our lives generously to God, for he gives us a great gift."

Tovar rode toward the Indians and attempted to speak with them. He was pulled from the mule, and a lance pierced his breast. The Indians made fun of him as they stripped his body and then filled it full of arrows. His corpse was never found. While this was happening, Tovar's companion escaped, and the Indians then successfully attacked Tepehuanes.

After destroying Tepehuanes, the rebels moved southeast some twenty miles to the mining town of Atotonilco. On the next day, the seventeenth, they attacked Atotonilco and killed two hundred people, including a Franciscan. The pattern of attack was the same in the different towns. When the Spanish and Christian indigenous sought protection in the strongest building, the Tepehuanes set fire to the wood or thatched roof. The people were forced outside and then killed.

Other Tepehuanes moved south and surrounded Santiago Papasquiaro on the night of November 16. Having heard rumors, the Spanish had gathered in the church, partially prepared to defend themselves. The next day, the Spanish held off the attack with the few harquebuses they possessed, and some Tepehuanes were killed. The church doors were twice set on fire, but the fire was put out.

On November 18, 1616, other Tepehuanes came from Atotonilco, and the attackers numbered about five hundred. After much negotiation, it was agreed that the besieged could leave unharmed and go to Durango. They came outside the church, where they were killed. There were a hundred people, including two Jesuits, Bernard Cisneros, thirty-four, from Carrión de los Condes, Spain, and James Orozco, twenty-eight, from Placencia, Spain.

On the same day, another group of Tepehuanes attacked Zape and killed eighty people, including two Jesuits. The people killed at Zape were Spanish and African, because some Spanish had come up from Durango with their slaves for the social and religious celebration. The Jesuits were Luís Alaves, twenty-seven, from Texestitlán, Oaxaca, and John Valle, forty, from Victoria de Viscaya, Spain.

The next day, Father John Fonte, forty-two, from Villa de Terrasa, Catalonia, Spain, and Jerome Moranta, forty-two, from the island of Mallorca, were traveling south from the Tarahumara mission. They were killed about half a mile north of Zape.

The last Jesuit to die, on Sunday, November 20, 1616, was the most famous. Hernando Santarén, fifty years old, was from Huete, near León in Spain. He had entered the Society at age fifteen, and as a young seminarian he came to New Spain. After doing tertianship, he was minister at Puebla. He then worked for many years with great success along the coast of Sinaloa and in the Sierra around Topia. He was coming from the west when he was killed at Tenerapa.

The Tepehuanes then moved south against Sauceda and Durango. They had a chance to destroy Durango because this administrative center contained only about five hundred people. However, there were about thirty Spanish farms in the area, and the settlers had time to gather in the city. The Tepehuán attack on Durango was repulsed, but the Tepehuanes still controlled the countryside. The besieged at Sauceda held out for forty-two days before they were relieved.

All of the north was now in turmoil, as the Tepehuanes tried to promote a general rebellion from the Gulf of California to the eastern Sierra. They sent envoys to all the nations, from the Yaquis in Sonora to the Laguneros at Parras, and all these nations considered the proposal. There was a peace party and a war party in every nation. The Jesuits were a strong influence in favor of peace, and one after the other, the nations opted for peace. Isolated, the Tepehuanes eventually withdrew to the mountains.

This uprising was a sad and destructive affair. The plot was kept secret, and the uprising was successful enough to kill hundreds of Spaniards, Africans, and Christian indigenous, including eight Jesuit missionaries. The Jesuits had lost another missionary in this area the previous year, when he drowned while crossing a river. So the Society lost nine missionaries within two years, which was a tremendous blow.

There were Spanish expeditions against the Tepehuanes for each of the next three years. After the leaders of the rebellion had been killed in battle or caught and executed, the Tepehuanes started to return to their land. Other Jesuits were sent to the area, and things were very good for a short time from about 1621 to 1631. Then a slow decline set in.

There is a description of the area north of Durango after the rebellion by Gerard Decorme, S.J., a French missionary in the twentieth century.

> There is little that we know about this mission. But we do know that, after a brief period of prosperity during which the populations were even dense in the villages, there began an era of decadence or ruin. The ranches of the Spanish multiplied more and more in that fertile region with an agreeable climate. Although the mines became less important, a great number of Indians were occupied on the haciendas and ranches with no small prejudice to religion and morality. The population was sucked from the missions which were a kind of reservation open to every wind.[8]

Decorme said that the Saxon race applies euthanasia to their Indians but that the Latin, prescinding from religion, is content with an interminable natural agony. In another place, he described the Native Americans of modern Mexico as a people still waiting for their redemption. Today, since so many people in modern Mexico are trying to survive on a minimum wage of four dollars a day, Decorme would be correct in writing that the people are still waiting for their redemption.

About 1752, the Jesuits handed the Tepehuán parishes over to the diocese and withdrew from the area.

CHAPTER 6

Sinaloa, 1594–1614

When Gonzalo de Tapia died in the summer of 1594, two new missionaries, Peter Méndez and Hernando Santarén, were traveling north through the State of Sinaloa.[1] They represented the beginning of a long expansion of Jesuit work in this area, in what was probably the order's most successful mission in North America.

There was now a team of five competent men on the river, two of them Americans. Martin Pérez was the superior, and he spent the rest of his seventy years on the river. The second was John Velasco, who was shocked when he first saw how Tapia and Pérez were living. He worked mostly on the Mocorito River to the south of the Sinaloa. He was friend, adviser, and confessor to the famous Captain James Martinez Hurdaide.

When John Velasco first arrived at Villa Sinaloa, he had a confrontation with some whites on a ship in the Gulf of California who were attempting to capture Indians in order to sell them as slaves. He and Tapia used threats to persuade the raiders to leave the area and not return. During his first year at the mission, Velasco lived through that epidemic of smallpox and measles, which caused enormous mortality to adults and children. He also mentioned in an early report that there were already *encomiendas,* or land grants, in the area.

The third member of the group was Brother Francis Castro, who built many churches and residences and taught catechism. He was much admired and loved by the people. He died in the area in 1627 at an advanced age.

The next missionary was Hernando Santarén, twenty-eight years old, from Spain. He was in Sinaloa for four years, and then he was sent

Principal Rivers of the Gulf Coast

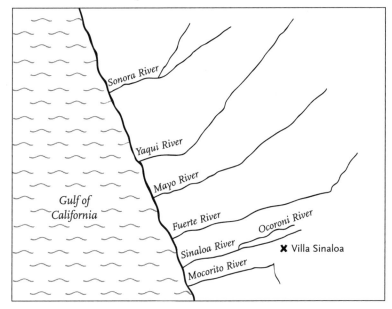

Fig. 13 Hernando Santarén and Peter Méndez worked only on the Ocoroni, Sinaloa, and Mocorito Rivers from 1594 to 1605.

to found the mission at Topia in the Sierra. He died in the Tepehuán revolt of 1616 while on his way to a religious celebration in the State of Durango.

The fifth member of the team was Peter Méndez. Born in Portugal in 1558, he entered a Spanish province of the Society when he was seventeen. When he was nineteen, he began an eight-year period of teaching Latin, and he also wrote good Latin poetry. After teaching, he returned to the seminary for philosophy and the beginning of theology. He finished theology in Puebla, was ordained, did tertianship, and reached Sinaloa at the age of thirty-six in July of 1594. Méndez was a missionary on the coast for forty-four years, including two sabbaticals in Mexico City. He left the area when he was eighty years old, then lived and worked for five more years at the professed house in Mexico, where he died.

In a report to the general, the provincial wrote that Pérez, Velasco, and Méndez knew Nahuatl quite well. Santarén had a moderate knowledge, and Brother Castro was not mentioned.

Hernando Santarén and Peter Méndez were coming north through Sinaloa when Tapia was slain in 1594. Because of the uncertain situation, Pérez instructed them to wait in the Culiacán area. They used part of their time there to meet the Tahue Indians on the Culiacán River. Arriving at the Sinaloa River, Méndez was assigned to Villa Sinaloa, and Santarén was assigned to the Mocorito River and later to the Guasaves, who were at the mouth of the Sinaloa River and south of the river along the coast.

Since so many Indians had fled the area when Tapia was killed, the Jesuits started work by traveling to the mountains to ask people to return to the villages. They worked for eleven years, 1594 to 1605, on the Ocoroni, Sinaloa, and Mocorito Rivers and made no further advance to the north during this time. Each Jesuit worked alone in a different village on the river. Each was instructing for baptism and preparing people for first Holy Communion and for marriage, as well as building churches, introducing domestic animals, and even trying to improve farming methods. Martin Pérez periodically sent a Jesuit down to Culiacán to give a mission in the town, as well as to instruct and have religious services with the Tahues on the Culiacán River.

On the Sinaloa River, some Indians found the changes hard to accept. Some left the area and joined other nations. Others were attracted by the gospel message and the more religious way of living. Some nations would be attracted by the progress, processions, and pageantry in the Christian villages, and many would ask for missionaries.

The twenty-four soldiers Tapia had requested arrived in 1595. These soldiers may have been Spanish, because they were coming from the interior. Later, it was the custom to recruit soldiers from the frontier. In this remote northwest area of New Spain, about 20 percent of the soldiers would be Indians; the remainder were mulattoes, mestizos, and whites. These soldiers were good horsemen because of their background on the frontier. They were paid three hundred pesos a year, but they had to provide some food and their own horses and equipment. They were allowed to marry while in the service.[2] They were also permitted to begin farms or ranches.

During the next ninety years, the number of soldiers at Villa Sinaloa would grow to forty-five, and there would be no more soldiers or other forts in the vast coastal region from Sinaloa to Arizona. However, detachments of soldiers from Sinaloa would be stationed more or less permanently in the north at different times and at different places. And there would also be companies of voluntary militiamen.

During these ninety years, there would be relatively few mines and Spanish settlers in the area. The Jesuit missions would expand to the north, and no Jesuit would die by violence in the coastal area during this time. In this isolated area, the captain at Sinaloa had both military and civil authority. If he was honest, things went well. If he was greedy, it led to discontent and disorder.

A second fort was finally established at Fronteras (near the present U.S. border) in 1689. But for fifty years afterward, less than a hundred soldiers were stationed in the whole region. Finally, starting in 1740, there were major Indian revolts. These revolts and also attacks by the Apaches resulted in the area becoming more militarized. After 1750, guerilla warfare began in parts of Sonora. Then, in 1767, the Jesuits were expelled.

At the same time that the soldiers came, some Mexicans and some Tlaxcalans from San Andrés, both groups being Nahuatl speakers, arrived in order to settle in Villa Sinaloa. The government, wanting an example of Christian living, had encouraged them to move north. When more Spanish moved to Villa Sinaloa in the same year, they and the Native Americans built a large adobe church, a granary, a Jesuit headquarters, and a school. The first school at Cubiri was abandoned, and the exact location of the village is not known.

In this same year of 1595, Peter Méndez was at Ocoroni on the Ocoroni River, a tributary of the Sinaloa. The Tehueco people came down from the Fuerte River and attacked Ocoroni when three soldiers happened to be visiting the pueblo. The soldiers helped the people drive off the Tehuecos.

During his years at Ocoroni, Méndez developed a fine orchestra.

In 1595, there were 6,770 Christians. These included 1,588 on the Mocorito River to the south in five villages, 3,312 on the Sinaloa River in thirteen villages, and 1,270 on the Ocoroni River in three villages.

This also included about 600 people scattered on the Fuerte River to the north. The Jesuits had made visits to the Fuerte and baptized some children, and some people had come down to the Sinaloa for instruction and baptism.

Luís de Velasco II ended his term of office as viceroy of New Spain in 1595. Two years later, Luís's nephew, Peter Velasco, fifteen years old, wanted to enter the Society of Jesus. Although his parents were not happy about it, they gave permission.

A new Jesuit arrived at Villa Sinaloa in 1598, and Martin Pérez assigned him to replace Hernando Santarén with the Guasaves. Since Pérez wanted to follow up the earlier work of Father Tapia in the mountains, he sent Santarén to found the mission among the Acaxées at Topia. From this area, Santarén would also be able to periodically visit the Tahues on the Culiacán River.

An estimated fourteen thousand Acaxées lived around Topia and San Andrés, two mining sites. Relatively advanced, they farmed in the valleys. Many had stone houses, and their clothing was made from the fiber of the agave plant. They were relatively chaste, and they did

Native People of the Sinaloa Region in the 1590s

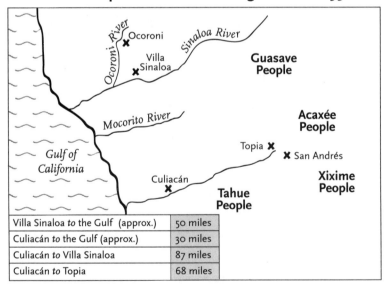

Villa Sinaloa *to* the Gulf (approx.)	50 miles
Culiacán *to* the Gulf (approx.)	30 miles
Culiacán *to* Villa Sinaloa	87 miles
Culiacán *to* Topia	68 miles

Fig. 14 Tahue, Acaxée, and Mocorito were similar languages. The Xixime language was different but still Uto-Aztecan.

not lie or steal. However, they had stone idols and were cannibals with their enemies. Their language was related to the Tahue and Mocorito languages. South of the Acaxées lived the Xiximes, who were not as numerous, and whose language was different, although still Uto-Aztecan.

Santarén first translated the catechism into Acaxée. Then, with catechists to help him, he began the work of evangelization. He had great success, and five thousand people became Catholic within three years and founded many Christian villages.

Santarén worked very hard, especially during Lent. Each week of Lent, he made a circuit on the very rough trail from San Andrés to Culiacán (seventy miles) and back to Topia and San Andrés. On Sunday, he started at San Andrés, where he preached three times during Mass in Nahuatl, Spanish, and Acaxée. He then made visits to the Tahues and arrived in Culiacán on Wednesday, where he preached during Mass in Nahuatl, Spanish, and Tahue. From Culiacán, he went to Topia for a similar service on Friday. Then he started again on Sunday at San Andrés. After two years, two Jesuits were sent to help him.

Meanwhile, in the Sinaloa area there was turmoil and danger from 1594, when Tapia was killed, until 1599. Tapia's killers had found refuge with the Tehuecos on the Fuerte River. When some of these refugees among the Tehuecos killed a Tehuecan, the Tehuecos handed

The Four Nations on the Lower Fuerte River

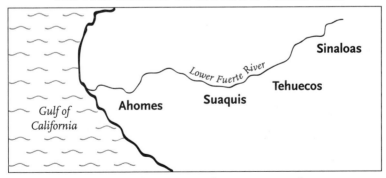

Fig. 15 The Fuerte and Sinaloa Rivers are forty to seventy miles apart at different points. Both are located in Sinaloa. The Cáhita languages predominate on the Sinaloa, Fuerte, Mayo, and Yaqui Rivers. Each nation on the Lower Fuerte River had about a thousand families.

the leader of the plot to kill Tapia over to the officer James Martinez Hurdaide, who was not yet captain of the area.

Here is a description of the nations farther to the north, starting with those on the Fuerte River, the first river north of the Sinaloa River.

The nation closest to the Gulf of California on the Fuerte was the Ahome Nation. Half of these people were fishermen and did no farming. They traded dried fish for corn. The Ahomes were friendly to the Spanish, partly because they were intimidated by the next nation on the Fuerte, the Suaqui. The Suaqui Nation began thirty miles from the gulf and extended for fifteen miles. This nation was hostile to the Spanish and had killed earlier Spanish settlers and Franciscan missionaries.

The Tehuecos were the next nation. They were also hostile to the Spanish. They started forty-five miles from the gulf and extended twenty miles along the river. The fourth nation was the Sinaloa, which began sixty-five miles from the gulf. Each nation had about a thousand families. The Fuerte River has tributaries that come from the Sierra. There were other smaller nations on these tributaries, and all of these people spoke Uto-Aztecan languages.

On the river to the north of the Fuerte were the Mayo people on the Mayo River. On the next river were the Yaquis on the Yaqui River. The languages of the Mayos and the Yaquis were almost the same as the Suaqui, so the Cáhita languages extended into the present-day State of Sonora.

How many people were there? Tapia had estimated 100,000 people in the north of Sinaloa on the Mocorito, Sinaloa, Ocoroni, and Fuerte Rivers. Also, farther north, in the present-day State of Sonora, which is much bigger than Sinaloa, there were 20,000 Mayos and 30,000 Yaquis. Beyond the Yaquis were the populous Pima and Opata Nations. So there must have been more than 250,000 people in the States of Sinaloa and Sonora when the Jesuits first arrived on the coast.

This was a big population, so dense as to seem as if the people had not been touched by epidemics. The epidemics may only have arrived after the people had direct contact with the Europeans and with their livestock, which can also carry human diseases. It seems that the Mayos did not have enough room for 20,000 people. They certainly felt hemmed in by the Suaquis to the south and by the Yaquis to the north, both of whom were their enemies. A Mayo male took as many wives as he could support, and the Mayos practiced abortion and some infanticide. They had more children when they were pagan than they later had as Christians.

Within seventy years of their conversion, the mission population of the Mayos dropped from twenty thousand to seven thousand. The main reason was disease. A lesser reason was that the Mayos liked to travel more than other people, and they would often go and settle in places that they had visited. Even before they were Christians and inside the Spanish Empire, they used to obtain safe-conduct passes from Hurdaide so that they could visit places like Culiacán. Also, many worked at mining sites and on Spanish ranches.

James Martinez Hurdaide made a trip to Mexico in 1599. He was named captain and was the highest civil authority in the area. He returned with ten more soldiers, making a total of thirty-four at Villa Sinaloa. While Hurdaide was away, a group on the Sinaloa River rebelled and went to the mountains. Hurdaide pursued them with allied Indians, captured the leaders, and punished them with death.

It was mentioned that there was danger, violence, and disorder in the area after 1594, when Tapia was killed, until 1599. At this time, Hurdaide made a bold and very violent move against the Suaquis on the Fuerte River. He chose twenty-four of his best soldiers and supplied them with rope and chains but told them nothing more. They went to the Fuerte without native allies, and there they camped and waited.

The Suaquis came around the soldiers and asked what they wanted. When Hurdaide said he wanted to catch some wild cattle and to share the meat with them, they wanted to know why he was waiting. He replied that he needed firewood. While the people went for wood, the caciques remained without fear among the few soldiers. Hurdaide had told the twenty-four soldiers that each was to seize two caciques when he gave the signal. He gave the signal, and they captured forty-three of them and tied them with ropes and chains.

The people hesitated to attack lest they hurt the caciques, and they were also without leadership. Hurdaide intended to hang the caciques, but he waited until Peter Méndez and John Velasco could be brought up to instruct and baptize them. After the Jesuits arrived, they had to wait two days before the last of the caciques agreed to accept baptism. Since two had died earlier in attempting to escape, and one was pardoned, forty were hanged.

Hurdaide was criticized for this extraordinary violence. The Suaquis were really not rebels as they were outside of New Spain, but Hurdaide considered them both rebels and criminals because of their conduct toward the Spanish and other indigenous. It was his custom to avoid the shedding of much blood by going after rebel or criminal leaders.

In 1601, the government sent Hurdaide to the Sierra along the upper Fuerte to prospect for precious metals. He took Peter Méndez and some Sinaloas with him. When the Sinaloas betrayed Hurdaide to the Chínipas people, they and the Chínipas besieged Hurdaide and his party for two days, but the Spanish were able to escape.

In the Sierra, the Acaxées rose in rebellion. There were five mining sites on their land, and mistreatment of the local Indians by the miners was the principal cause of the rebellion. The rebels attacked the mining sites. They wiped out some of them and destroyed property in all of them, including mining machinery and chapels. They killed over two hundred people—Spanish, Christian Indians, and Africans. The Tlaxcalans of San Andrés were able to hold out until the governor arrived with soldiers from Durango.

A big battle took place in January of 1602. It lasted most of the day and pitted three hundred rebels against the governor of Durango, his soldiers, and allied Indians. About 130 rebels were slain before the rest surrendered. The governor acted with restraint, and Father Santarén was sent alone to discuss peace with the rebels. He was successful, but it was another year before there was real peace in the area. In the end, the people handed over forty-eight rebel leaders to the governor, and they were executed. By 1607, seven Jesuits were at work in these mountains, and the mission spread to the Xiximes, south of San Andrés.

At Villa Sinaloa, there were thirty boys up to the age of thirteen living and studying at the school in 1602. Music was always important, and the instruments they had by this time were flutes, horns, and tambourines.

About this time, the Ahomes on the Fuerte River asked for help. The Suaquis were occupying Ahome land and kidnapping women and children. Again, Hurdaide went north with a small force. He seized a principal cacique when the cacique, thinking he had things under control, entered Hurdaide's camp. But this time the Suaquis attacked. When Hurdaide seized one of the attackers and hung him, the act shocked the Suaquis and they withdrew.

Hurdaide went downstream and surprised a Suaqui village. When the men fled, he captured three hundred women and children. He returned the captives when the Suaquis agreed to make peace with the Spanish and to return occupied Ahome land. He then went farther downstream and surprised another village, where he seized a great quantity of corn. Again the Suaquis made peace in return for their supplies.

So there was peace along the Fuerte River in 1602. The people accepted that they would be a part of New Spain, and they also had respect for Hurdaide. The captain had conquered the river by acting decisively with a small number of soldiers. He had hung forty leaders, but he had destroyed no property or food supplies and had taken no slaves.

By this time, the people knew Hurdaide and his lifestyle. James Martinez Hurdaide, born in Zacatecas, was married with at least one son. He lived simply, even poorly, and did not exploit native labor. The people also knew that he kept his word. He could send an official messenger anywhere without the messenger ever being molested.

In 1604, Hurdaide again made the long journey to Mexico. With the continuous disorder in the area, the government had been thinking of holding the line at the Sinaloa River or even of withdrawing to a river in the south. The operation in Sinaloa was costing the government seventeen thousand pesos a year, and there was no tax income from the area. However, Hurdaide wanted to advance to the Fuerte River. The government accepted his proposal and gave him permission to build a fort on the Fuerte River, although it was not constructed until 1610. The government also gave him ten more soldiers, making a total of forty-four, and authorized two more Jesuits for the area. The provincial assigned two Jesuits to return with Hurdaide. They were Andrew Pérez de Rivas, a future provincial and historian of the missions, and Christopher Villalta.

While Hurdaide was away in Mexico, a disastrous flood, the flood of 1604, struck Sinaloa. There was torrential rain for five days. The Ocoroni and Sinaloa Rivers rose, joined together, and wiped out everything downstream.

There was a Jesuit downstream named Hernando de Villafaña. Arriving in 1598, he had replaced Santarén and worked six years with the Guasave people on the lower Sinaloa and along the Gulf of California. The Guasaves were Uto-Aztecan but not Cáhita people. Father Villafaña and the Guasaves had built three adobe churches, the first in the area since the one at Sinaloa. With axes and hatchets, they felled and trimmed trees for vertical and horizontal support beams. The walls, several feet thick, were made of adobe blocks, but the people had trouble with the roof because they could not produce boards and planks. They made osiers for the roof, which were big mats woven with pliant twigs or thin branches. The osiers were attached to the roof and covered with mud or clay.

They had just finished building the churches, which were not yet dedicated, when the rains and the flood hit and everything was destroyed. Peter Méndez, who was down from Ocoroni to help with the project, sought safety on a high hill, but it was not high enough, so he spent twenty-four hours in a tree.

The floodwaters also entered Villa Sinaloa, which was well upstream. The granary and some houses were destroyed, but the church and school survived because they were on higher ground. On the Mocorito River to the south, John Velasco was trapped for five days in his church.

In the Jesuit Province of New Spain at this time, not counting those in the Philippines, there were 290 priests, brothers, scholastics, and novices. One-quarter of the total had been born in New Spain. Of the 113 priests, 64, or over half, were proficient in at least one native language. So the language situation had greatly improved, because twenty years earlier, in 1584 and before the missionary move to the north, only 18 had been proficient in a native language.

Hunger and some rebellion followed the flood in Sinaloa. Hurdaide put down the rebellion when he returned. At this time, trade began with the south when some merchants arrived, offering blankets for cotton and food products.

There were now ten thousand baptized people on the Sinaloa River, and caciques came from all four nations on the Fuerte to ask for missionaries. It was a new beginning, a time for building. It was 1605, eleven years after the death of Gonzalo de Tapia, and the Jesuits had spent fourteen years on the Sinaloa River.

Three Jesuits were assigned to make the move to the Fuerte River. The first was Andrew Pérez de Rivas, who left in the company of a group of Ahomes. He would be missionary to the Ahomes and Suaquis, the nations closer to the gulf on the Fuerte River, for eleven years. Peter Méndez, who was named superior of the three Jesuits on the Fuerte, went to the Tehuecos because it was correctly believed that this nation would be the hardest to work with. Christopher Villalta went to the Sinaloas.

The friendly Ahomes gave Rivas a big welcome. A blind Indian from the Sinaloa River had already gone from house to house teaching the prayers and the catechism. Rivas found the people warm and affectionate. Bigamy was rare among them, and medicine men were also rare. The Ahomes had always been friendly to the Spanish and attracted to Christianity.

What happened with the hostile Suaquis is more surprising. Rivas won the medicine men for Christ, and the whole nation was transformed. It was a miracle of grace. Despite all this success, however, Pérez de Rivas got sick about halfway through his eleven years on the Fuerte River with some kind of a depression. He was alone too much. The regional superior at Villa Sinaloa sent another Jesuit to help with the work and serve as a companion. Rivas recovered his enthusiasm, and later he founded the mission to the Yaquis beyond the Mayo River.

Peter Méndez was missionary to the Tehuecos, next upriver after the Suaquis. Hurdaide accompanied Peter Méndez to the Tehuecos, who received them with great joy. It was thought that there might be trouble, but Méndez had made trips here, and there were Christians in the area. Méndez had no trouble with the language because it was the same as the language at Ocoroni, where he had been working.

Peter Méndez was with the Tehuecos for at least six years. He was very successful in teaching at his village school and in fostering the musical talent of the people. He translated the lives of the saints and other books into Tehuecan, and the students read the books to the people in the church. Although things went well, there were medicine men whom Méndez never won over. In confrontation with these men, Méndez destroyed some idols and won their lasting enmity. Since his life was in danger, the superior at Villa Sinaloa replaced him with another Jesuit. In 1612, Méndez went to Mexico for a rest. He was fifty-four years old and had been in the area for eighteen years. He would return by himself in 1614 to found the mission on the Mayo.

Christopher Villalta spent twelve years with the Sinaloa people. An outstanding young cacique facilitated the conversion of these people, who were talented and quick to learn. They were skilled in woodworking and produced flutes and church furnishings, such as altars. They made rosaries and sold them to neighboring peoples, and they were the first to wear the rosary around the neck. Their religious devotions included our Lady, the Blessed Sacrament, and prayers for the deceased.

When the Jesuits moved to the Fuerte River in 1605, the Mayos on the next river north sought an alliance with the Spanish. They wanted missionaries and protection from the Yaquis, so Hurdaide signed a formal peace treaty and military alliance with them. A large number of Mayos then moved south and joined the Suaquis on the Fuerte River. The Suaquis had been their enemies, but now they were becoming Christian, and they spoke the same language as the Mayos.

Father Peter Velasco, twenty-six years old, arrived at Villa Sinaloa in 1607. In that same year, his uncle, Luís de Velasco II, was named viceroy of New Spain for his second term of four years. Peter Velasco was assigned to work with new people on the upper Sinaloa River and had fine success. Within a few years, he had baptized six thousand people, and in 1611, another Jesuit was sent to help him.

That same year, some Ocoronis rebelled and went far north to join the Yaquis. The major rivers are about sixty miles apart. From south to north they are the Sinaloa, Fuerte, Mayo, Yaqui, and Sonora. Hurdaide decided to go to the Yaqui River to deal with the Ocoroni rebels. He took forty soldiers and a hundred Indian allies. They made the long journey to the Yaqui and met with the leaders of the Yaqui Nation. The Yaquis refused to turn over the Ocoronis, and there was nothing Hurdaide could do but withdraw. However, two Yaquis asked to go with him in order to be instructed and baptized.

The next year, 1608, the Yaquis said that they would return the rebels, so Hurdaide sent some Christian Suaquis to accept the Ocoronis from them. The Yaquis killed the Suaquis and took their horses and baggage. Since this was conduct Hurdaide would not accept, he prepared for war. He moved north with an army of forty soldiers and two thousand indigenous allies, pagan and Christian.

In hostile encounters with the indigenous, the soldiers had the advantage that they sometimes wore metal armor, including metal headpieces. However, it was more common for a soldier to be protected from arrows with five or more layers of cowhide which left his arms free. A soldier carried a leather shield, a sword, and a musket. His horse was protected by two layers of cowhide and went into battle carrying about twice the weight of the soldier. Also, each soldier had extra horses. A soldier was more like an immovable fortress than a mobile cavalryman, and it seems that Hurdaide's soldiers in this battle fought mounted rather than on foot. An Indian would sometimes try to bring a soldier down by slashing at the feet of his horse.

Shoulder guns were available at this time—harquebuses and primitive muskets. The harquebuses were very heavy, one-shot guns that had to be fired by lighting a fuse. The harquebus was also called a swivel gun because it could be rotated around a barrel support on the ground. The muskets were lighter and were also fired with a lit fuse. One-shot, flint-fired muskets would not be mass-produced in Europe until about sixty years later.

Hurdaide needed room in order for his army to be effective. He seems to have lined up the forty soldiers in a semicircle, spaced, mounted, and in front of the two thousand native troops armed with bows and arrows. The Yaquis met Hurdaide with four or five thousand warriors. The firearms of the soldiers helped prevent the Yaquis from overwhelming the less numerous allies. Also, the allies could see the mounted soldiers, which would have given them confidence that the line was holding.

The two armies fought all day, resulting in many dead and wounded on each side. The Yaquis were not as intimidated by the guns as other nations had been. While warriors fell around them, the Yaquis, wearing orange war paint, kept coming, and they fought in silence without the usual war cries. The next day both sides withdrew, and the Yaquis left the area. Since Hurdaide had exhausted his supplies and had many wounded, he began the long retreat to the Sinaloa.

But Hurdaide was not finished. In 1609, he gathered thirty-seven soldiers and four thousand allies, many of them Mayos, which was a formidable army for that time and place. He moved two hundred or so miles north from Villa Sinaloa with cattle and other supplies for the army. He did not yet have the fort on the Fuerte River as his base. This time, the Yaquis did not allow Hurdaide time to deploy his army. They caught him in a narrow place with thousands of warriors. When the captain realized he had to retreat, he ordered half of the soldiers and all of the allied troops to retreat with the baggage and supplies. He himself remained with nineteen soldiers and an allied cacique as a rear guard. When the allies panicked and fled, the soldiers who were with them also fled. The supplies were in Yaqui hands, and Hurdaide was trapped.

Hurdaide and his squad found a high place and fought all that afternoon. He was wounded five times, and an arrow even pierced his metal helmet. When the Yaquis started a fire in order to burn him out, he started a backfire. When his fire had burned off the vegetation and the ground had cooled, Hurdaide moved his squad onto the burned ground before the Yaqui fire reached them.

The day was very hot, and Hurdaide gave no water to the spare horses. That evening, the Yaquis withdrew, but the soldiers were still trapped. In the middle of the night, Hurdaide released the thirsty spare horses, and they headed straight for the river with a tremendous racket. The Yaquis assumed that the soldiers were attempting to escape, and converged on the running horses while Hurdaide and the others escaped by another route.

The Yaquis had won a great victory. They had defeated the best that the Spanish could bring against them, and they had captured the Spanish supplies. However, they had failed to take down the great captain even when they had him trapped, and they didn't bring down a single mounted soldier.

Hurdaide hurried back to Sinaloa before the report could spread that he had fallen. He had to nurse his wounds. It was the third time he had retreated from the Yaquis. Hurdaide never lost a Spanish soldier in battle in twenty campaigns during his twenty-seven years as captain in Sinaloa. He also lost few allied soldiers except in these two battles with the Yaquis.

Next, some ships hunting for pearls appeared off the Yaqui River. Hurdaide spread the word that he was considering a three-pronged attack against the Yaquis, as he actually was, from ships at the mouth of the Yaqui River, as well as overland from the Mayo and Sinaloa Rivers.

The Yaquis decided to discuss peace terms. Actually, there was a peace party and a war party. The Yaquis sent some women to test the atmosphere. The Mayos met them and took them farther south to see the captain. The women were well received, but the captain said that the caciques would have to come down. He guaranteed them a safe return even if they rejected the peace terms.

Two caciques came down, and again they were treated well. Hurdaide gave a horse to one of them, but he wanted all the caciques. Subsequently, 150 caciques and members of the peace party came down to Villa Sinaloa, arriving on April 25, 1610, and there was a great festival and celebration.

Hurdaide met with the delegates and proposed these terms: that they attack no people under the protection of the Spanish government, that they deliver the Ocoroni rebels, and that they return the supplies they had captured. In return, the Yaquis would have the assistance of the Spanish government if they were attacked.

The caciques returned and informed the others of the terms. They also related the impressive things they had seen. The war party lost influence, and it was decided to accept the terms. They could not return the horses, which they said were running wild. The Yaquis also sent fourteen boys to Sinaloa to attend school.

In Sinaloa, it had usually been the people under thirty who were attracted by Christianity, as the older people found it harder to change their ways. With the Yaquis, it was somewhat different. The younger people made up the war party, and the older caciques made the commitment to an alliance with the Spanish. The people later made a strong commitment to Christianity, and there was now nothing holding up the evangelization of southern Sonora except the lack of missionaries.

Hurdaide started construction of a fort on the Fuerte River in 1610. Many Mayos volunteered to help build the fort. A detachment of soldiers would be kept at the fort, but Villa Sinaloa remained the headquarters. The fort grew into a modern town, called Fuerte, a stop for the railroad coming from the Sierras.

In 1611, the bishop of Guadalajara came to administer the sacrament of confirmation. It was the first visit by a bishop, and it was a big event. The people were impressed by the bishop, and the bishop was impressed by the devotion of the people. He confirmed eight thousand people over a five-day period at Villa Sinaloa.[3]

The Jesuits had their annual meeting at Sinaloa in July of 1613. John Velasco was sick, but he felt obliged to go. By the time he arrived from Mocorito, he was dying. He was placed in one of the rooms on the straw sleeping mat that he had brought from Mexico twenty years earlier. He received the last sacraments, insisting that he get on his knees to receive the Eucharist. The other Jesuits gathered around him to say the prayers for the dying. When he asked if he would be saved, they said yes, suggesting that he entrust himself to the Divine Mercy. Before he died, he mentioned that he had never committed a serious sin against chastity. He is buried in Sinaloa beside Gonzalo de Tapia, the young superior who had thought him lacking the right stuff.

John Velasco had written a grammar of the Cáhita language as it was spoken on the Sinaloa River. He was also writing a grammar of the Tahue language, probably as it was spoken on the Mocorito River. The manuscripts were very valuable to new Jesuits, but they were not published.

In 1613, Peter Velasco had trouble in the mountains on the upper Sinaloa River. There were two enemy factions within the Camanito

Clan (or small nation), but they had reconciled and become Christian. One day an angry dispute erupted during an athletic contest. Velasco was present and was able to calm the situation, but one group decided to leave the mission. They attacked the other group and killed two people before they left. The group that left then harassed Christian villages as far south as Topia.

In 1614, the two groups fought a pitched battle, and Velasco thought the whole mission was breaking up. He asked Hurdaide for help, and the captain came with seven soldiers and fifty Indian bowmen, an action that brought some stability. Hurdaide left the seven soldiers in the area, but it was another two years before there was real peace.

At this time, after nine years on the Fuerte River and twenty-three years in Sinaloa, the Jesuits decided to send a missionary to the Mayo Nation on the next river to the north.

CHAPTER 7

Sonora, 1614–1767

Peter Méndez was in Mexico for a rest, and he wanted to go to the Mayo River. In fact, superiors had promised him that he could go when the time was right, so he returned to Sinaloa. He was in such a hurry that he did not stay long enough at Villa Sinaloa to see the other Jesuits in the area. He went to the Mayo early in 1614, and he would be the only Jesuit there for a few years.

Méndez left a description of his first days.

> The Mayos were advised of our coming to give the holy baptism, which they had many times requested, and that they should come together in order to receive it. Although they were scattered because of hunger, they responded to the message by coming together in selected pueblos. About 20 miles before coming to a pueblo, the cacique would meet us and inform us of the preparation. Further along, 15 principal people received us. Before arriving at the first pueblo on the river, 400 Indians came out with their women and children to meet us with joy, adorned with multicolored feathers. They had erected crosses along the way which made us shed tears of devotion.
>
> They had erected arches, not triumphant like those of Mexico, but they well proclaimed the glorious triumph of Christ, King of kings and Lord of lords, over His enemies. A great number of people came out on horseback and on foot. They arranged themselves in lines to be counted, the men and boys in one line, the women and maidens in another. They had put up bowers of vines and branches, made like chapels, where the little ones would be baptized.
>
> We arrived at the pueblo. From here to the sea, in 45 miles, there are some 20,000 people in seven pueblos. A great number of people are missing because they are in the mountains looking for food since the hunger is great. This does not count other people spread along the Gulf of California.

The caciques from along the shore came at the command of the captain. They promised they would settle in the town which the captain designated because it was close to their fisheries. So altogether there is a great population.

In the first 15 days, to the glory of Our Lord and the consolation of superiors who sent me, I have baptized 3,100 children and 500 adults, not counting a great number of old people. There are more than 500 other children and adults who have died after being baptized. They have gone to enjoy the company of Our Lord with the guarantee of salvation.

I had arrived on foot and was very tired. However, before the Indians could scatter, I baptized 500 or 600 without stopping until I finished all of them. The patience of Captain Hurdaide edified me very much. From there I baptized others including 17 principal people. It appears to me that these are the best Christians I have encountered in all the missions in which I have been.

During Lent of that first year, many people made their first confession and first Holy Communion, and during Holy Week there were penitential processions of blood. The following year, Méndez wrote with the same enthusiasm.

Never have I instructed people who are so quick to learn so much doctrine. They do not tire of prayer. Those who are catechumens one moment, are teachers of the catechumens next moment. For this they hurry to the church as if there were a meal waiting for them. At night in the houses nothing is heard except those who have come together in order to say the prayers.[1]

It should not be assumed that Méndez was baptizing without instruction. In the beginning, he was baptizing mostly children, old people, and people in danger of death from hunger and disease. Also, many people had already been prepared for baptism by catechists, and people would receive further instruction before making their first Holy Communion. Within four years, sixteen thousand had been baptized.

In 1616, the Jesuit superior in Sinaloa sent Andrew Pérez de Rivas, who had been on the lower Fuerte River for eleven years, to Mexico to obtain permission from the viceroy and the provincial to advance to the Yaqui River. Rivas obtained permission and returned with Thomas Basilio, an Italian Jesuit. On the way back, Rivas heard about the revolt of the Tepehuanes. He and Basilio made a big detour in order to avoid the rebellious area.

The rebellion of the Tepehuanes meant great danger for the mission of Peter Velasco, which bordered on Tepehuán villages in the mountains. The Tepehuanes came to Velasco's mission when he was absent in order to ask the people to rebel. They also approached the people of Topia and San Andrés and sent envoys as far as the Yaquis. When the Tepehuanes were rebuffed, they became hostile. The Acaxées fought a battle to drive the Tepehuanes from their area. South of San Andrés, the Xixime people fought a battle with a war party, influenced by the Tepehuanes, within their own nation.

The influential family of Peter Velasco was very worried about his dangerous position. When his family asked the provincial to transfer him to Mexico, Peter argued against the move. He said that he had influence with the people as founder of the mission and as a longtime missionary. He said he knew two languages and was working on a third. If he were replaced, the new Jesuit would have to start all over. So he was left on the river for another five years. When he was recalled (forty years old, after fourteen years at the mission), he taught at the Colegio Maximo. Later, he had two separate terms as provincial.

There were three Jesuits on the Mayo River by 1617. Fathers Andrew Pérez de Rivas and Thomas Basilio now traveled north past the Mayo to the Yaqui River, and Rivas described their entrance to the Yaqui Nation.

> The two of us left the Mayo on Ascension Thursday, 1617, with four Suaquis. We had in our company neither soldiers nor other Spanish. The Suaquis would be catechists, would help with the Mass, and would be god-parents of those who were to be baptized. We had previously advised the Yaqui caciques of our entrance. They brought their people together in certain pueblos. As we entered their land, we noticed that men, women, and even children were holding in their hands small crosses, made of cane. This encouraged us. It indicated that they really did wish to become Christians. We were received at the first pueblo with arches, although triumphant and attractive, yet humble, made from the branches of trees.[2]

The people gathered around the two Jesuits. Rivas began to speak in their own language, which was almost the same as Suaqui, which he knew. He taught the existence of a creator God and of a future life that the people would have, receiving the reward or punishment that they merit in this life with good works or bad. He taught the necessity of holy baptism for the salvation of souls and mentioned that many nations, who dwell in neighboring regions, had received baptism.

Finally, he said he would begin the work of conversion, which they had requested, by baptizing the smaller children. He put on the surplice, stole, and white cope that he had brought for the occasion, and began the ceremony. There was a group of two hundred children of seven years or less. He baptized them, giving much joy to the parents and to himself, and so concluded the mission of this blessed day.

Rivas later mentioned a female hechicero, or medicine woman. She told one of the Jesuits that the reason they had not been killed was because of the good they did for the people. She also believed that the prayer of the Mass gave the Jesuits protection.

Rivas's companion, Thomas Basilio, spent thirty years as a priest with the Yaquis.[3] In the beginning, he was almost killed when a man's child died after being baptized, and the father blamed Basilio and shot him in the chest with a poisoned arrow. Another Yaqui sucked out as much poison as he could, and Basilio recovered. Later in life, Basilio published *El Arte y Catecismo en Lengua Cáhita*.[4]

In 1619, Father Martin Bourgeois and a companion went to Movas and Onabas in the vicinity of the middle Yaqui River in order to start work among the Pimas Bajos (Lower Pimas), who were very friendly to the Spanish. Some of them had gone down to the Sinaloa River, even before the Jesuits arrived in Sinaloa, to establish the village of Bamoa, downriver from Villa Sinaloa. After the Jesuits arrived at Villa Sinaloa, other Pimas from the middle Yaqui went to join their relatives at Bamoa. Others came to visit, but they could not stay because the land would not support more people. They were promised missionaries on the middle Yaqui as soon as possible.

Hurdaide wanted missionaries with the Pimas Bajos to help check any possible trouble with the populous Yaqui nation on the lower Yaqui River. The Jesuits had originally planned to recall Hernando Santarén from Topia so that he could found the mission with the Pimas Bajos at the same time that Rivas and Basilio went to the Yaquis, but Santarén was killed in the Tepehuán revolt of 1616.

When the Jesuits advanced to the Mayo and Yaqui Rivers, they were moving into the present-day State of Sonora. In comparison to Sinaloa, they found the Sonoran land more attractive and fertile. Five valleys run from north to south in the center and western parts of the state. The streams and rivers also flow from north to south before coming together and flowing west to the gulf. However, although there was more water and fertility, the climate was still very hot, and there could be drought and famine just as in Sinaloa.

In Sinaloa, the rivers run from east to west, and the Jesuits had worked a long time on each river before advancing to the next one. In Sonora, however, it was possible to work up the rivers toward new people without a lot of red tape with officials in Mexico.

The Jesuits found it easier to relate to the people in Sonora. The four principal nations were the Mayo, Yaqui, Pima, and Opata. The Yaquis lived on the lower Yaqui River. The Pimas lived on the middle Yaqui River and in the north and northwest of the state. The Opatas lived in the center and northeast of the state. The Mayo, Yaqui, and Opata languages were Cáhita languages; the Pima language was different but

The Pimas Bajos in the State of Sonora

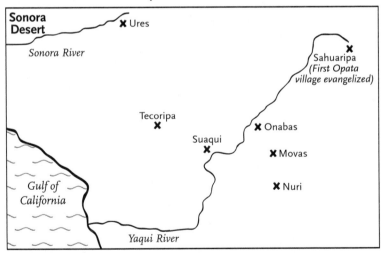

Fig. 16 The Pimas Bajos had about ten villages near the middle Yaqui River, separated from the Pimas Altos by the large Opata Nation. The Pimas Altos lived in north central Sonora and in Arizona. The Opatas had fifty or more agricultural villages in central and northeast Sonora. Ures was an important Pima Bajo pueblo upriver from present-day Hermosillo. Ures, Suaqui, and Sahuaripa are now *municipios,* similar to county seats in the United States.

still Uto-Aztecan. A smaller nomadic people, the Seris, with a language related to the Yuma of Arizona and to the California languages, lived along the gulf in the desert area of northwest Sonora.

The people of Sonora were progressive. When the Jesuits arrived, they were in the process of building adobe houses in place of palm huts. Also, better dressed than the people of Sinaloa, they used the fiber of the maguey cactus and the cotton plant to spin and weave cloth. They had their own method of spinning and weaving, and they were slow to adopt the more efficient European method. It was the custom among the Pimas Bajos for the men to produce cloth, as it was among the Pueblo people of New Mexico, but among the Opatas, the women did this work. The cloth was used to make blankets, loincloths, skirts, and shawls. Apparently, because the people wore more clothes, they used less body paint and had fewer tattoos. They were also accomplished in making baskets, some of which could hold water, and they had shoes.

They grew the usual foods, and there were wild grapes in the area. The grapevine and the cotton plant were native to the Americas. However, it turned out that the grapevine did poorly in Sonora, and expensive altar wine had to be brought in.

In 1620, Peter Méndez, now sixty-two years old with six years on the Mayo, was recalled to Mexico for the second time. But Méndez was not ready for semiretirement, and he asked to go back. When the provincial agreed to his proposal, the Jesuit set out for the third time on the three-month journey to the northwest coast. When he arrived, he was assigned to work with the Yaquis on the Yaqui River, where there were now six Jesuits.

In 1621, the Jesuits decided to establish a second regional superior, who would be independent of the regional superior at Villa Sinaloa. The new superior would live at Torin, a principal Yaqui village, and he would be superior of the Jesuits on the Mayo, the lower Yaqui, and the middle Yaqui.

In May of 1622, Captain Hurdaide reported that there were 80,000 Christians among the 185,000 people who were under his authority. At that time, after thirty-one years on the coast, there were thirty-one

Jesuits, four of them brothers. Sixteen of the priests were in Sinaloa, and eleven were in Sonora.

Two important people died in 1626: Father Martin Pérez, founder of the mission with Gonzalo de Tapia, and Captain James Martinez Hurdaide. The next year, Brother Francis Castro died. The first phase of the mission effort on the coast was ending after thirty-five years.

James Martinez Hurdaide had been captain for twenty-seven years, and his administration had facilitated the work of the Jesuits. During his years of service, he went on twenty military expeditions, and the expense of these expeditions was a heavy burden on Hurdaide. When he went to Mexico the second time, in 1604, the government was spending seventeen thousand pesos a year for the administration of Sinaloa. This included a salary of two thousand pesos for Hurdaide. There were thirty-four soldiers before 1604, whose total yearly salaries were about ten thousand pesos. The soldiers also had to be fed and housed, although they supplied their own horses, equipment, and some food. Six Jesuits each received three hundred pesos a year. So there was almost no money left over for administrative expenses.

Hurdaide had been given a land grant, or an *encomienda*, and he was an *encomendero*. It seems that Hurdaide himself was expected to finance the administration of the province, but there were no big markets on the coast where he could sell cattle and horses. He was probably raising horses, as he seems to have had a lot of them. For example, when he went on an expedition in 1612 with two thousand non-Christian Indian allies, he promised them a horse for every prisoner whom they did not kill, especially for women and children.

By 1615, over halfway through his term of office, Hurdaide was in debt for forty thousand pesos. He reached the point where interest on the debt must have been taking his salary. He tried to get relief a few times, not by applying for an emergency appropriation, but by asking for an advance on his salary. On the other hand, the government in Mexico did pay for the construction of the fort on the Fuerte River in 1610, with a grant of two thousand pesos.

Many later governors would solve these financial problems by not providing police protection for the people of the region. For example, one governor used the soldiers to hunt for pearls in oysters along the coast, and some later governors would be indifferent to raids by nomadic people like the Seris and the Apaches on Christian villages.

When Captain Hurdaide died in 1626, Father Peter Méndez was a pastor with the Yaquis, with whom he had been for four years. Two years later, the Jesuit superior asked Méndez, now sixty-nine years old, to begin the mission to the Opatas by moving to the village of Sahuaripa on the upper Yaqui River. Sahuaripa was beyond the Pimas Bajos and is as far north as the modern city of Hermosillo on the Sonora River. At Sahuaripa, Méndez was 240 miles north of Villa Sinaloa, where he had started, and he spent eleven years with the Opatas. When he was eighty years old, he was sent for retirement to the Casa Profesa in Mexico. However, he was still alert and zealous, and he worked five years in Mexico, where he died when he was eighty-five years old on July 23, 1643.

The Jesuits had moved 240 miles in thirty-seven years, but the next advance of 240 miles, to the vicinity of Tucson, would take them another 139 years. Except for the Pimas Altos, the Opata Nation was the last that they evangelized in this area, and the Jesuit missions never linked up with the Franciscan missions in New Mexico.

The advance of the Jesuits was similar to the advance of the Spanish. The Spanish people had quickly expanded over New Spain during the first hundred years of their presence. Their principal motive was mining on the northern plain. They were also into New Mexico relatively early, but after the first hundred years, their expansion almost stopped. However, around 1700, they did move into eastern Texas because of the French presence in Louisiana, and it was after the expulsion of the Jesuits that the Spanish colonized upper California, for fear that the Russians would move down from Alaska.

When Peter Méndez moved to the Opata village of Sahuaripa in 1628, he had little trouble with the new language because the Opatas spoke a Cáhita language, although it was modified by the Pima languages. Méndez also found a people who were more developed in culture and agriculture than any other nation on the coast. In fact, the Opatas were considered the most advanced people between the Mexicans of Mexico

City and the Pueblo people of New Mexico, and they treated their women almost as well as the Spanish treated theirs. The old missionary was also pleased to find that he could get a good night's sleep because the people were not singing and making a lot of noise during the night.

In their religious beliefs, the Opatas had little idea of a creator or supreme being, and there were few traces of idol worship. They did venerate the sun and moon as "brothers," and they had a dance to welcome the new moon. However, they had many superstitions, including rites to placate angry natural elements like thunder, lightning, and hail.

The Opatas lived together in villages and went out to work the land. This was different from the custom of the Yaquis, who lived on the land and came together in the villages for social and political events. Another difference between the two nations was in their dress. The Yaqui men sometimes dressed elaborately, and the women dressed simply. With the Opatas, the men dressed simply, and the women often dressed elaborately. With their clothes and ornaments, the Opata women made as much noise in church as did the Spanish women.

In time, the Opatas became part of the modern Mexican people, and there is no remnant of the nation that still speaks the Opata language. In contrast, there are Yaqui people today who speak the Yaqui language. They live on the lower Yaqui River, and some live in Tucson, Arizona.

Although few new missionaries came in the 1630s, there was an advance to the Sonora River around 1635, when Father Lorenzo Cárdenas went to the Pima Bajo village of Ures, above present-day Hermosillo.

In 1644, there was still just the one fort at Villa Sinaloa for the greatly expanding mission area, and it had been there for fifty years. At this time the captain (or governor) at the fort caused a great deal of trouble. He was abusive not only to the Indians but even to his own soldiers. The local Indians got fed up and left the Villa, but about 160 Nahuatl-speaking Indians stuck it out with the whites who were there.

In the 1640s, two Jesuits died on the Yaqui River during epidemics.

The missionary work continued during the next two decades, and we get a detailed look at the situation in 1662, after seventy-one years on the coast, in a report by a Jesuit visitor to the area. Some of the following information is from his report.

In Sinaloa in 1662, sixteen Jesuit priests served 18,912 people in sixteen parishes. It is better to speak of parishes than of villages because each Jesuit lived in one village and was responsible for one to three other villages. The three or four villages made up a parish, and each parish had a school.

In Sonora, sixteen Jesuit priests served 17,990 people in seventeen parishes, and each parish had a school. A total of 36,902 people were under the pastoral care of the Jesuits in Sinaloa and Sonora, with an average of 1,118 people in each of the thirty-three parishes. Most of the thirty-two Jesuits (compared to fifty-one Jesuits 105 years later when they were expelled) received 350 pesos from the government rather than 300. The decline of the population is obvious, because forty years earlier, Captain Hurdaide had written that there were 80,000 Christians among the 185,000 people who were under his authority.

Also, at this time (1662) in the Sierra around Topia, another twelve Jesuits served 3,851 people, with an average of only 321 people to a parish. Five of the twelve parishes were Acaxée, but Nahuatl, more than Acaxée, was spoken in these parishes (in 1598, there had been an estimated 14,000 Acaxées in the area). Spanish was now being taught in many of the parish schools, but there was no uniform policy with respect to teaching Spanish. Many Jesuits thought the Indians should not be taught Spanish because it made it easier for them to leave the missions.

There was a shortage of vocations to the priesthood and to missionary work at this time. Spain had always tried to keep non-Spanish people out of her colonies, including non-Spanish priests. In 1664, Spain gave permission for non-Spanish Jesuits to enter New Spain, but the non-Spanish Jesuits could not make up more than one-third of the total sent. Most of the non-Spanish Jesuits came from Germany, Italy, and Czechoslovakia. So there was a new missionary expansion from about 1675 to 1730, which included the evangelization of all of the Sierra Madre.

The Jesuits in Europe now started to complain about the expense of educating Jesuits who would work in the missions. It cost about a hundred pesos a year to support a seminarian for six years—two years of novitiate and four years of theology. Around 1700, it was agreed that the Jesuits in New Spain would reimburse the European provinces six hundred pesos for every Jesuit they sent to New Spain.

How were the mission parishes financed? A good description of the economics of the Sonoran parishes was left by a German Jesuit, Ignaz Pfefferkorn, who had eleven years of experience in northern Sonora before the expulsion. He later wrote about the missions when he was back in Europe.[5]

He wrote that the parishes were basically supported by efficiently managed communal agriculture and by the compulsory labor of the Indians. The government contributed 350 pesos. However, the Indians and the Jesuits were mostly on their own in a far-off place where everything manufactured was very expensive. European goods were expensive to start with in Mexico, and then they had to be transported to Sonora on mules at the cost of six pesos per twenty-five pounds. The cost of transportation could be almost as much as the cost of the goods themselves.

The Indians were already farmers before the arrival of the Jesuits, but they tended to be improvident and disorganized. For example, they often did not plant enough food to last from one harvest to the next. This meant that they had to hunt and to search for wild fruit and edible roots in the mountains. It also meant that in a serious emergency they might be forced to consume the corn that they were saving as seed for the next planting.

The Jesuits insisted that the people in the Christian parishes plant enough food on their own plots to last from one harvest to the next, and they often had to provide seed to the Indians. The Indians were also required to work three days a week on the communal land, although three or four weeks would sometimes pass without any required work.

When working on the communal land, the workers received three meals a day, a vegetable-and-meat stew, but no other remuneration. The full-time workers in the parish also had to be supported, as well as widows, orphans, the old, and the incapacitated.

The Jesuits received and disposed of the products of the communal fields. Some goods were stored for future use and for emergency, and the surplus was sold at mining sites for raw gold and silver (not coins). The products sold included corn, vegetables, strips of dried meat, molasses from sugarcane, and tallow for making soap, margarine, and lubricants. The gold and silver were sent to a Jesuit brother in Mexico, who purchased goods for the missions and arranged for their transportation to Sonora. The goods requested by the missionaries included cloth, tobacco, tools, chocolate, knives, scissors, needles, glass beads, medicines, candles, and wine.

The churches were made of adobe with flat log roofs, and their interiors were beautiful, with fine altars, paintings, and valuable chalices and ciboria. Although candles and wine were very expensive, the divine worship was splendid with music, silk vestments, and many lighted candles. A one-pound candle in Sonora cost as much as two sheep or three pounds of chocolate.

Father Ignaz Pfefferkorn, describing the situation before the expulsion of 1767, had interesting things to say about health, disease, and population in Sonora.[6] He wrote that the Sonora Indians were a sturdy people with erect, healthy bodies, who held their heads high. He thought they were healthier than the Spanish because they consumed simple and natural foods and because their bodies were not weakened by venereal diseases, which were very common and widely distributed among all other classes in America. It was rare to see a feeble or deformed Indian, and they suffered much less than the Spanish from things like fevers, back pain, and strokes. It was not rare for an Indian to live to an advanced age.

A pregnant woman avoided neither danger nor heavy exertion, yet the birth of a dead or deformed child was extremely rare. An Indian woman would go off by herself and give birth unattended. After she washed herself and the infant, she returned to her normal duties. Infants were allowed to lie and roll about naked on the ground like puppies, and the father seemed indifferent to his own children.

The people seemed stoic and fatalistic. For example, it was the custom to shun or almost abandon the sick, and people seemed insensitive to the sufferings of those closest to them. A sick person would be left to lie alone with the hard earth as his or her bed, and a spouse would visit twice a day to bring water and food. The Indians died as they had lived, with tranquillity and indifference.

Father Ignaz Pfefferkorn described many natural remedies for sickness in Sonora, which he himself administered. For example, the juice from mescal leaves cured scurvy. He mentioned that the medicine men sometimes brought real relief by administering herbs but that in general they were quacks. He added that some of the Spanish doctors were also quacks. He gave credit to the Spanish women of the area for caring for the sick of both races.

He said that it was the opinion of the Jesuits of his time that the Indian population had decreased by more than half in Sonora during the sixty-seven years before the expulsion (during the 1700s). The main reason was smallpox, which assaulted the area every nine or ten years, but this was not a sufficient explanation. He said that the fertility of the Indians was in general not exceptional, but he did not know whether their gradual decline in numbers resulted from infertility or from other causes.

It is often assumed that the Jesuits increased the mortality of epidemics by bringing people together into larger villages, but the opposite is probably true. There would have been better sanitation and greater cleanliness in the mission villages, and during epidemics, food and nursing care were available. Some people recovered and probably helped build up resistance to the diseases in the general population. There was certainly a great decline of the Indian population in the Jesuit area, but at least on the gulf coast it did not implode as in other parts of North America.

As more Spanish homesteaders moved to Sonora, a great antagonism developed between the Jesuits and the white ranchers and farmers. The efficient missions were in direct competition with the settlers when it came to selling food products to the miners. The settlers also resented the fact that the missions had the best land and water, and both settlers and miners saw the Jesuits as an obstacle to the exploitation of native labor. Nevertheless, until the king turned on them at the end, the Jesuits continued to have the support of government officials in Spain, who saw the missions as an inexpensive way to secure the frontier.

Here is a summary of the founders of the missions on the different rivers.

- 1591, Sinaloa River, Gonzalo de Tapia and Martin Pérez
- 1605, Fuerte River, Peter Méndez and two companions
- 1614, Mayo River, Peter Méndez
- 1617, Yaqui River, Andrew Pérez de Rivas and Thomas Basilio
- 1619, the Pimas Bajos on the middle Yaqui, Martin Burgensio and companion
- 1628, the Opatas on the upper Yaqui, Peter Méndez
- About 1635, Sonora River, Lorenzo Cárdenas
- 1687, the Pimas Altos, Eusebio Kino

The Jesuits were on the Sinaloa River fourteen years, 1591–1605, before they moved north; on the Fuerte River nine years, 1605–1614, before they moved north; on the Mayo River three years, 1614–1617, before they moved north; and at the Yaqui River a long time, eighteen years, before moving to the Sonora River.

CHAPTER 8

The Tarahumaras, 1611–1767

The city of Chihuahua, the capital of the State of Chihuahua, is in the center of the state and 220 miles directly south of El Paso, Texas. The ride south from El Paso is through a harsh desert where bare hills and mountains rise up here and there on the desert plain. About forty miles outside the city, a few trees appear, and then there are farms and apple orchards.[1]

The northern boundary of the Tarahumara Nation was a line through the modern cities of Chihuahua, Cuauhtémoc, and Guerrero. The Tarahumaras lived well south of this line on the plain and also southwest of the line in the Sierra, and they still live there.

At Chihuahua, there were mines and Spanish people after 1700, but Cuauhtémoc is a new city, founded about 1910. Presently, thousands of Mennonites from Canada and Germany live on farms around Cuauhtémoc. The city itself is Mexican and relatively prosperous,

Upper Boundary of the Tarahumara Nation

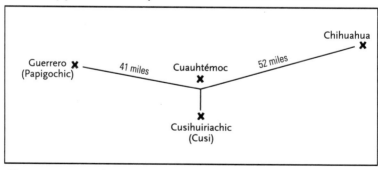

Fig. 17

although there are thousands of poor workers in the city. Some Tarahumaras also live in the modern city, some working and some begging.

About ten miles south of Cuauhtémoc is a little place called Cusihuiriachic, where fifty or so Mexican people dwell near a mine. The place is on a small stream within a circle of hills in the middle of flat farmland. Now called Cusi by the inhabitants, it is the place where the upper Tarahumara mission began.

There was a silver strike at Cusi at one time, and the native people left. When the whites left, the natives returned. Then, when there was a second silver strike, the Tarahumaras left and did not return.

Guerrero is on the site of the former village of Papigochic, and the Papigochic River runs north through the site. It then turns west and becomes part of the Yaqui River, which flows into the Gulf of California.

A railroad comes down from the Texas border to the city of Chihuahua. The train continues from Chihuahua to Cuauhtémoc, and between these cities the land rises from 4,800 to 6,800 feet. The train continues west toward Guerrero before turning south into the higher Sierra. For forty miles south of Cuauhtémoc and Guerrero there are farms, but the farms become fewer as the train goes higher. Tall pine trees appear at about 7,300 feet, and the train goes as high as 8,000 feet, where the land is broken by deep gorges. Magnificent tall pine trees extend about a hundred miles along the rail line until the altitude starts to decrease. The train stops at a spot overlooking the Copper Canyon, which is bigger and deeper than the Grand Canyon.

The train finally stops at a town called Témoris, which was part of the Jesuits' Chínipas mission. Then it comes down from the Sierra in three great concentric circles within the mountains around Témoris. The rail line then follows the Fuerte River across Sinaloa to the Gulf of California.

Also coming down from Texas is the Continental Divide, which runs between Chihuahua and Cuauhtémoc. Here, at the top of the continent, four Jesuits were martyred along the Papigochic River at the northern border of the Tarahumara Nation.

The Sierra runs to the southwest from the city of Chihuahua, but directly south of Chihuahua is the plain. Some 125 miles south of Chihuahua is the city of Parral, on the plain and still in the State of

The Baja Tarahumara

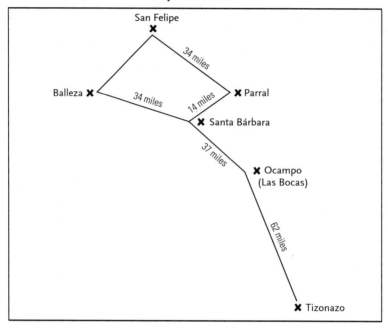

Fig. 18

Chihuahua. To the west and northwest of Parral was the mission of Baja, or lower, Tarahumara, founded before the mission of Alta Tarahumara. The land around Parral is fairly fertile, and the Baja Tarahumara mission, although the number of people was never great, was fairly prosperous, with farm products, chickens, and livestock.

Some small rivers around Parral flow north to the Rio Grande, but north of Parral and extending to Texas, the main feature is a desert. To the east and southeast of Parral are mountains and more desert, in which is located the huge Basin of Mapimí, which was a refuge for a hostile and warlike indigenous people. The desert extends east of Parral to the Sierra Madre Oriental in the State of Coahuila. This eastern Sierra runs south through the State of Coahuila. Then it widens out and extends to Zacatecas, where it meets the Sierra Occidental.

The principal hostile nation in the desert, the Toboso, was joined by individuals who left the Concho, Cabeza, and Salinero Nations. None of these people survived as distinct nations, and little is known of their languages except that the Conchos were Uto-Aztecans, and the Tobosos are thought to be related to the Apaches. The Franciscans had missions with the Conchos, some of which were east of Parral, as well as to the north of the Tarahumaras, even north of Chihuahua City.

Sometimes scholars guess at the languages of a place from scant evidence, such as place-names. However, it is accepted that the original languages of northeastern New Spain were related to the languages of Baja California. In other words, the original inhabitants of northern New Spain must have been separated in the distant past by expanding Uto-Aztecan people. Other languages related to the languages of Baja California (a new family of languages) are most of the languages of the Pueblo people of New Mexico, the Yuma language on the Colorado River in western Arizona, and the Seri language on the Gulf of California at the Sonora River.

The first contact that the Jesuits had with the Tarahumaras, not counting the Chínipas area near Sinaloa, was in 1604 when Father John Fonte visited them from the Tepehuán area. This Jesuit, who was mentioned earlier, arrived at Durango in 1600 to help Jerome Ramirez. In 1607, Fonte made a second visit to the Tarahumaras as far as Papigochic, or present-day Guerrero.

Later in the year, when Fonte was back with the Tepehuanes, other Tepehuanes came south from the area around the future pueblo of Balleza and requested help for a war against the Tarahumaras. The Tepehuanes who were with Fonte suggested that he be consulted, and he counseled peace. When his counsel was accepted, Fonte went north with the Tepehuanes to the area around Balleza, where he met and established friendly relations with over eight hundred Tarahumaras, who invited him to establish a mission village in their country.

Fonte went south to Durango in the spring of 1608, as was also mentioned earlier, to seek support for a permanent move to the Tarahumaras. The governor promised support, but permission had to come from the viceroy. Fonte wrote from Durango:

> I am in a happy and enthusiastic frame of mind, seeing the door now open for numerous conversions. I am in good health (thirty-four years old), and I shall go forward without the aid of soldiers, whom I have always avoided.

> The natives are happy to see us in their country unaccompanied, for at the sight of soldiers and other Spanish they flee.

It was almost three years later, in January of 1611, before Fonte could go permanently to the north. He went with four Tarahumara caciques, and he was well received everywhere. He went about fifty miles beyond Balleza and met many people. He wrote:

> Many of the Tarahumaras live in caves, some of which are large enough to hold several small dwellings for a related group. Unlike other nations, they bury their dead in cemeteries apart. Alongside the deceased they place household furnishings and food for the journey. The dwelling of the deceased is destroyed or burnt, and the relatives of the deceased cut their hair in mourning.
>
> The women are good weavers, making cloth from the fiber of the agave. At first, the women shrank from me in bashfulness. Later, seeing their men in easy conversation with me, they came up and spoke as with their father. They, as well as the men, asked me to return again to their country. I preached about the necessity of holy baptism in order to be saved.[2]

Fonte was told that there were 3,170 Tarahumaras in the general area. At this time, he and the people, both Tepehuanes and Tarahumaras, founded the pueblo of Balleza, about thirty-four miles northwest of Santa Bárbara. One of the first things they did was to visit the Spanish at Santa Bárbara in order to establish good relations. The caciques insisted on an armed escort of thirty braves in order to show the Spanish their esteem for Fonte. John Fonte and another Jesuit worked in this area for five years until they were killed in the Tepehuán revolt of 1616.

The Jesuits returned to the Tepehuán area after the revolt, but it was twenty-three years before they reestablished the Tarahumara mission. They did visit the Tarahumaras from the Tepehuán area, and sometimes a Jesuit would stay a few months with the Tarahumaras.

In 1623, the Tarahumaras themselves decided to establish the pueblo of Ocampo (called Las Bocas during the colonial period), about thirty-five miles southeast of Parral. They also founded other pueblos near Balleza, and in 1626, caciques of the Tarahumaras went down to Durango to request permanent missionaries. In 1631, mines were discovered at Parral. The Spanish had been at Santa Bárbara, about fourteen miles southwest of Parral, for a long time before this date.

Two Jesuits reestablished the mission in Baja Tarahumara in June of 1639. The superior and second founder, after John Fonte, was Jerome Figueroa. Originally from Spain, Figueroa had spent seven years in the Tepehuán area. The first thing he did in the Tarahumara was to travel around to meet everyone and to see the country. Then he established his base on the Concho River in the new village of San Felipe, about thirty-four miles northwest of Parral. This village would be the headquarters of the lower mission, and within a few years there were five Jesuits in the area.

The 1640s were a time of general disorder in this area. A great number of Spanish had been attracted to the area by the mines, and there were at least ten mining sites north of the city of Durango. Thirteen hundred indigenous Sinaloa Christians worked in the mines, and the Spaniards did not allow the Jesuits to approach them.

The Spanish took natives both from the missions and from pagan villages for work in the mines. The people were promised food and eight yards of cloth for two months of work. At the end of two months, they would often be told that they would have to work two more months before being paid. Also, children were sometimes kidnapped in order to be adopted or to be used as servants.

Mining was labor intensive, and there were two methods for refining the ore. In both methods, the ore was crushed into a powder by animal-driven machines. The first method then used stone furnaces, billows, and fire. The silver formed into marbles, or kernels, in the ashes, and the ashes then had to be sifted and washed. This method was fast, but a lot of the silver was lost. Charcoal was needed, and many mining sites became denuded of wood. The second method used mercury imported from Europe. A slush was made with the crushed ore, the mercury, and water. The slush was spread over a big, flat rock or a cement surface. Then the mixture had to be kept moist and stirred for over two months. This method was more efficient, and about 60 percent of the mercury could be recovered.

Unskilled workers, carrying ore to the surface, were often exploited. But the skilled workers had to be paid, or they would move on. In fact, the skilled miners were the best-paid laborers in New Spain. At the end of the workday, a miner could fill a small bag with ore, which was worth five to eight pesos at a time when unskilled laborers made less than one peso a day. The Hispanicized Indians from the center of the country may also have done well, but the northern Indians were being paid with the promise of eight yards of cloth. The Jesuits called it slavery and said the wage was an unjust pittance. The local civil authority did nothing about the injustice, and the civil authority was also rather indifferent to the raids by the Tobosos, which were particularly bad during 1644 and 1645.

The Tobosos, like the later Apaches, usually attacked pagan or Christian indigenous villages instead of Spanish towns because the Spanish towns were better defended. However, isolated Spanish farms and ranches were often attacked, and the livestock outside Spanish towns were sometimes taken.

The Franciscan missions suffered more than the Jesuit missions from the Toboso raids. They were more exposed in the east, and the Franciscans also extended to the north as far as New Mexico. Still, the Tobosos attacked as far south as the Jesuit missions of the Lagoon area in the south of Coahuila, and many of the Cabeza people in one Jesuit village, Tizonazo, joined the Tobosos.

The Tobosos were defeated in one battle in 1646. Then, in 1648, some of the Tarahumaras rose in rebellion for a short time.

In 1646, the Jesuits were removed from the Lagoon area and replaced by diocesan clergy. It was really too early for this move, which weakened the general structure of the missions and made the south of Coahuila more vulnerable to Toboso raids. Also, the Spanish were after the land in the Lagoon area. There was a lawsuit by the Indians against the white settlers concerning land and/or water rights, and the Jesuits were involved on the side of the Indians. The Indians won the lawsuit, as they usually did, but in time they still ended up losing the land. After the Jesuits left, the Christian indigenous villages greatly declined, and many of the Laguneros joined the Tobosos. The Jesuits did retain their church and college in Parras. During these years, there was also a struggle between the Jesuits and some of the bishops in Mexico over jurisdiction.

Father Cornelius Beudin came to the Tarahumara in 1648. From Belgium and thirty-three years old, he had taught for some years in Europe. After arriving in New Spain, he learned Nahuatl with more-than-usual ease and then spent some time at San Felipe learning the Tarahumara language.

The governor had sent some settlers and soldiers north to the Papigochic River. The Spanish founded a village called Villa Aguilar, a few miles from the Tarahumara village of Papigochic in the present-day city of Guerrero. When the governor asked the Jesuits for a missionary to attend to both the Spanish and the Tarahumaras, they sent Cornelius Beudin. This was unusual because the missionaries usually went to a mission only after visiting and being invited by the indigenous. But Beudin was very successful, for he had those gifts for language and music that were common to many Jesuits who stayed in the missions.

Beudin traveled around and invited more people to come together. Six thousand Tarahumaras congregated at or near Papigochic. Living at Papigochic in the company of one soldier, Beudin built a temporary church with the help of the people.

As time went on, the people started to turn against Beudin because the Spanish were forcing the Tarahumaras to work for them, and there were other unspecified injustices. Father Beudin went down to Parral to seek relief, but the governor did nothing. One of the Spanish at the villa threatened Beudin's life because of his interference. This Spaniard may even have been making an attempt on Beudin's life when the priest's soldier companion walked in.

The Tarahumaras now became more suspicious of Beudin. He had obtained no redress for their grievances, and he was in continual contact with the Spanish at Aguilar because he was also their pastor. So the Tarahumaras decided to do away with Beudin and the soldier. Before dawn on Saturday, June 4, 1650, the house where Beudin and the soldier lived was set on fire. When they came outside, they were shot with arrows and clubbed to death. One of the leaders of the attack, Tepóraca, was a Christian, a ladino (a person who understood and spoke Spanish), and a former good friend of the Spanish.

The Spanish soldiers marched after the people, who all fled from the area to the mountains. The Spanish were beaten back on two occasions, but after continuous harassment, the Tarahumaras accepted peace and returned to the river. When many Jesuits asked to take the place of Father Beudin, Anthony Basile, forty-one, was chosen. From Naples, Italy, Father Basile had entered the Society at age twenty-one and had come to New Spain in 1642. He had taught five years at Tepotzotlán and for some time at St. Gregory in Mexico and had been asking for the mission for eight years. He was soon in Papigochic, where so much needed to be done. Wounds had to be healed, the church rebuilt, and contacts made again with surrounding villages.

While Basile was busy with these tasks, Tepóraca was planning to drive the Spanish not only from the Papigochic River but also from the whole State of Chihuahua and as far south as possible. He worked quietly for almost two years and successfully kept his plan hidden. Finally, Tepóraca and some of his followers clashed in a careful and deliberate way with some Spanish soldiers. When the report spread that the Tarahumaras had risen, the Spanish rushed to Aguilar from five or so ranches. It is not certain how many Spanish were in the area, but as there were no mines, it would have been scores rather than hundreds.

The Spanish used the residence of the captain in Aguilar as a kind of fort. On Friday, March 2, 1652, Tepóraca attacked Aguilar, but it was only to keep the Spanish occupied while a band of Tarahumaras gathered the livestock as well as other useful goods from the farms and took them to a safe place. Tepóraca then withdrew to regroup his forces.

While this was going on, Father Basile was at a village twenty miles to the south. A cacique came from Papigochic to tell him that Aguilar was under siege, and he offered to accompany Basile to Sinaloa or Parral. The Tarahumaras in the village urged Basile to go with the cacique or to remain with them, but Basile decided to return to Aguilar, where there would be people who would want to receive the sacraments before dying. He went back on Friday evening.

The accounts differ as to what happened next, but it seems that Tepóraca attacked before dawn on Saturday when Basile was in the church, and he and his Tarahumara interpreter were killed. The attackers then set fire to the captain's house and killed the people as they came out.

Tepóraca then led his soldiers on an invasion of Baja Tarahumara, killing Spaniards and Christian Indians and destroying villages and churches. The Christian Tarahumaras in the lower area barricaded themselves in two villages and were threatened with extermination if they did not kill the missionaries. When they refused to do the bidding of Tepóraca, he went alone to the east to confer with the Tobosos, who had also rebelled. When the soldiers caught them together and defeated the Tobosos, Tepóraca escaped, and the hostile Tarahumaras withdrew to the Alta Tarahumara. After two or three battles, Tepóraca was captured in February of 1653. He refused the sacraments before he was executed.

During these years, there were five parishes in the Baja Tarahumara. A resident pastor lived in each of the five villages, but each pastor also served two or more other villages, which were called *visitas*. There was a shortage of priests and no expansion of the mission during these years.

The Tobosos continued to raid during these years. They usually did not attack villages, but they raided livestock and killed any isolated Tarahumara. For example, it is reported that over the years, about fifty people from San Felipe were caught and killed as they worked away from the village on farmland or with the livestock. There was a devastating epidemic in 1662.

Roderick Castillo (Rodrigo del Castillo) was captured by the Tobosos in 1667. From Puebla, he had entered the Society when he was seventeen and had been a missionary for twenty years. He was pastor at Ocampo and forty-five or forty-six years old. His own account about what happened has been published by a modern historian.[3]

A sick person had been restored to health after praying to St. Francis Xavier. This person wanted to give thanks for the miracle by holding a fiesta in the big church in the village of Tizonazo. Father Castillo was invited to give the sermon because he had been pastor for a year at Tizonazo before moving sixty-two miles north to be pastor at Ocampo. Both places are northeast of Durango. The people at Tizonazo were Cabezas, and the people at Ocampo were Tarahumaras.

After the celebration in Tizonazo, Castillo was returning to Ocampo in a party of sixteen. With him were three Spanish soldiers, two Spanish men with muskets, one Salinero, two Tarahumara choirboys, and seven Tarahumaras armed with bows and arrows, apparently young men or teenagers who were musicians or part of the choir.

When they were halfway home, they dismounted for a rest. It was noon, perhaps on Friday, June 17, 1667. Nearby was an arroyo (a streambed that is usually dry). Suddenly, 150 indigenous who had been watching and waiting appeared from the arroyo.

The first flight of arrows did not injure anyone, and the Christians formed a defensive line. When the Tarahumaras told Castillo to leave the group, he went with the two children to the arroyo, where he pleaded for the lives of his companions. But the cacique said they had to die because they were soldiers. A Toboso then took charge of Castillo.

At that moment, another indigenous came up and asked, "Do you know me, Father? I'm Juanillo, the brother of Augustina."

Four Forts (Two Built Later) between Parral and Durango

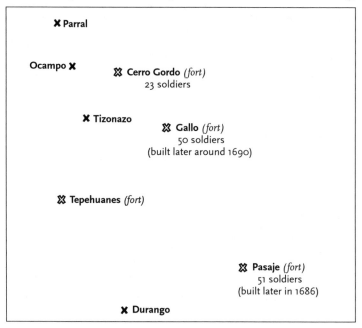

Fig. 19 Pasaje is very near Cuencamé.

Juanillo was a Cabeza from Tizonazo, the place from which Castillo was coming. Juanillo's sister was married to a Tarahumara, apparently at Ocampo. Juanillo was captain of a squad, and a squad must have been twenty-five warriors, because the raiders were operating in six groups of twenty-five.

Juanillo told Castillo not to worry. He said that Castillo would not be harmed because his squad was ladino and Christian. Juanillo then took Castillo's hat and rosary. By this time, Castillo's thirteen companions had been killed, and the clothes were being taken from their bodies. Then a native approached and told Castillo to strip. Castillo gave up his shirt, but he was allowed to keep his undergarments and cassock.

The attackers were coming back to the arroyo, and they were in a very good mood because none of them had been wounded. Each came up and bowed his head so that Castillo could put his hands on his head as a sign of benevolence or blessing.

The two boys were beside Castillo, clutching his cassock in fear. The warriors were friendly to the boys, and they wanted them to join their company. When one of the boys refused, he was shot with an arrow. Castillo removed the arrow, but he could do nothing to stop the bleeding. The boy died rather quickly, and the other boy was taken away.

The group then started toward the mountains to the east. Castillo was on foot, but they later put him on a horse. After they had stopped at a temporary camp to cook some meat, they went much higher into the mountains to a more permanent camp, where they had boys to help with the livestock.

That evening they talked together. They warned Father Castillo, whom they considered to be an *hechicero*, not to call down any sickness upon them. They said that they had captured some Franciscans, but they let them go when they called down an epidemic on the people.

They traveled all day Saturday in the mountains. At 5:00 P.M., a scout reported seeing a squad of soldiers on foot who were separated from their horses. There were only two soldiers with the horses, about two shots of a musket from the main group. These soldiers must have been from the nearby fort at Cerro Gordo. At this time, there were only two forts between Durango and Parral, a distance of about 225 miles, at

Cerro Gordo and Tepehuanes. Two other forts were built later, after the 1680 revolt of the Indians of New Mexico, in order to protect the trade route between Durango and Parral.

Father Castillo's group had been making a sixty-two-mile trip from Tizonazo, which was southwest of Cerro Gordo, to Ocampo, which was between Cerro Gordo and Parral. So the Tobosos had penetrated the defensive line of the Spanish, and they were operating very close to the garrison at Cerro Gordo.

The raiders divided into six groups of twenty-five and quietly descended to lower ground. When they revealed themselves, they had the soldiers trapped. They sent Castillo and some of their own to talk to the soldiers. They told the soldiers that if they gave up their horses, they would be allowed to go free, but the soldiers refused the offer. So both sides prepared for battle, and Castillo was very upset. He wrote that most of the soldiers were boys, presumably meaning teenagers, and that the three soldiers killed the day before were also boys.

Castillo had a mule, which the raiders had given him because they were planning to set him free, and he rode the mule between the indigenous and the soldiers. When the Tobosos asked what he wanted, Castillo pointed out that they had already captured the horses, and he asked them again to let the soldiers go. They agreed and let him go as well.

The whole experience seems to have shattered Castillo both physically and psychologically. His new church, which they had been building for at least seven years, was dedicated in May of the next year, and he died a few months later on August 15, 1668.

In a book of documents edited and published by Luis Gonzalez, there are two earlier reports by Roderick Castillo about Ocampo. He writes that Ocampo is an attractive place on the Florida River, with willow and poplar trees for many miles around. He says that there are 150 people at Ocampo and that there had once been many more, but many had died from the epidemics. He mentions that a previous pastor had died of the contagion after nursing the sick. But the next year he writes that there are four hundred people at Ocampo and also many more Spanish and Tarahumaras on five neighboring haciendas.

He writes that most of the Tarahumaras are ladinos, because of much contact with the Spaniards. Besides their own language, the knowledge of Mexican is common, and there are few born in the pueblo who do not understand or even speak Spanish. He describes the people as enthusiastic and with a lively and deep faith. They send all of their children for catechism both morning and afternoon, and the children learn quickly. The people have a great devotion to the Blessed Sacrament and to our Lady. There is a painting of Our Lady of Guadalupe in a separate chapel. The people attend Mass on Sunday, and on Saturday in honor of our Lady. Their songs, including Christmas carols, are in their own language.

In 1669, the year after Father Castillo died, the Jesuits established a residence and parish in Parral. Since more missionaries, including foreigners, were starting to arrive, it was decided to hold an organizational meeting at Parral in 1673, about evangelizing the Alta Tarahumara.

At the meeting were the governor, caciques of the Tarahumaras and Tepehuanes, businessmen of Parral, civil and church authorities of the city, and several Jesuits. One of the Jesuits was Jerome Figueroa, who founded the Baja Tarahumara mission at San Felipe in 1639. Also, before he went to the Tarahumara, he had spent seven years with the Tepehuanes. He was a veteran of forty-one years and had written two treatises in the Tepehuán and Tarahumara languages that were a great help to new missionaries. Each unpublished treatise included a grammar, a dictionary, a catechism, principal prayers, and the manner of going to confession.

At this meeting, Father Figueroa spoke plainly about the causes of the problems in the past. He said that Spanish greed was the principal cause of Indian revolts and of a twenty-year delay in the advance of the missions. One reason for the Indian revolts was the unjust treatment of the Indian by miner and soldier alike. The just treatment of the Indians, their conversion and pacification, is actually linked to the safety and prosperity of the whole area.

There was general enthusiasm when he finished speaking. Everyone promised to make a fresh start and to help with the establishment of a new mission in the Alta Tarahumara. The meeting ended when the governor from Durango knelt and kissed the hands of the old priest.

Jerome Figueroa was a heroic person. It was a hard mission. He had asked for a new assignment after ten years in the Tarahumara, but superiors had asked him to stay. There were the problems caused by the Europeans, the continual attacks by the Tobosos, and the diseases that seemed to undermine so many of the positive accomplishments. Although the later Baja California mission would be physically more difficult with its severe heat and lack of material things, the Tarahumara mission was the most discouraging.

On the other hand, it should be mentioned that the people of the lower Tarahumara mission were friendly and even enthusiastic. They had come down to settle these villages. The people in the upper Tarahumara would be more reserved, and many would be indifferent. Now it was time to go to the Alta Tarahumara.

Two Jesuits went to Cusi in the Alta Tarahumara in November of 1673. With foreign Jesuits now permitted to enter New Spain, this was

The Jesuit "Upper Mission" of the High Sierras

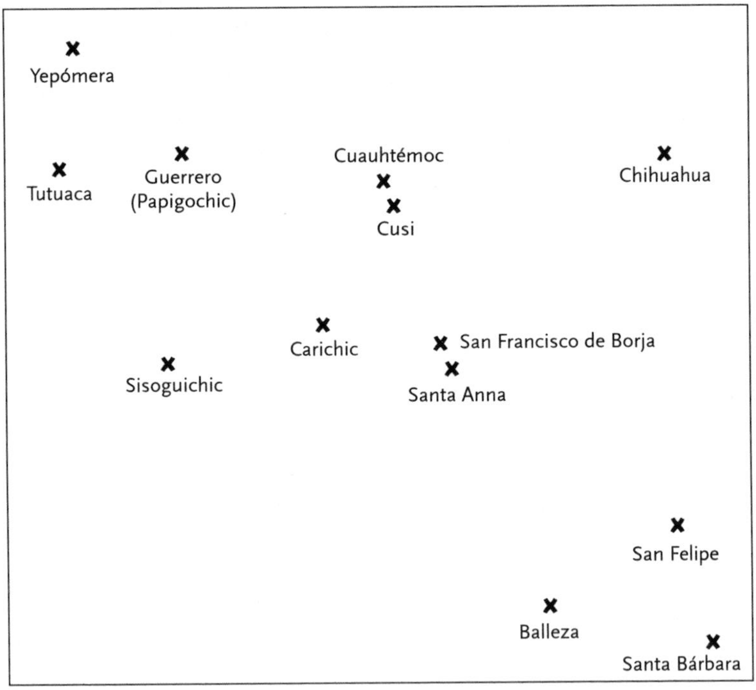

Fig. 20

the beginning of an extensive expansion of the Jesuit missions that included the upper Tarahumara, a renewal of work in the Chínipas area, a move to the north of Sonora and into southern Arizona among the Pima people, and Baja California.

The two Jesuits went to Cusi with about twenty Tarahumaras from the lower region. One of the Tarahumaras was Cacique Don Pablo, a devout Catholic of great prestige. Don Pablo went in order to introduce the Jesuits and to assist with the work. The group was well received at Cusi, and within a year, over three hundred people had become Christians.

However, the two Jesuits found life in the high Sierra too difficult, and within a year, they were replaced by two other Jesuits. These two new Jesuits, Joseph Tardá and Thomas Guadalajara, are considered the founders of the upper mission. Tardá and Guadalajara established their base of operations at Santa Anna, which was closer than Cusi to the Baja Tarahumara. There were a few Spanish and also some Baja Tarahumaras at Santa Anna. From there, they organized the village of San Francisco de Borja, some miles north of Santa Anna. Borja was usually served by a priest from Santa Anna, but Father Joseph Tardá lived there for a while before moving on to Cusi.

Tardá and Guadalajara made a first journey deeper into the Sierra in 1675. They went to Carichic and Papigochic, where they were denied entrance to the villages. They had to be conciliatory, respectful, and patient because there had been so much bloodshed in this area twenty-five years earlier. However, they wanted to see the land, to meet the people, and to let the people get to know them. A ladino told the people that if they accepted the missionaries, soldiers and Spanish would enter the area in a short time, which was more or less true and also inevitable. In fact, there were already Spanish as far north as Chihuahua City. On the other hand, the people knew that their kinfolk were doing well in Baja Tarahumara, and this could always be mentioned by the Jesuits.

The two Jesuits decided to return in September of the same year. Don Pablo and other Tarahumaras went ahead of them to Papigochic, where the Jesuits found some people who were friendly and others who were hostile. They were told that this was not a good time but that they should return on another occasion. When they left Papigochic, they continued to the northwest as far as Yepómera. They met a few people who were Christian and baptized a few others. When they returned from Yepómera along the Papigochic River, they stopped again at Papigochic, and this time they found a friendly reception.

After the Jesuits returned to their home villages, people came to Santa Anna from Carichic and asked Thomas Guadalajara to visit them. When he visited along with some Christian Tarahumaras, the people of Carichic killed two sheep and had a festival for their guests. A hundred people were baptized that day. It was a touching experience for Father Guadalajara, who wrote that he was moved to tears. He appointed catechists, and the people said they would build a chapel and a house with a straw roof for a priest, which they did in fifteen days. It was November 9, 1675.

The Tarahumaras grew corn and beans, and they had sheep, chickens, and horses, but no cattle. They used the horses for travel, and they also sold them to the Spaniards for cloth, tools, and trinkets. The wild animals in the Sierra included bighorn sheep, deer, black bears and grizzlies, pronghorns, wolves, and mountain lions.

Families were united through the female line, with the man becoming part of his wife's family at the time of marriage. Men wore loincloths and no shoes, often wrapping themselves in a square rug. The children went naked and were not punished for wrongdoing, and the people did not understand how God could be good if he punished wrongdoers.

But people responded to God's grace and also to the personalities of the two Jesuits. Thomas Guadalajara, in particular, was much loved. Born in Puebla, New Spain, he had a bachelor's degree when he entered the novitiate at the age of nineteen. After theology and ordination, he was minister at Tepotzotlán. He was sent to the upper Tarahumara, arriving there in August of 1675, when he was twenty-seven. He spent the next forty-five years in the northern area.

After nine years in the Tarahumara, Father Guadalajara was made superior of the college in Durango. During this three-year period, he was also visitor to the Alta Tarahumara, which means that he was the representative of the provincial in the area. He would have visited and talked to every missionary in the area. A visitor usually had the power to make changes of personnel and to name local superiors. During the next three years, he was superior of the residence in Parral, and it was about this time that the Jesuit college was founded there.

During the next six years, Father Guadalajara was superior of the Tepehuán mission. For the next twenty-four years he was in the Baja Tarahumara, where he died in 1720. He was a very spiritual person who lived with particular attention to the vow of poverty. Thomas Guadalajara's writings are abundant and for the most part unpublished. He himself published in Puebla, in 1683, *Compendio del arte de la lengua de los Tarahumares y Guazapares*. In the same year, he published a similar book in Tepehuán.

So it was in November of 1675 that the people of Carichic welcomed Father Guadalajara. In 1676, he was sent to a place far to the northwest between Yepómera and Papigochic to introduce the faith, and in 1677, four more Jesuits were sent to the Alta Tarahumara.

By 1678, when the mission was five years old, there were two more Jesuits (for a total of eight), with five thousand Christians in the upper area. With four thousand Christians in the lower area, there were a total of nine thousand Christian Tarahumaras out of an estimated forty-five thousand people.

At this time, Joseph Neumann and Eusebio Kino were waiting in Spain to go to New Spain. Newman would work in the Tarahumara for fifty-one years, and Kino would be in Sonora and Arizona with the Pima people.

Joseph Neumann arrived at Parral in January of 1681 with a Jesuit companion. Neumann was a thirty-three-year-old German, born in Brussels and reared in Austria, and he was a member of the Jesuits' Bohemian Province. His Jesuit companion was Joseph Ratkay, a baron of Hungary, who died after two and a half years in the Tarahumara. After a few months of language study, Ratkay was assigned to Carichic and Neumann to Sisoguichic. Sisoguichic was thirty miles west of Carichic and on the mission frontier, where the people had little contact with Europeans. A Jesuit had been there a few years earlier, and a primitive church had been erected.

Neumann went with another Jesuit who would introduce him, and he was followed in a short time by a gift of thirty cattle from Carichic. They were met a day's journey from Sisoguichic by five caciques, and when they arrived, there was an arch to welcome them. The people gathered around, and Neumann's companion listed conditions to be met if the Jesuit were to stay. The people had to build a house for the priest, send their children for instruction, and bring in people from the area who had not been baptized. They agreed, and the other Jesuit left after one day because of worry about sick people in his own village. Neumann was on his own with a weak knowledge of the language and with sixty families living along a stream in a valley. He was also pastor of the people in four other valleys rather distant from Sisoguichic. He described the people and his first days.

> They are simple of nature and unpolished, swarthy of color but not black, of good height and solidly made, but extremely unwilling to work. They always go armed with bows and arrows, and these are their only weapons. Their arrows are envenomed with a deadly poison, and for this reason they are much feared by other tribes. Yet they are naturally peace loving, and never quarrel among themselves.
>
> Twice daily I gathered the children into the church. In the morning after Mass I repeated with them the Pater Noster, the Ave Maria, the Credo, the precepts of the Decalogue, the Sacraments of the Church, and the rudiments of the Christian doctrine. I had brought these with me in a translation into Tarahumara, and I repeated them from the written text. In the evening I reviewed the lesson and also asked the children questions from the Catechism. At the same time I gave instruction to those who were still pagan, acquainting them with the principal mysteries of the Faith, and preparing them to receive baptism. The rest of the day was spent in visiting the sick and hearing confessions (although, to be sure, I heard but few), or in assisting the builders and directing their operations. For in these countries, the fathers themselves are the only architects and the Indians the only masons.[4]

His house had three rooms with the bare earth as a floor. The center room was a dining room and office, with a storeroom to one side and a bedroom to the other. A woman came once a week to cook enough tortillas for the week, and Neumann had two boys living with him to serve Mass, to help with the work, and to lead religious services if he was absent. The new or rehabilitated church was finished in March.

The Easter Mass was celebrated there, and the people slaughtered two of the cattle for a big feast.

The first few years were the most difficult for Neumann. The Jesuits considered it essential that the people be drawn together into villages if any progress at all were to be made, even if this made it easier for the Spanish miners to impose on them for work. Many Tarahumaras resisted coming together because it meant giving up their freedoms and accepting a more regimented work schedule. At a later time Father Neumann wrote:

> The people are stony-hearted. The seed of the gospel does not sprout, or if it sprouts, it is spoiled by the thorns of carnal desire. The people are also less gregarious than other nations in New Spain, and each hut is some distance from the others along a steam. They live in low hovels which seem more suitable for catching birds than for human habitation. Of the fourteen Jesuits in this mission there are only two who have not at some time asked for another assignment. They had dreamed of winning many nations for Christ, but now they feel that they are wasting the best years of their lives.
>
> As wandering sheep, or like wild beasts, the people live in lairs and caves. Unless one makes an effort to tame them in these hiding places, and draw them forth, attempts to win them to baptism are in vain.
>
> What is wanted is not the zeal of Elias, but the gentleness of Our Savior. For it is not sublime theology nor subtlety of doctrine in any of the other sciences that is needed in the work of instilling Christian doctrines into these people; there is need only of the gentleness of the Lamb in directing them, of invincible patience in bearing with them, and, finally, of Christian humility, which enables you to become all things to all men, to disdain no one, to perform without shrinking the meanest task, and, if the barbarians scorn you, to endure their contempt to the end.[5]

In 1681, the Jesuits had been in the Alta Tarahumara for eight years. Despite the difficulties, things were going fairly well under the guiding hand of Father Thomas Guadalajara, for whom the Indians had great affection. But it was difficult for these people, who had always enjoyed so much freedom, to adapt to a new way of life. Back in 1652, for example, when they believed themselves oppressed, they had wiped out the Spanish on the Papigochic River.

Two civilizations were meeting, and the Indians were being asked to make most of the changes. This complex situation is well described by a modern historian:

Missions were successful to the extent that the initial enticements of food, clothing, and supplies led to richer benefits of education and incorporation into the comparative opulence of Spanish society. Indeed, the Spaniard saw the mission as a means of acculturating and pacifying fiercely independent peoples. The religious considered the mission as the only reliable stepping stone to salvation. The Indian saw the mission as a tolerable, if threatening, means to enter a new way of life. In other words, the mission was a complex social reality that served multiple purposes and was perceived according to very different scales of value.[6]

The year before Father Neumann arrived at Sisoguichic (1680), the Pueblo people of New Mexico had rebelled and driven the Spanish south to El Paso. During the 1680s, there were continual rumors of imminent insurrection in the Alta Tarahumara, and a few plots were nipped in the bud.

A blizzard buried Sisoguichic in February of 1682. Neumann survived several days in his house without heat, and the people and the mission lost all their livestock.

In 1683, Father Thomas Guadalajara published his Tarahumara grammar in Puebla, and at the end of the year, Father Joseph Ratkay fell sick and died at Carichic. He was replaced by a very competent Sicilian, Francis Píccolo, who would later be one of the founders of the mission in Baja California.

Mines were established near Cusi in 1684 and three years later in Cusi itself. Many more whites were coming to this border area of the Tarahumara, and the people of Cusi were angered when the miners started to take the wood, to use the grazing land, and to force people to work in the mines. About this time, gold was discovered near Sisoguichic, but almost all the rest of the mines were to the north between Cusi and Chihuahua.

By 1686, when the upper mission was thirteen years old, there were more than sixteen thousand baptized Tarahumaras in nine parishes, and already the mission was about as big geographically as it would get.

Two Jesuits were killed in 1690 north of Guerrero along the Papigochic River, and again the trouble was at the northern border of the mission. John Ortiz de la Foronda, from Toledo, Spain, and stationed at Yepómera, died April 1, 1690. His village was attacked by Conchos, and he was killed by them at a mission station near Yepómera. There was an alliance of many nations in this rebellion, including non-Christian Tarahumaras and some Christians.

About April 11 of the same year, Father Manuel Sanchez, thirty-eight, from Marchena, Spain, was killed in the countryside. He was stationed at Tutuaca, which is south of Yepómera and on a level line with Papigochic. Both John Ortiz and Manuel Sanchez had arrived in New Spain together in October of 1675, along with John Salvatierra, who would found the mission of Baja California. Both of the slain Jesuits were at remote spots deep in the Sierra.

At this time, some other missions and parishes in the north were also destroyed. After some inconclusive battles, a peace of sorts was established. Few of the Tarahumaras had actually been involved in the rebellion. However, in 1697, half of the Alta Tarahumara rose in rebellion against both the Spanish and the Jesuit mission system. The stage was set for this rebellion by a devastating epidemic in 1693, which included both smallpox and measles. Father Joseph Neumann wrote from Sisoguichic:

> This pestilence destroyed a great number of children and many pregnant women; indeed hardly any of the latter escaped. It took the young, the flower of our reductions, whereas old people and a small number of mature men and women were untouched. Forty in Sisoguichic took sick within four days and most of them died. It is miraculous that none of the Jesuits died from exhaustion. Only one Jesuit took sick from the plague.

Two years later, in 1695, another epidemic struck, and again it carried away mostly the young. After this, a conspiracy started to form, and the people became reserved and even hostile to the Jesuits. In 1696, there was an earthquake and an eclipse of the sun. People told the Jesuits that a rebellion was coming and that the rebels were gathering supplies and congregating at a place northwest of Papigochic. Neumann was now superior of the Jesuits in the Alta Tarahumara, and he informed the governor in Parral of the rebellion. A Spanish captain with troops came up to Papigochic in the spring of 1697.

The captain made excursions from Papigochic, capturing and executing over a hundred rebels. However, he ended up more or less besieged in Papigochic while the rebellion spread, and one pueblo after another was captured by the rebels or went over to them. Mission property was burned in all of these pueblos.

The rebellion was centered in the area northwest of Papigochic, and the people farther south at Sisoguichic and Carichic did not rise. Joseph Neumann was pastor in Sisoguichic, and Francis Píccolo had been pastor at Carichic. Píccolo had built in Carichic the most beautiful of the Jesuit mission churches in the Alta Tarahumara, but just before this rebellion, he had been sent as one of the founders of the mission to Baja California.

The rebels, who were at least a few hundred in number, now bypassed Papigochic and moved south. They destroyed mission property in some villages and moved toward Sisoguichic. Father Neumann, the women, the children, and most of the men fled from Sisoguichic to Carichic. The Spanish captain in Papigochic was informed of the movement of the rebels, and he surrounded them in Sisoguichic. Some of the rebels slipped away, but most occupied a hill near Sisoguichic where they fought to the last man. The captain lost one soldier and four allied Tarahumaras. Fifteen others were wounded by poisoned arrows, but remedies were applied without delay, and they escaped death.[7] The heads of thirty-three rebels were struck from their bodies, set on spears, and exposed on a hill near the ruins of the church.

The battle at Sisoguichic was the turning point in the rebellion, but it still dragged on for another year before it was ended by further military expeditions and by famine.

After the rebellion of 1697, there was a military stalemate in the Alta Tarahumara, and the Spanish, including the Jesuits, backed off with two healthy changes of policy. It had been considered rebellion if the natives left the Christian villages, and often it was. But after 1700, the people were left alone. It was discovered that the Tarahumaras were not rebelling but that they wanted more freedom. The Jesuits discovered that they were welcome when they went to visit these people who had left the missions. In fact, the people even built chapels and small residences for the visiting priests. There was also a practical reason for this change of policy. The Spanish government had much less money to spend in New Spain during the European War of the Spanish

Succession in the early 1700s.

The second change of policy had to do with the administration of justice in the mission pueblos, where the Jesuits had had a lot to say about crime and punishment. A Jesuit could tell a local native official that so-and-so should be punished for such and such a crime. After 1700, the Tarahumara governor of a town was given authority by the Spanish governor to administer justice. This authority even included capital punishment, and the Jesuits were no longer involved in the administration of justice.

There were also significant changes in the country as a whole. Before 1700, about two hundred thousand Africans had been brought into the country as slaves. After 1700, few were brought in.

Before 1700, continuing economic development meant upward mobility by people of different races. After 1700, there was less economic growth, and the social structure became more rigid as people tried to hold on to what they had. There was more racial prejudice and discrimination, but there was still upward mobility on the frontier. Mining started to require huge capital investments to reach the ore in deep mines.

Before 1700, there was less conflict over land because so many indigenous had died from diseases. After 1700, there was more pressure on Indian lands. The white population started to expand in the Jesuit area, except in the Alta Tarahumara. North of the Tarahumara, the city of Chihuahua was founded about 1700. But in the mountains southwest of Chihuahua, there were not many Spanish because mines were few and the land was not good (though the Mennonites have made it productive in modern times), so the mission character of the Alta Tarahumara remained until the expulsion of the Jesuits in 1767. However, in the rest of the Jesuit area, the expanding white population started to see the Jesuits as an obstacle to the economic development of the region. The Indians had the best land and water, and the Jesuits resisted the exploitation of native labor.

After 1700, there was also a change of dynasties in Spain. The earlier Hapsburg kings had been more or less paternalistic, but the later Bourbon kings were more autocratic.

Here are some notable events of this period:

- In 1715, the bishop of Durango visited the Tarahumara in order to administer confirmation. He reported that the churches were clean; that the people were well fed and clothed; that the young people could read, write, and speak Spanish; and that many could play musical instruments, including the violin and the organ.
- In 1718, a mission school was established at Cusi. In the same year, ground was broken for a Jesuit college in the city of Chihuahua.
- In 1720, Thomas Guadalajara, the founder of the upper mission, died. He is buried at a village called Huejotitlán near Balleza.
- In 1725, the provincial sent a visitor to the Tarahumara, who reported that some of the Jesuits did not know the native language. The provincial wrote to the Jesuit superior in the Tarahumara that all of the Jesuits would have to learn the language even if they had to be removed from their parishes until they did so.
- In 1732, Father Joseph Neumann, eighty-four years old, died after fifty-one years in the Alta Tarahumara, first as pastor at Sisoguichic and then at Carichic. He is buried at Carichic, as is Joseph Ratkay, the Hungarian baron with whom he arrived.

In the Baja Tarahumara, the missions did not survive until the expulsion in 1767. In this area near Parral, the Tarahumaras were leaving the missions to work on the Spanish farms and ranches, which is hard to understand. The missions and the indigenous had good land, but the natives and the Jesuits did not make a go of it in the long run. The native farms and ranches may not have been large enough. Much of the land in northern Mexico is similar to the land in central and west Texas, where it takes twenty or twenty-five acres to support one steer, and a rancher often has to purchase feed in the winter. In Texas, they speak of sections rather than acres. A section is a square mile and supports about twenty-five steers. But this land can be very productive when it is irrigated. For example, the United States has turned the lower Rio Grande valley into a garden with a huge dam farther up the river.

Modern Mexico has also built dams, especially along the west coast. There are dams on the Sonora, Yaqui, Mayo, and Fuerte Rivers. There are no dams on the Sinaloa and the Mocorito, but there are other dams farther south in Sinaloa. At the present time, Sinaloa produces one-quarter of the agricultural products that the country exports.

Some questions about the missions seemed to have no solutions. One question was, "Integration or separate development?" In Baja Tarahumara, the people chose integration. In the Alta Tarahumara, they chose separate development. The people in the Alta Tarahumara avoided contacts with the Europeans more than any other people in North America. Of course, they were able to do this in the vast western Sierra with its deep canyons.

The Jesuits hated to see people leave the mission. The native people went to the mines for two things—horses and cloth. This means that their own farms were not generating enough cash. After a while, only a few missions were left in the Baja Tarahumara. The last of the parishes were handed over to the diocese around 1750.

In the Alta Tarahumara, the people tended to wander. The missions were like community centers for fiestas and religious celebrations. Seventeen Jesuits were working in the Alta Tarahumara when the expulsion came in 1767.

As has been mentioned, the Jesuits found this mission discouraging. The people were more reserved than in other places. Some of them held on to past practices like communal drinking. Also, life in the high Sierra, though healthy, was rigorous and difficult. Still, the missions were a source of support for the people materially, culturally, and spiritually.

After the expulsion of the Jesuits, the Franciscans were assigned to replace them. However, before the Franciscans arrived, government officials had disposed of mission property and lands, and the people were left in great poverty.

In modern Mexico, Jesuits are once again serving in the Alta Tarahumara.

1745: Nayarit

Nayarit is a small, mountainous state south of Sinaloa and Durango on the Pacific Ocean. In 1721, soldiers entered the mountains of Nayarit. In 1722, the Jesuits entered to work with the Cora Nation. Franciscans worked with the Huicholes. These two nations speak very similar Uto-Aztecan languages, and the two languages are closer to Nahuatl than to the Cáhita languages of Sinaloa. A Jesuit, Joseph Michael Ortega, published a vocabulary and grammar of the Cora language in 1729.

Farming can be done year-round in these mountains because the temperature is mild. But there is a scarcity of water, and the soil is thin and not very fertile. Nonetheless, by 1745, seven Jesuits served eleven mission villages. There were also forty-four soldiers at three forts, with half at the main fort.

At the present time, thirty thousand Cora and Huichol Indians live in the mountains of Nayarit and extend east into the State of Jalisco. They continue a traditional way of life, eating little meat, living dispersed in small communities, and doing traditional crafts such as weaving and pottery making.

CHAPTER 9

Chínipas, 1626–1638

Chínipas is a town and a *municipio* in the extreme west and toward the south of the State of Chihuahua. A *municipio* is similar to a county in the United States, and the county seat is also called a *municipio*. Chínipas Municipio, or County, is fifty miles from north to south and sixteen miles from east to west, and it borders southern Sonora between the Mayo and Fuerte Rivers.

The mountains in this part of the Sierra (including neighboring *municipios*) are only 4,500 feet high. But the area was, and still is, one of the most inaccessible regions in North America because there are no convenient valleys through the mountains. The vast area is drained by

The Chínipas Area in Southwest Chihuahua State

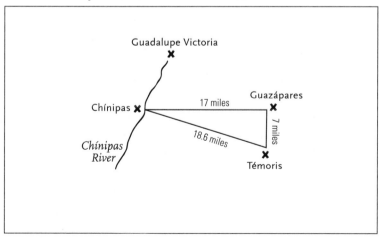

Fig. 21

tributaries of the Mayo and Fuerte Rivers, but the rivers flow west from the Sierra through deep chasms. In this part of the Sierra, it never snows except on the highest mountain peaks, and the land is covered by bushes rather than trees. There are also some tall cacti. Before the Spanish arrived, the people both at Chínipas and in the surrounding area irrigated their crops with canals or ditches. This was unusual because no other nations irrigated in the Jesuit area except in the north of Sonora and in Arizona.

The three towns of Chínipas, Guazápares, and Témoris form a right triangle and, with nearby Guadalupe Victoria, are all important in the story of the Jesuit missions. Chínipas is on the Chínipas River, a tributary of the Fuerte River. The hills pull back from the river at Chínipas and create a beautiful spot where crops can be grown. The indigenous village of Témoris was on top of the mountain, though now it has an addition about a thousand feet below, where the train station is located.

When the Jesuits first entered the area, there were two to three thousand Chínipas people, and about a thousand of them formed the pueblo of Chínipas. The Témoris and Guazápares seem to have been fewer in number than the Chínipas. The Jesuits distinguished the Chínipas Nation and language from those of Témoris and other places, but all of these people spoke dialects of Tarahumara.

Even in the dry season, the Chínipas River has a good quantity of water moving briskly in the middle of its sandy riverbed. It is possible in the dry season to walk the ten miles upstream from Chínipas to Guadalupe Victoria on the riverbed, but the river sweeps against the bank, forcing a traveler to climb over boulders.

A fourth nation, called the Varohío, was on the Chínipas River about a half-mile south of present-day Guadalupe Victoria. This nation had fewer people than the Chínipas Nation, and the people of all of these nations tended to be scattered in the mountains rather than congregated in their principal towns.

Peter Méndez was the first Jesuit to visit the Chínipas area. In fact, he was the first Jesuit to visit any of the Tarahumara region. In 1601, he went with an exploratory party of Captain Hurdaide, who had been instructed to search for precious metals. They were ambushed on this trip and were lucky to escape with their lives.

The next Jesuit to visit Chínipas was Michael Wadding, from Waterford, Ireland. He had studied two years in Spain before entering the Society at age twenty-one. After a year of novitiate in Spain, he did the rest of his studies in New Spain. In 1618, he was assigned to the upper Mayo River four years after Peter Méndez had established the mission on the Mayo.

Wadding visited Chínipas from the Mayo River in 1619. The trip from the Mayo to Chínipas is long but is less rugged than the approach along the Fuerte and Chínipas Rivers. Wadding was well received by the Chínipas and baptized eighty children.

Michael Wadding was on the Mayo from 1618 until 1625. These were very difficult years because in the early twenties there were five years of drought, hunger, and diseases. In 1620, knowing that there was famine in Sinaloa, the Chínipas carried a great quantity of corn, beans, and squash down the Fuerte River. They asked Father John Castini, from northern Italy and stationed at Toro on the upper Fuerte, for a missionary.

John Castini responded to their request by making a visit to Chínipas in 1621, accompanied by a hundred of the Chínipas people. He was welcomed at the village with arches of flowers and with crosses, and found that the people had built a chapel. Castini baptized 362 children, and he asked that they burn or destroy any scalps and bones of their enemies that they might possess, as well as idols and any objects of superstition. They agreed willingly. He also asked them to make peace with the Témoris and Guazápares.

At this time, a messenger arrived from the Guazápares requesting both peace and the Christian religion. So the Guazápares were invited to Chínipas, and more than a hundred came. Then Castini asked that boys return with him to Toro to study the usual subjects of letters, catechism, and music. Twenty-four were chosen to go, and they all returned to Toro.

Later, representatives came again from the three nations to see Father Castini and Captain Hurdaide and to request a permanent missionary.

Castini made a second trip to Chínipas, visited Témoris and Guazápares, and met people from the north who came to Chínipas to invite him to their villages. Castini left a catechist, married to a Chínipas woman, in Chínipas to instruct the people.

In 1624, Father Julio Pascual, from Brescia, Italy, arrived in Sinaloa. He was assigned to Chínipas, but for two years he had to replace a sick missionary on the Fuerte River.

Michael Wadding left the Mayo in 1625, after seven years there. He would teach in Puebla, Guatemala, and Mexico until he died at age fifty-eight. Wadding wrote a book, *Práctica de la Teología Mística,* which was published in Puebla after his death. This book was reprinted many times in Europe during the next hundred years, in Spanish, Italian, and Latin. In this book, Wadding described missionary life on the west coast.

> I worked many years in Sinaloa in the ministry for the conversion of the gentiles, and I can testify as an eyewitness to the immense labors of body and soul which the first missionaries endured. The work of those teaching the converted is a bit softened by temporal comforts, of which they have few enough.
>
> The land is exceedingly hot and the missionaries walk about at every hour of the day and night, accompanied by naked savages, surrounded by wild animals, sleeping in deserted places—the ground often serving as a bed, the shade of a tree as a house. Their food is a little corn, roasted or boiled. Their drink is any water they find. Their clothes are torn, poor, mended, and remended. They never see bread, meat, fruit, or preserves.
>
> Their lives are up for sale among the hechiceros, who have a pact with the devil, and who make crude war on us, preaching the devil and the opposite by night of what we preach by day. They wounded two of my companions with arrows. I escaped two times through the mountains although they killed a servant of mine. And people whose children I baptized at Chínipas killed two religious.
>
> Those first missionaries proceeded ragged, hungry, sad, weary, persecuted, swimming rivers, on foot through lofty and rugged mountains, through woods, valleys, thickets, and canyons—lacking many times the things necessary for human life, weighed down by sickness, without doctors, medicines, comforts, and friends. And with all these labors God was served and many gentiles were converted. Just one of them, the holy martyr Father Santorén, learned eleven languages and built fifty churches.

When we came together once a year where the superior lived, we reported the number of baptisms and the more notable dangers and successes which had occurred. The number of baptized was never less than 5,000 each year during my time, and some years it reached 10,000. In 1624 there were more than 82,000 Christians. Later it passed 120,000.

It is true that afterward there were diseases which killed thousands but we worked very hard for the sick.

I knew some missionaries to whom God communicated high levels of infused contemplation. I knew one person who was in ecstasy three days and three nights. There were others who, from four to six hours, enjoyed heavenly favors in a high contemplation. But those were few and veteran soldiers, for the very good are always very few.[1]

Julio Pascual went up to Chínipas as the first resident missionary the same year in which Captain Hurdaide and the elderly Martin Pérez died. When Pascual arrived in Chínipas on March 6, 1626, there were twenty children living of the eighty whom Wadding had baptized seven years previously. Pascual started classes for children and adults. Thanks to the catechists who had preceded him, he was able to baptize almost all the adults after two months. He and the people spent the next three months building a church. It was no doubt of adobe and quite an effort because logs had to be brought down from higher places. The church was finished in August. At this time, there were a few Spanish prospectors who had come into the area after Pascual, but there were no soldiers.

In December of 1626, Pascual went up the Chínipas River to the people called the Varohíos, south of present-day Guadalupe Victoria. He also visited Témoris and Guazápares, where there were catechists at work. The catechist at Guazápares was married to a woman of the Guazápares.

The cacique of the Guazápares, named Cobamea, was a big man in his fifties and was very influential. Cobamea had held himself aloof during the first visit of Castini, but during Castini's second visit, he requested baptism. He also made a long speech, encouraging others to be baptized and talking about peace and a new way of life in the Sierra.

Cacique Cobamea later went back to pagan ways, which probably means bigamy. Cobamea now started to plot against Pascual, and we can only guess at his motives. There were no soldiers and very few

Spanish in the area. In other places, Jesuits would be killed in riots or rebellions, but it seems that Pascual would die more for religious reasons.

Cobamea could have been annoyed at the changes that were taking place. A catechist in the village was teaching a way of life that Cobamea had accepted and then rejected. The catechist's brother was also living in the village. The catechist may have been from Sinaloa or perhaps was one of the twenty-four Chínipas boys who had gone down with Castini to study.

There could also have been a resurgence of hostility toward the Chínipas that was motivated by jealousy. The Chínipas were changing. They were in close contact with the Native Americans of Sinaloa and with the Spanish. They had their church, a choir, and perhaps a school. They may have been doing better than others with domestic animals, and they had a beautiful setting for their pueblo. They were moving ahead into a new way of life, so, whatever his motives, Cobamea decided to kill Julio Pascual, and he brought some of the Varohíos into the plan.

The Chínipas heard of the plot and warned Pascual. When he did not take the warning seriously, they warned other missionaries and the captain in Sinaloa. The captain sent six soldiers to the area, but when things quieted down, Pascual thought it had all been a mistake, and he sent the soldiers back to Sinaloa in January of 1632. Pascual had been six years at Chínipas without any Jesuit help, but now he was expecting assistance.

Cobamea decided to act, but he had to get Pascual away from Chínipas. So Cobamea went to the Varohíos, and they sent a message to Pascual that there was a sick person there. Pascual made the sick call, but he did not stay two or three days as was his custom. He hurried back to Chínipas because he was expecting Father Manuel Martinez, a thirty-one-year-old Portuguese. Martinez had come to New Spain with an uncle at age nineteen. After a year of study at Puebla, he entered the Society. After completing his seminary studies and ordination, he arrived at Chínipas on Friday, January 23, 1632. He would be a missionary for nine days.

Two days after Martinez arrived, the two Jesuits went up to the Varohíos with nine carpenters and eight choirboys. The boys would have been from Chínipas, but the carpenters could have been from Chínipas or Sinaloa. On Thursday, the catechist from Guazápares arrived and reported that his brother had been killed and that a big crowd of warriors was on its way to Varohío, but Pascual did not believe things could be that bad. The next day the reports were confirmed. He believed it now, but it was too late. He sent to Chínipas for help. Although most of the men were away from Chínipas, probably hunting, those who were there came up. When they ran into a great number of Guazápares and Varohíos, they retreated.

On Friday night, the church was burned as well as part of the house in which the Jesuits and the Chínipas were trapped. On Saturday morning, Pascual went out to talk, and it seemed to do some good. All day Saturday and Saturday evening they remained in the house surrounded by the indigenous under Cobamea. On Sunday morning, February 1, 1632, there was great shouting, and the house was attacked. Doors and parts of the adobe walls were broken down, and the attackers started shooting arrows. After one of the arrows pierced Pascual's stomach, Manuel Martinez said, "Let us not die like sad cowards. Let us give our lives for Jesus Christ and his holy law." They went outside. Martinez's arm was fixed to his breast by an arrow, and they both fell to their knees. Their bodies were covered with arrows. The carpenters and choirboys also died, except for two who managed to hide. The village was then abandoned.

The Chínipas went up and brought the bodies back to Chínipas for burial. But when the nearest Jesuit on the Mayo was informed about what had happened, he thought it better to bury the Jesuits at his place, which was done on February 14, 1632.

Into the Sierra now came the captain, the successor to Hurdaide, with soldiers and native allies. From the Sierra, many indigenous, probably Chínipas, joined him. However, the captain could not reach the Guazápares and Varohíos, who were in deep canyons or on high peaks, so he sent the allied soldiers against them. It is reported that the allied indigenous killed eight hundred of the enemy. The Spanish put the blame for all this killing on the natives, saying that they were new Christians. This is the sort of thing that did not happen under

Hurdaide. Four hundred of the enemy were taken as prisoners and were settled in Sinaloa. All of the Chínipas then left their beautiful valley and settled on the Fuerte River.

During the next twenty years, Jesuits sometimes visited these areas, mostly to encourage the Christians who were there. They were always escorted by soldiers or natives from Sinaloa. At the end of twenty years, or around 1653, the captain appointed some residents of those places as governors of the towns. The Guazápares and Varohíos then returned the stole, cassock, and chalice of Father Pascual, and many Chínipas returned to the area.

For another twenty years, there was a lot of contact between the Chínipas and the people of Sinaloa. The Chínipas and Varohíos, for example, would go down to visit their relatives on the Fuerte. Some of these people received instruction and returned to their home villages as catechists. During these years there was also a shortage of Jesuits. But in 1664, the Spanish government lifted the ban against foreign missionaries, and many foreign Jesuits came from Italy and southern Germany. It was a new beginning.

Two Jesuits entered the high Sierra south of Chihuahua City in 1673, and three years later two Jesuits returned to Chínipas, where many people had been asking for them. Others in the area were tolerant. It was at this time that the pueblo of Guadalupe Victoria was founded north of Chínipas, and the Jesuits would be in the area for almost a hundred years until their expulsion in 1767.

Since the founding of Guadalupe Victoria, the people there have been using the martyrdom site (downstream a mile or so) as a cemetery. They inter bodies within the outline of the church that was being built at the time of the martyrdom. Part of the adobe wall of one of the original buildings is still standing.

Six years after the death of Pascual, there was an interesting meeting of the Jesuits in Mexico City. The government, considering the appointment of a bishop for Sinaloa, put out a report concerning conditions in Sinaloa and asked different groups for their responses. The Jesuits met to discuss the proposal, and Peter Méndez, just returned from his forty-two years on the coast, was at the meeting.

The Jesuits' opinion was that a bishop should not be appointed on the coast at this time. Their report gave a good description of conditions in Sinaloa in 1638.

> We have one ranch on the coast at Villa Sinaloa where there are less than 8,000 cattle. The majority of these are running wild and are of little use. The cattle are used for barbecues at various fiestas throughout the province. Other missions sometimes have small herds for milk.
>
> The native products were corn, beans, squash, and some other seeds and vegetables, and droughts are frequent. The indigenous often have to search for edible roots in the forest and to hunt wild animals. The fathers often have to look beyond Sinaloa for provisions for themselves and the people. The land is not suitable for growing wheat. Some cotton is grown, but its yield is small and the quality poor. A cotton garment means wealth. Grass and deerskin are still common clothing in Sinaloa.
>
> In all of our mission fields in the northwest, including the central plain in the north of New Spain, the baptismal records show that 300,000 people have been baptized. In this year of 1638 there are about 100,000 Christian natives under the pastoral care of the Jesuits.
>
> We do raise various crops with the help of the people but there is no personal profit in this since there is a sizable group of native helpers who must be fed. The indigenous should not be expected to pay tithes for the support of a diocesan organization. They are already exempt by law from paying tithes on native products. The Spanish in the area pay tithes regularly although they are only a little better off than the natives.
>
> The indigenous in the north do not pay taxes to the state and should not be expected to do so. First, they are too poor and could hardly pay them. Second, they are not accustomed to paying taxes. The people in the south had been accustomed to paying taxes by the Aztecs, but the situation is different in the north. If taxes are imposed, there would be danger of revolt. The people on the coast are very numerous. Remember how much damage was done by the small nation of the Tepehuanes.

Other respondents agreed with the Jesuits, and no bishop was appointed at that time.

CHAPTER 10

Eusebio Kino, S.J., 1681–1711

Eusebio Francis Kino was born in the mountain town of Segno, near Trent, Italy, on August 10, 1645.[1] His family was Italian, but the area was part of the Holy Roman Empire. Kino attended the Jesuit school in Trent, where the Jesuits were German, but instruction and conversation were in Italian. After Trent, he studied in Germany.

As a student, Eusebio became very sick, and he prayed to St. Francis Xavier, promising he would go to the missions if he recovered. When he recovered, he added Francis to his name and entered a German Jesuit province when he was twenty years old. His natural abilities were scientific, and he concentrated on mathematics and cartography with the hope of going to the China mission. Despite being offered the chair of mathematics at the University of Ingolstadt, he left Genoa, Italy, with other Jesuits in June of 1678, bound for Spain and New Spain. In July, they missed their connection with the fleet sailing from Cádiz, Spain, so they went to Seville to study Spanish, to make other preparations, and to wait for a ship.

One of the German Jesuits described Seville at that time, saying that the French and Dutch had a monopoly on industry and commerce. There were forty thousand French in the city, an amazing number of clergy and monasteries, and a multitude of beggars—the archbishop regularly fed twenty-two thousand people. Kino was in Seville for two years. When he finally left Cádiz in July of 1680, his ship grounded. He finally got away in January of 1681 and reached Vera Cruz, New Spain, on May 1, 1681.

A Jesuit just ahead of Kino described the trip by mule from the coast through Puebla to Mexico City. They were received at an hacienda of the college in Puebla, which had eighty thousand hogs, twenty thousand sheep, and many thousands of cattle. Forty Jesuits lived in Puebla. This Jesuit wrote that in Mexico City the Jesuit church at the professed house shined with gold and contained so many fine pictures that there was hardly any empty space on the walls. The Colegio Maximo had 2,500 students. Although highly endowed, it had a debt of forty thousand pesos. He said that the Spaniards formed the ruling class and that the Mexicans were considered their serfs.

When Kino arrived in Mexico City, he was assigned to Baja California. Attempts to colonize Baja California had been unsuccessful, and now a new effort was being planned by the archbishop of Mexico City, who was filling the vacant office of the viceroy. The plan, approved by the government in Spain, looked more toward evangelization than economic profit. Isidro Atondo was in command of the expedition, with the title of admiral for California. He was also governor of Sinaloa, and he retained that position so that he could more easily obtain supplies.

Atondo built ships of sixty and seventy tons, with a launch for each, on the Sinaloa River, as well as a third smaller ship called a sloop. He was taking over a hundred people on the expedition, including thirty soldiers, twenty-four seamen, four pilots, three carpenters, two caulkers, one gunsmith, a surgeon, and a master bloodletter. There were Mayo workers, both men and women. Also included were two Jesuits— Eusebio Kino, as the superior of the two and as official mapmaker for the government, and Matthew Goñi, who had experience as a missionary in Sinaloa.

The people of the expedition were forbidden under pain of death to take anything from the natives, to trade with them, or to enter their houses. They could keep any gold, silver, or pearls that they found, but one-fifth of the value had to go to the king as tax. The armament of the expedition included eight canons and fifty muskets.

The ships were finished and pushed into the Sinaloa River on October 28, 1682, but it was several months before they reached California. They sailed south of Sinaloa State to the port of Chacala, near Compostela, where supplies were being sent from Mexico and Guadalajara. When they left Chacala, it took two weeks to get up to Mazatlán. Then it took a month to sail to the Sinaloa River. Perhaps they were experimenting with the new ships.

At the Sinaloa River, they spent eight days taking on horses, cattle, fowl, and other supplies. They sailed at last on March 18, 1683, and were immediately becalmed for five days. Two days later they could see both shores, but it took another six days to reach the large bay at La Paz, Baja California. By this time, Kino had been in New Spain for almost two years.

That first night, everyone stayed on board. When some rowed ashore on Thursday morning, April 1, they found an area covered with reeds, human footprints, plenty of wood, and a spring. They returned to the ship.

On Friday, almost all the men went ashore. They fashioned a large cross and explored a little, but they returned to sleep on the ships that night. On Saturday, Sunday, and Monday, they went ashore and

Area Explored by Kino and Goñi with Expedition of Isidro Atondo, 1682–1685

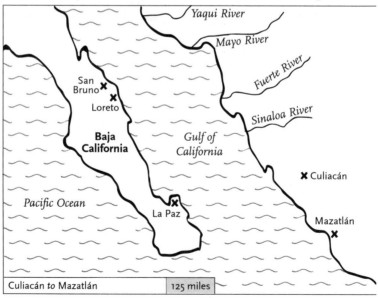

Fig. 22

unloaded supplies. That Sunday, April 4, 1683, was Passion Sunday, two weeks before Easter. On Sunday, they explored the estuary of the bay. They saw smoke in the distance, and that evening they caught a great quantity of fish in a dragnet.

On Monday, Atondo took formal possession of the country in the name of the king, with as much pageantry as possible. Kino and Goñi took spiritual possession in the name of the bishop of Guadalajara. They then began to build a fort and a small church, and that night they remained on shore. Tuesday morning, while the crew was clearing a small elevation, they heard the shouting of native Californians. People appeared with war paint, bows, and arrows, and they made signs that the strangers should leave. The Spanish made signs that they had come in peace, and they offered to lay down their weapons. The native people refused to lay down their weapons.

The two Jesuits approached the people and offered crackers and necklaces. The Californians, who spoke the Guaicura language, gestured that they should put the gifts on the ground. The Californians then offered the Spanish men gifts of small, well-woven nets, some feathers, and roasted *mezcales,* which were the vegetable hearts of a species of cactus.

On Wednesday and Thursday, the Spanish felled trees and tall palms. They had seen deer and rabbits, and they caught enough fish on Thursday to last three days. On Friday, eighty people came to visit. Kino made them welcome and offered corn, which was much appreciated. He showed them how to make the sign of the cross. When he gave a rubber ball to some of the children, they were frightened at first because they thought it was alive.

The people in Baja California did not farm. They ate wild seeds, worms, some insects, mice, bats, snakes, some wild plants, roots, and the fruit of some species of cactus. There were fish and oysters in the gulf, but only the people at the southern end of the peninsula had canoes for fishing. The other people had rafts made from bundles of canelike grass or from the light, pithy trunks of a local tree. They also hunted rabbit, squirrel, deer, and fowl. They had neither dogs nor pottery, but they made wooden bowls. With the heat and the scarcity of water, the people must have been among the poorest on earth.

Friday evening, the native people went inland to sleep, and they returned on Saturday. In order to impress their guests, the Spanish set up a leather shield. An arrow could not pierce the shield, but a bullet from a musket could.

On Palm Sunday, Kino offered Mass and blessed and distributed palms.

On Tuesday, the admiral sent some soldiers to explore. Traveling six or seven miles, they found no rivers or native settlements, but from a hill they saw a lake, an attractive plain, and columns of smoke. On Wednesday, when forty Californians came to visit, many of them were new, and the Spanish offered them *pozole* (a corn soup or stew) and *pinole* (a cookie). In order to make *pinole,* corn was ground or at least pounded and crushed. It was mixed with sugar, and the dough was then fried or toasted over a fire.

On Wednesday and Thursday, many in the party went to confession, and they received Holy Communion on Holy Thursday. On Good Friday, some natives visited and brought a small load of wood because they had noticed that the Spanish gave gifts to those who brought wood. That evening, one of the priests gave a sermon in Spanish about the passion of our Lord.

On Holy Saturday, presumably late in the evening, they sang the litanies and celebrated the Mass of the Resurrection. They fired muskets and rang bells at the Gloria and at five other times during the Mass. On Easter Monday and Tuesday, they planted seed for corn, melons, and watermelons, and the two Jesuits started to study the language. The people of the area were the Guaicuras with the Guaicura language, and Kino eventually compiled a list of five hundred Guaicura words, ascertaining their meanings as best he could.

The people were poor because of the heat and lack of rain. The Baja receives only three or four inches of rain a year, as compared to twenty-three inches in Mexico City, and more than forty inches along the east coast of the United States. However, there is more rain in the north of Baja California, especially on the Pacific side, and there is also more rain at the southern end of the peninsula.

In Baja California, the men went naked, and the women wore skirts of reeds or skins, in the front and the back, from the waist to the knees. On the mainland, in contrast, the men usually wore at least loincloths, and the women wore fiber, skins, or cotton from the waist or shoulders. In Baja California, infants were powdered with wood ash or partially buried where a fire had been, in order to keep them warmer. In the north, where it was colder, a person might have a shawl made of sea otter or rabbit skin.

In Baja California, the people were living without huts or any shelter, and this fact surprised the Jesuits more than anything. Besides the warm weather, a second reason for the lack of shelter was that the Californians had to keep moving in order to find food, staying a week or so at each location. If there was a cool wind, they made a windbreak of rocks and slept behind it, and they often kept a fire going during the night.

A chain of mountains runs down through Baja California, from half a mile to over a mile high, with a few peaks in the north at ten thousand feet. This mountain chain is along the gulf side, and most of the Californians lived in the mountains.

The Spanish had first gone ashore on April 1. They caulked one of the ships, and on April 25, the admiral sent the ship to the Yaqui River for more horses and other supplies. Meanwhile, they made two exploratory trips of about twenty-five miles each, and they met a new people to the south, the Pericús, who were enemies of the Guaicuras.

As summer came on, the Spanish became worried because supplies were running short. Their crop had probably failed for lack of water, and the ship had not returned from the Yaqui River. Their third smaller ship had not sailed with them, and it was still trying to find them. Moreover, relations with the Guaicuras had deteriorated.

There was some stealing by the Californians. Then, when a mulatto cabin boy, John Zavala, disappeared, the people to the south informed the Spanish that the Guaicuras had killed him. When a Guaicura shot an arrow at a soldier, the admiral took him prisoner. The Guaicuras were angered by this, and 150 of them came armed to the camp. However, there was no fighting.

Next, fifteen Guaicuras came to the camp with signs of peace and sat down to eat. The admiral thought they had come to rescue the prisoner, and since he believed that they had killed John Zavala, he ordered that a canon be fired at them. He killed three people and wounded others. These murders ended all relations with the Guaicuras, and it was difficult for the Jesuits to relate to the people of La Paz for many years to come.

The Spanish now had fear of the Guaicuras to add to their worry about supplies. The soldiers asked to return to Sinaloa because they did not want to remain while the last ship went for supplies. The admiral finally agreed, and they left on July 14, 1683. They had been three and a half months at La Paz, and it took a week to sail back to the new port of San Lucas, north of the Fuerte. Kino sent a map of part of the California coast to the viceroy.

They found out later that the Guaicuras had not murdered John Zavala. When Zavala had met some sailors, probably pearl fishermen, he traded a pearl for a canoe. He then paddled, apparently by himself, 120 miles across the open Gulf of California to the mainland.

The admiral started to gather supplies for another attempt to colonize Baja California. He replaced some soldiers with fifteen others from the fort at Sinaloa. In the same area, he recruited thirty-eight civilians, including some female slaves. Native Americans could be legally enslaved if they were involved in a rebellion. They could also remain slaves with the Spanish if they had been slaves within one of the indigenous nations.

It was on Wednesday, September 29, 1683, that they departed the second time for California. This was a dangerous time to leave, because during August, September, and October there were often sudden, destructive windstorms on the gulf. By the evening of the next day, they were only fifteen or twenty miles from shore, but they could see California. They then went across rather quickly and spent some days looking for a port, as one ship was leaking. On Tuesday, they anchored at a spot they called San Bruno, fifteen miles north of the present town of Loreto. They were about 165 miles north of their first settlement at La Paz.

On Wednesday morning, October 6, 1683, they went ashore. There was a river, but it had no water because it was the dry season. They did find water by digging in the sandy riverbed, and then twenty

Californians appeared who were very friendly and more relaxed than the people at La Paz. These Californians were Cochimís, members of the third language group in Baja California, who extended far to the north. They were much more numerous than the Guaicuras and the Pericús.

On Thursday, fifteen horses were put ashore. When ninety Californians appeared, they helped the party to unload, and they brought water. They were curious about the Spaniards and wanted to board the ship, so some went in the launches. That evening, the party slept on shore, and a small group of Californians, men and women, slept nearby with their children.

During the following days, the Spanish were getting organized. They built a primitive chapel, and on Sunday, two hundred Californians were at Mass. They were attracted by the paintings in the chapel, especially that of Our Lady of Guadalupe, and they invited the newcomers to visit their village.

During this week, there were also some unsettling events. On Monday, a dog with the party bit a Californian. Then, that evening, a Sinaloa man disappeared. His wife was worried and weeping, but he returned after a few days. It seems he was angry about something. Then, on Thursday, two Californians shot arrows at a horse. They wanted to see if an arrow could pierce the skin of a horse—it could. When a whole village came to stay on Friday, October 22, Kino had to tell them that things were not yet ready.

On November 8, the first Catholic marriage was celebrated in Baja California, between two Native Americans from Sinaloa.

The settlers had come ashore on October 6. They spent all of October and November building shelters. Later in November, the admiral sent a ship to the mainland for supplies. Blessed with favorable winds, it went over in three and a half days and returned in thirty hours.

Eusebio Kino and Matthew Goñi had started work on the languages. Actually, there were two different languages at San Bruno and to the south. The language at San Bruno was Cochimí, which Kino studied, and this language extended through the central and northern part of Baja California. Eventually Kino produced a short vocabulary, grammar, and catechism.

These languages were difficult because the different dialects of the language could differ from one village to another, as much as Spanish differs from Portuguese. For example, in four different Cochimí villages, the word for people was *tamo, tama, tomo,* and *tamoc.* This is only one word, but it appears that the consonants were fixed more than the vowels.

Matthew Goñi was studying Monquí, a Guaicura language found to the south of San Bruno and south along the coast to La Paz. In the middle of the next August, Goñi went with a ship to obtain supplies. He returned with a new Jesuit, Augustine John Copart, who worked on the Guaicura language for four months. He put the extensive notes of Goñi into a treatise with the grammar, vocabulary, prayers, and so on.

After the first two months, on December 1, 1683, Admiral Atondo and Kino set out to explore Baja California. They took provisions for twelve days. Also in the party were twenty-five soldiers as well as five Mayos, six Cochimís, and six Guaicuras. They took six pack mules and fourteen horses, five of which were armored.

On the first day, they traveled to the northwest about eight miles to a site that was later called San Juan Londó. There was water here and good pasture. In fact, they later set up a second base here, mainly for the care of the animals. That evening nine new Cochimís joined them, and some of the other Californians returned home.

On the second day, for the first time on this second trip to the Baja, they saw flowing water. On the third day, they reached the wall of a mountain that the horses and mules could not climb. So they left six soldiers with the animals and proceeded on foot, carrying as much food as they could.

Very early the next morning, they climbed the mountain. They had to use ropes to haul up the weapons, the food, the admiral, and a few more people. At the top, they looked out over a beautiful plain. They then walked about ten miles to a water hole, where they rested and took a nap. In the afternoon, they went a few more miles. They saw some villages, but the people had fled in order to avoid contact. Then they came to a lake and made camp.

The admiral decided not to go farther. The next morning he stayed by the lake while Kino, five Mayos, and fourteen soldiers and ensigns carried provisions for two days. They found another lake, and they met some armed Californians who were reserved but not hostile. There would be a future mission in this area called Purísima, and Kino noticed that the language was Cochimí, the language he was studying at San Bruno. They then returned to San Bruno.

Two weeks later, Kino rode with twelve others, soldiers and Mayos, up the coast. They were looking for a pass through the mountains that horses and mules could manage. After traveling a great distance in three days, they found a pass and also a large settlement of Californians. They returned in time for Christmas.

During the next twelve months, work went on at San Bruno. Over three thousand adobe blocks were made. They were putting up buildings, and during this time there was only one light rain shower. They did grow some melons, but the results of farming were meager or a failure. They planted in the riverbed. These crops were covered by windblown sand, and they had to carry water to their other plants.

The admiral kept discipline at San Bruno. A soldier stoned an Indian for a small offense, and the admiral caned the soldier. A native stole a sheep and was caned by the admiral. Atondo had a Mayo woman flogged, and Kino protested. When some natives chased a soldier, the admiral pursued them and killed a native. Kino, upset by the conduct of the admiral, wrote that the admiral regarded what he had done as a courageous and manly deed.

The next December, on the fourteenth, they set out to explore across the peninsula to the Pacific Ocean. They were forty-three in number, including nine Mayos and a few Californian guides. They had ninety-one horses and mules. Among the horses, thirty-two were armored with bull hides and five were armored with metal; there were twenty-nine soldiers with leather jackets for protection.

They first had to get over the Sierra, which blocked the coast from the rest of the peninsula. The Sierra in this area is three hundred miles in length, and it is called the Sierra de la Giganta, going as high as six thousand feet. It can be seen from the Yaqui River in Sonora, but only at sunset. They went up the coast to the pass they had discovered the previous year, but it was still very difficult with the heavily laden mules. Some of the animals fell, and it took three days to descend from the pass.

It took two weeks to cross the Baja. The way was rough and stony, and the horses often went lame. A lot of time was spent in repairing the horses' shoes, and the men often had heavy work in preparing a path by clearing away bushes and filling in holes.

As they proceeded across the peninsula, the native people sometimes disputed their passage. However, with conversation and presents the native people were won to friendship and acted as guides. The party came to a riverbed. There had been virtually no rain at San Bruno, but at this spot there were springs that fed water into the riverbed. They continued their journey in the middle of the boulder-strewn riverbed between canyon walls, arriving at the Pacific on December 30, 1684. After exploring north and south along the ocean, they arrived back at San Bruno on January 13, 1685, after a trip of one month.

In the middle of December, just as Kino and the others left for the Pacific, one of the ships went to obtain supplies on the mainland. The other ship had been away for a whole year. It had gone for repairs, and the captain of this ship was also communicating with the interior of New Spain in order to obtain pearl fishermen. The smaller, third boat was also away, so the party at San Bruno was marooned.

During these months, the situation went from bad to worse. Supplies were very low, and many soldiers had swollen gums from scurvy. The water holes that they had dug in the sandy riverbed were turning foul.

In February, the admiral made a long trip down the peninsula looking for a better spot. He was also looking for an easier way through the mountains to the west. He found neither. At the end of March, one ship and the smaller boat returned to San Bruno. There was good food now, but the water kept getting saltier. In April, there was an appalling epidemic. Some of the party died, and others were paralyzed. The majority were sick.

Atondo asked the opinions of the others, and all were for leaving except Kino. Kino thought that the sick should be taken to Sinaloa but that the colony should be maintained. During the year and a half that they had been at San Bruno, Kino and Goñi had baptized only eleven people because they thought that they might not be able to stay.

The admiral decided to leave because he believed that the land was too sterile to support a colony. Also, it was impossible to remain so dependent on Sinaloa and Sonora, and money was running out. The whole effort had cost 225,000 pesos.

They packed up. Getting the livestock on board was a huge effort, but the Californians helped, and many of them wanted to go along. The admiral refused all except for two boys to study more Spanish and to go north by ship with Kino to look for a better site for a colony. After they left on May 8, 1685, there was a reaction among the Californians against those who had been friendly to the Spanish, and some of the friendly Californians were killed.

Kino was on the second ship back to Sinaloa. They dropped the sick off at the Yaqui River and were there a month before they sailed for further exploration. They went over to the California coast and then north before returning to the Sonora mainland. They had contrary winds for a month. Kino visited the Seri people at the Sonora River. The Seri language was related to the Cochimí language, and the Seris could have come across the gulf at some time in the past over a chain of islands. The chain ended at the Sonora River with the very large island of Tiburón.

Kino's ship returned to the Yaqui and took on board some of the recovered soldiers. They were going to take them south, but first they stopped back at San Bruno to leave off the two boys. Everything was green at San Bruno because it had rained. They then went to warn a ship from the Philippines that there were pirates in the area, and finally Kino was back in Mexico City.

Kino recommended that the next effort in California be made with smaller ships and a small garrison. He thought that Loreto, south of San Bruno, would be a good location because it had more water, and he suggested an agricultural base on the mainland for the support of California.

Kino thought he was going back when the government promised thirty thousand pesos a year for California. When the money was used for something else, he asked to work with the Seris because he saw their land as a stepping-stone to California. However, he was assigned to the Pimas, with whom he would do the great work of his life. He was forty-one years old, and he would serve in the Pimería for twenty-four years.

Kino was a person to whom the Pimas responded with confidence. He was physically tough, prayerful, and very disciplined. He slept on some sheepskins on the floor of his room, with his saddle as a pillow. His diet was plain, and he used neither tobacco nor alcohol. A Jesuit who worked with him said that Kino spent a lot of time in prayer.

During his twenty-four years in the Pimería, he made more than thirty-five expeditions. He could ride for sixty or more miles a day for weeks on end. He spread horse and cattle ranches among the Pimas over the north of Sonora and the south of Arizona. He baptized forty-five hundred people and would have baptized fifteen thousand more if he could have provided the people with priests.

He did this while often having to refute false charges brought against both himself and the Pimas. He was sometimes criticized by fellow Jesuits, who may have been jealous of his success. And he was always defending the Pimas against calumnies. If the Apaches did some raiding, people would accuse the Pimas. It would have been an excuse to dispossess them and to use them as slaves in the mines and on the haciendas.

He sometimes traveled with Europeans, but more often with the Pimas. He rode with up to 120 horses, mares, and colts. With many horses, the riders could easily take fresh mounts, and the horses were an emergency source of food. Also, Kino left the mares and colts in different villages to start herds. The idea was that the people were preparing to receive a missionary.

The horse was as highly valued by the Native Americans as it was by the Europeans. The Indians would go to the mines to work for two things—horses and cloth. They used the horse for travel rather than as a farm animal, and some preferred the meat of horses and mules to beef. It may have been closer to the taste of the game to which they were accustomed.

Kino disposed of thousands of animals as if they were his own, but there was a more communal notion of property. The idea was that mission property was for the use of the native people and in trust for them. He shared livestock with villages all over the Pimería, and he sent great numbers of cattle and horses to the later mission in California.

Kino was often away from his home parish at Dolores, but the people at Dolores went on producing a great deal of wealth. Kino also traveled beyond the Pimas to the Yumas on the Colorado River, and he crossed the Colorado and met some of the people on the other side. The Colorado, running south to the gulf, is almost the boundary between Arizona and California.

All of these people asked for missionaries. One time a group came from Upper California. They traveled down the gulf to a spot opposite Dolores, where Kino was located. Since they were afraid to cross the 170 miles of unknown land to Dolores, they sent a message asking Kino to come to them. He was away at the time and received the message too late. The visitors, who were living on what fish they could find in the gulf, started to go hungry, and they finally went back to California.

Kino was situated at Dolores, once called Cosari, in the Parish of Our Lady of Sorrows, in a corner of the Pima territory. To the south and to the east were people who spoke Cáhita languages, and farther east were the Apaches. So Kino looked north and west. This suited him, because he was also interested in helping the missions in Baja California, although he never succeeded in making contact with Baja California by land around the gulf. He dreamed of winning the whole desert area for Christ, including Upper California. There were about thirty thousand people in the rectangle from Dolores north to Tucson and west to the Gulf of California and the Colorado River.

Kino was positive and optimistic in his writings. He promoted the importance and dignity of the Pimas and the need for more missionaries. He did not discuss any internal problems at Dolores.

Kino left Mexico for this new mission on November 20, 1686. In Guadalajara, he spoke with public officials. Other Jesuits had told him that the recently converted were being enslaved and forced to work in the mines. He wanted as much relief from this abuse as he could obtain for any people he worked with. He found that a decree had arrived from the king granting an exemption for the recently converted from twenty years of any forced labor. He took with him an official copy of the decree.

Kino arrived at Conicari on the Mayo River on February 15, 1687. At the end of the month, he went to Moctezuma, then called Oposura, on a tributary of the Yaqui and two hundred miles upriver from where the Yaqui empties into the gulf. The vice provincial, the elderly Manuel Gonzalez, was here. He was Jesuit superior of the whole Sonora area, and the two men would work together for fifteen years. By chance, Father Joseph Aguilar, also elderly, was visiting at Moctezuma. He was the missionary who was working farthest to the north.

The three Jesuits mounted and set off. They first stopped at the mining site of San Juan, only a few miles west of Moctezuma, where Kino was introduced to the Spanish governor of the area and where there was a garrison. They went farther west about thirty miles to Huépac on the upper Sonora River to visit the Jesuit who would be Kino's local superior, an Irish Jesuit working under a Spanish name, John Muñoz de Burgos. Going farther west to the San Miguel River a tributary of the Sonora, they rode north about thirty-five miles through

The Pima Area, Where Eusebio Kino Worked for Twenty-four Years

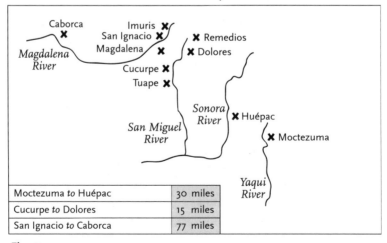

Moctezuma *to* Huépac	30 miles
Cucurpe *to* Dolores	15 miles
San Ignacio *to* Caborca	77 miles

Fig. 23

villages attended by Father Aguilar to Cucurpe. This village, where Aguilar lived, was the last Christian village, and none of the people in this village were Pimas. They all spoke a Cáhita language.

To the west of Cucurpe, stretching 120 miles to the gulf, is a desert. To the east were mountain chains, tributaries of the rivers to the south, and many people. To the north were the Upper Pimas with no missionaries. However, this would not be the first Jesuit missionary work with the Pimas. There was a Pima village far south on the Sinaloa River whose people Tapia and Pérez had met when they first came to Sinaloa. Several villages of people—called Lower Pimas, or Pimas Bajos—were located on the Yaqui River above the Yaqui Nation. Further, there were a few villages of Pimas on the middle Sonora, and all of these people were called Pimas Bajos. It was the Spanish who called them Pimas; their name for themselves was Ootam.

Father Aguilar had contacts with the Upper Pimas, or Pimas Altos, and they were waiting for a Jesuit. The three priests set out from Cucurpe on March 13, 1687. It was only about fifteen miles up the San Miguel River to Dolores, then called Cosari. Cosari was the home of Cacique Coxi, who had prestige and some authority over all of the Pimería. The cacique was away at the time, but the people gave the three Jesuits a warm welcome.

The next morning, Gonzalez returned to Moctezuma, and Kino and Aguilar set off on a seventy-five-mile circular trip through the villages for which Kino would be responsible. They rode west eighteen miles in this mountainous country to San Ignacio on the Magdalena River, which flows directly west and is a tributary of the Concepción River. They went upriver to Imuris, then to Remedios on the San Miguel, and then down to Dolores.

Protected by mountains, Dolores was in a river valley with good land. Kino had seed and stock from other missions to sow fields and to start herds. He also started to build and to instruct in the catechism. For this work, Kino had the help of two brothers who were Pimas Bajos. They were Francis Pintor, a catechist and an interpreter, and Francis's brother, who was blind and an excellent catechist.

That first spring, Kino and a hundred people from Dolores went to Tuape to celebrate Easter. At the end of April, Kino made a circuit of the other villages of San Ignacio, Imuris, and Remedios. He did not travel much farther than this during his first four years. He was also learning a completely new language.

The two children of Cacique Coxi were among the first who were instructed and baptized. Cacique Coxi and his wife were baptized on July 31 of that first year, the feast day of St. Ignatius of Loyola. It was a big occasion, and five caciques came for the ceremony and celebration.

There were many Spanish in the area at mine sites and haciendas to the east and south. From the beginning, there were rumors and calumnies about the Pimas, which Kino had to refute. Kino was not specific about who started the rumors, but in general, it was said that the Pimas did not need missionaries, that they were few, that they were moving away, that they stole horses, or even that they were rebelling.

Almost from the beginning, Kino asked for more Jesuits. The first help arrived at the end of 1689 with three Jesuits, but new Jesuits did not always stay. They might have trouble learning the language, or the whole situation might be more than they could manage.

At this time, the provincial sent Father John Salvatierra to be visitor, or regional superior, and he asked him to investigate Kino and the Pimería because of the contradictory reports he was receiving. The meeting of Kino and Salvatierra was important, and Salvatierra would be the founder of the permanent California mission.

John Salvatierra was born in Milan, Italy, on November 15, 1648. His father was a Spanish official, and his mother was from a noble Italian family. Salvatierra had traveled to New Spain as a seminarian before Kino, and he did his theology at Puebla. He was ordained, did tertianship, and was sent to the Chínipas area in 1680, still a year before Kino arrived in New Spain.

Salvatierra spent ten years in the Sierra Madre, from 1680 to 1690. Then he was named vice provincial, or superior, of Sinaloa and Sonora for three years, and it was at this time, Christmas Eve 1690, that he and Kino met. He was three years younger than Kino.

The two Jesuits decided to see the situation in the Pimería firsthand. They started from Dolores on a trip of some 225 miles. They rode west to visit a new Jesuit at Imuris, where there were seventy families, then to San Ignacio on the Magdalena River, and then farther west another forty miles to visit the Jesuit on the Altar River, which, like the Magdalena, is a tributary of the Concepción River. Kino was now in new territory, and it was his first long journey in the Pimería.

They went farther to Tubutama, where there were five hundred people and a new Jesuit. At a fiesta on January 6, 1691, the Feast of the Epiphany, there were in attendance many chiefs of the Soba people, who made up the western part of the Pima nation and extended to the Gulf of California. The goodwill of these people would later make it possible to explore the west of Arizona to the Colorado River. The Jesuits continued up the Altar River and were invited to visit some villages across what is now the international border in Arizona. Here they were again approached by Pimas and invited to go another forty miles to San Xavier del Bac just south of Tucson, Arizona. They did not go to Bac but returned to Dolores.

Salvatierra was impressed by everything he saw. He saw the goodwill and peaceful nature of the people. He saw their desire to become Christian and the need for more missionaries. Also, on the trail together,

The Upper Pimas, or Pimas Altos

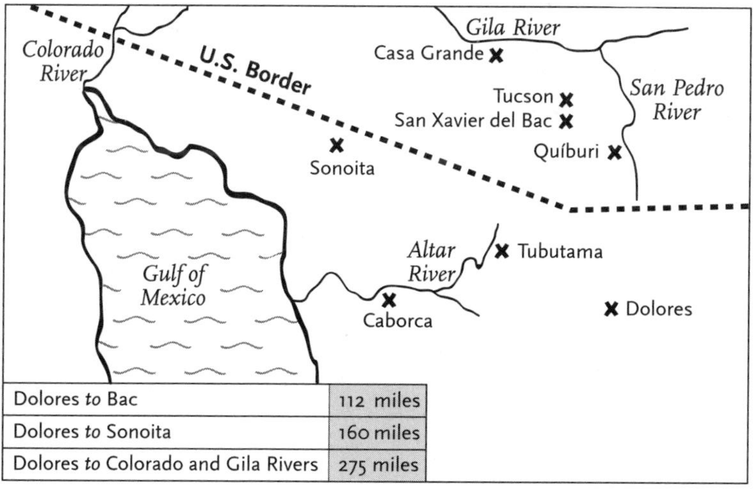

Dolores *to* Bac	112 miles
Dolores *to* Sonoita	160 miles
Dolores *to* Colorado and Gila Rivers	275 miles

Fig. 24

Kino shared his enthusiasm for California, and it was to Baja California that Salvatierra would go, almost seven years later, in October of 1697. He would work there for twenty years, except for a three-year term as provincial. Salvatierra would die on a trip from California to Mexico in 1717, sixty-eight years old, six years after the death of Kino.

The next year, in the summer of 1692, Kino made his first journey to San Xavier del Bac, south of Tucson, where there were eight hundred people. Then he went southeast to visit the important Cacique Coro at Quíburi on the San Pedro River, about thirty-five miles north of the border. The San Pedro River, which flows north to the Gila River, was the Pima front line, facing the Apaches. All of these people were part of the eastern Pimas.

Kino was kept busy building, and also helping missionaries. In April of 1693, the adobe church at Dolores was dedicated, and many Spanish and Native Americans came for the celebration. The Irish Jesuit who was the local superior sang the Mass.

Toward the end of 1693, Father Augustine Campos arrived and would spend several decades in the area. He was the most important Jesuit after Kino. In order to introduce him to the people, Kino invited Campos to go with him on a long trip to Cacique Soba, ruler of the four thousand Soba people, or western Pimas.

At this time, Kino proposed a peace treaty between the warring eastern and western Pimas in order that there might be a united front against the Apaches, and the peace proposal was accepted. Kino and his party then went many more miles west, and from a hill they saw the Gulf of California. The people at this spot were friendly, but some were frightened because it was the first time they had seen Europeans.

After his return to Dolores, Kino talked to civil authorities in Sonora about building a ship at Caborca in order to explore the gulf. He was given a new arrival as a companion, Lieutenant John Manje, who would write many fine journals of his explorations with Kino in the Pimería.

Manje and Kino left Dolores in March of 1694 with supplies to build the ship. There were about a thousand people in the area around Caborca. Except for the Concepción River and its tributaries, they were in a vast desert. However, Kino thought that Caborca would support three thousand or more people. During their stay at Caborca, Manje and Kino went sixty miles farther west to the shore of the Gulf of California.

They left the logs for the ship at Caborca to season, and on the way back to Dolores they came across the remains of a prehistoric site called Trincheras. In June, thinking that the timbers would be seasoned, they returned to Caborca. Manje went north to explore while Kino worked on the ship. A letter came from the local Irish Jesuit superior telling Kino not to continue with the shipbuilding. He probably thought Kino was too often away from his parish duties at Dolores. Kino obeyed, although he did have permission from the provincial.

During 1694, as was typical, there was continual warfare between the Opatas, Pimas, and Spanish on the one hand and the Apaches and other nations to the east and northeast on the other. The Opatas, Pimas, and Spanish were farmers, and the people to the east were nomadic.

In March, some herds of horses were stolen from the Sonora missions. The Pimas north of the future international border on the San Pedro were suspected. A lieutenant, not Manje, took a squad of soldiers to hunt for the horses and the thieves. Toward Bac they discovered Pimas cooking what they thought was the stolen horsemeat. They killed three Pimas and captured two, but it turned out that the Pimas were cooking deer meat.

In May, this lieutenant led 240 armed men against the Apaches. There were 90 soldiers and civilians, as well as 150 Opatas and Pimas. They killed sixty of the enemy and captured thirty as slaves for the mines and haciendas. Then at Tubutama, a village near Caborca, a Jesuit sent word of trouble. Two Pimas were haranguing the others. The lieutenant went with thirty soldiers, and he punished the ringleaders. Several Opata villages in the mountains to the east were attacked by the Apaches during this year. At one mission village, the grain fields were burned, and some old men and women were killed.

At a place called Cuchuta, east of Dolores, six hundred Apaches launched a massive attack. However, the Opatas, Spanish, and Pimas had been warned and were waiting for the attack. They ambushed the attackers and killed twenty-five. One Spanish soldier was killed. They later heard that many more of the attackers had died because the Pimas had used poisoned arrows. This was part of life on the frontier. It was more dangerous than it once was because the Apaches and others had horses even if they did not yet have guns. However, all of this violence in 1694 was typical because there was really a continual state of war in the northeast of Sonora.

In the middle of October 1694, two new missionaries arrived at Dolores. One was Francis Xavier Saeta. Born in Sicily, he came to New Spain in 1692 and did his last year of theology. He was sent to Caborca. There were now six Jesuits in the area. A new rectorate was established with the superior at Cucurpe. Father Kino went with Saeta to Caborca to introduce him and to help him get started.

Toward the end of November, Kino made his first visit to Casa Grande on the Gila River northwest of Tucson. It is an ancient ruin, and Kino described it as a four-story building as large as a castle. Scholars believe that Casa Grande was built by the ancestors of the Pimas.

When Kino went on these trips, he took mares and colts. The people would have to wait a while, but this was one way to start a herd. Kino eventually established nineteen ranches in the Pimería as far as Sonoita and Bac. Meanwhile, Saeta made an enthusiastic beginning at Caborca. He and the two hundred people at Caborca were founding and building the future town. Within a few weeks they had made five hundred adobe bricks.

Kino had promised Saeta a hundred cattle, a hundred sheep and goats, saddle and pack animals, twenty mares with their colts, 120 bushels of wheat and corn, and household effects, all of which he would deliver a little at a time. Kino asked Saeta to consider about 10 percent of the stock as in trust for the California mission, which did not yet exist.

Kino had also asked Francis Pintor to go with Saeta to help him. Pintor was the catechist who had been with Kino since he arrived. He and his blind brother were Pimas Bajos from Ures on the Sonora River. Pintor had ridden with Kino and Manje on some of their expeditions.

Saeta soon realized that the supplies from Kino would be insufficient. So at the end of November, he made a begging trip around the missions. Kino headed the subscription list, promising another sixty cattle, sixty sheep and goats, 120 bushels of wheat and corn, and more mares. Hogs are not mentioned. Kino had attempted to introduce hogs at Dolores, but the men did not wish to care for them. They assigned the task to the women, who could not manage the animals, and one woman was hurt.

Saeta was not neglecting religious instruction. He wrote:

> My children attend Mass every morning and catechism twice a day, adults as well as children. They work with all love. I have planted a very pretty garden plot in which the little trees [a gift from Kino] are set out and the vegetable seeds planted for the refreshment of the sailors from California.

Kino invited Saeta to Dolores for Holy Week services and for a rest, but Saeta begged off. Later, he suggested to Kino that they meet halfway. He wrote to Kino on April 1, 1695, and the next day he was dead.

The trouble started at Tubutama, about fifty miles upstream from Caborca. This is the place where two people were punished and probably hanged the previous year. The Jesuit there was Daniel Januske. With him he had two Spanish and three Opata overseers, as it was the custom to employ experienced cowboys and herdsmen as overseers in new areas. There was great tension at Tubutama between the Pimas and the newcomers.

Things blew up on March 29. Father Daniel had left to observe Holy Week at Tuape. An Opata herdsman knocked down and kicked the Pima overseer of the farm. The Pima shouted to his friends, "This Opata is killing me." They attacked the Opata and killed him. The two Spanish fled, and the Pimas killed the other two Opatas.

The Pimas burned the church and the priest's house, desecrated sacred articles, and slaughtered mission cattle. They then started for Caborca to clear all foreigners from the area. It was not an organized revolt but a group of angry people.

Saeta received word of the destruction, and he thought it was a deep raid by some group from far to the east. He heard that a man and a boy from Dolores had been killed. They were returning to Dolores after having brought cattle to Saeta from Kino.

Others—a group of more than fifty—joined the Pimas as they came south on Holy Saturday, April 2, 1685. They went to Saeta's quarters and talked with him, acting peaceful. When he went to the door with them, they shot him with two arrows. He went back inside, picked up his crucifix, and fell on the bed, where they shot him with more arrows.

They then killed Francis Pintor, who, as much as anyone, had been evangelist of the Upper Pimería. They also killed the two Opatas who were overseers at Caborca. After they sacked Saeta's house and stampeded the cattle, they returned upstream. Francis Xaxier Saeta is buried at Cucurpe.

During this time, Kino was suffering with a fever at Dolores, but he arranged with the Spanish that there would be peace if the Pimas handed the ringleaders of the group that killed Saeta and the Opatas over for punishment. However, some people in the government thought that rebellious Indians should be soundly punished. The governor was persuaded, and he broke his agreement with Kino.

The Pimas and the soldiers met at El Tupo, about twenty-five miles west of Dolores, on June 9, 1695. The ringleaders were handed over. The soldiers then surrounded the fifty Pimas who had brought the ringleaders in and were unarmed. Three other Pimas started to point out accomplices of the ringleaders. This was not part of the agreement. Manje, who was an eyewitness, wrote that the lieutenant drew his sword and struck off the head of one of the accused. This act of violence panicked the Pimas. They tried to escape, and the soldiers shot them down, killing forty-eight. Kino wrote that thirty were innocent of any complicity in what had happened to Saeta and the Opatas.

The lieutenant in charge was the same person who had killed one of the three people who were cooking deer meat near Bac by mistake. He had also punished and probably hanged the two people at Tubutama the previous year.

Later, when the soldiers left the area to continue their struggle against the Apaches, the Pimas rose in fury. They destroyed what was left of the buildings at Caborca. They burned the churches and houses at Imuris, San Ignacio, and Magdalena, but they did not attack Dolores, Remedios, and Cocóspora, which were under the care of Kino.

The soldiers returned to put down the rebellion. The Spanish feared that it would engulf all of Sonora and that the Spanish would be driven out, as they had been from New Mexico only fifteen years previously. However, the Pimería was not isolated like New Mexico. Also, the uprising was not an organized rebellion. The people were enraged about what had happened at El Tupo, and bands of Pimas were destroying the establishments of the five Jesuits in the area. However, the records do not mention that they actually killed anyone, and the caciques, including pagan ones, were not committed to a rebellion.

An army of a few hundred Spanish and Native Americans gathered to put down the uprising. The army marched west, but the soldiers found no army to fight, although they attacked Tubutama, killing twenty-one people and destroying the crops in the area.

The army then moved south to Caborca, where the people had had nothing to do with anything that had happened. Their food supply had been damaged by the raiders from Tubutama, and then it had been destroyed by soldiers who came after the death of Saeta. These people were scattered in the mountains and deserts, and some of them were begging for food in different villages. They feared to reassemble at Caborca until Kino was called in to reassure them. Finally, there was a big meeting, and peace was reestablished.

On November 16, 1695, Kino, fifty years old and now seven and a half years in the Pimería, set out on a trip to Mexico. He rode with young Pimas, including the son of the cacique of Dolores. They rode the twelve hundred miles to Mexico in seven weeks instead of the usual three months, and Kino was able to offer Mass each day of the trip.

This trip was crucial because of the uprising and the massacre at El Tupo and because the mission was in danger of being abandoned. Kino's ideals and vision for the area are described in a book he wrote, just before leaving Dolores, about Father Francis Xavier Saeta, the slain missionary. He attributed to Saeta the qualities that a missionary must have: a sincere affection for the people, a boundless generosity toward them, heroic endurance of the inevitable hardships, frequent prayer and meditation, avoidance of idleness, and the good example of a profound and well-ordered religious life. The Indians must see that the missionary is personally interested in them and that he will spend himself for their welfare, both temporal and eternal. He must not just direct others, but personally share in the work of instruction, visiting the sick, constructing buildings, farming, and so on. The missionary life is a supernatural calling, and although divine assistance is more important than human effort, the former will not be forthcoming unless man does his part.

It is also important not to offend anyone, because the Indians make public whatever they know about someone. "On journeys to very distant regions I have met Indians whom I had never seen. They come up and say they already know me. This would happen even as I traveled farther from home."[2]

As much as possible, there should be no military presence. Sometimes the soldiers are summoned to a disturbed area. By the time they arrive, the guilty have disappeared, and the innocent are often punished. The soldiers do not have to return with prisoners as evidence of their success. Law-abiding natives should see the soldiers as their protectors, not their persecutors. Also, as much as possible, the missions should be self-supporting.

One of the main purposes of both the trip and the book was to defend the Pimas. Kino said that there was not a general revolt but a raid on Caborca by a few people who had been abused. He described the cooperation of the Pimas to punish the guilty—cooperation that resulted in the massacre of innocent people at El Tupo and the consequent attacks on other missions.

Father Kino had a vision of a Christian and prosperous civilization that included Baja and Alta California, the Pimería and the Yumas, and all the people to New Mexico and beyond. He was thinking of the evangelization of California when he started to build that ship, and he persisted in his effort to find a trail through the desert to Baja California for livestock and people. On his journeys, he explained the faith and the sacraments. He also relied on trained catechists to spread the message. Lieutenant Manje was well educated and well read. If he was exploring on his own, he too would explain the faith. They used the cross and what pictures they had when they taught.

Kino wrote:

Many of these poor people, despite their humble condition, on seeing and experiencing kind treatment will come to rely on the missionary with deep attachment, sharing with him the best of their possessions and food. Gradually they will place themselves and their families at the disposal of the missionary. These newly converted Christians, with striking simplicity and with less reluctance than other Indians and older Christians, hold in high esteem and awe what they had not heard before, such as the more extraordinary doctrines of our faith—for example, the resurrection of the dead, the never ending torture of hell for the wicked, the everlasting happiness of heaven given in reward to the good, and the divine creation of the universe, including all peoples, the sun, moon, heaven, earth, and all else.[3]

During his stay in Mexico, Kino met Salvatierra, who was stationed at Tepotzotlán. They still could not obtain permission for the evangelization of California, but the provincial did promise five Jesuits for the Pimería.

Kino arrived back at Dolores in the middle of May 1696. He sent word of his coming to caciques and Pima officials, and they had a big meeting and fiesta at Dolores in June. Kino brought greetings to the people from different officials in Mexico. These Pima leaders then helped Kino to harvest the ripe grain, as it seems they did every year.

Some were baptized at this time. Others were denied baptism as not sufficiently prepared. In order to show the loyalty of the Pima Nation, Kino sent the minutes of this assembly to officials in Mexico, together with a list of the Pimas who participated. He kept up with the paperwork.

The next spring, 1697, word came that Kino was going to California with Salvatierra. Civil officials protested loudly that Kino could not leave the Pimería. So he stayed, and the vice provincial asked him to prepare the way for new missionaries on the San Pedro River, east of Tucson.

That same spring, the cacique of Bac and two of his children came to Dolores to be instructed and baptized, and around that time Kino sent an oven to the people of Bac as a present.

In the fall, Kino and Lieutenant John Manje made plans to explore the San Pedro River. They and ten Pimas set out from Dolores after Mass on All Souls' Day, November 2, 1697, with sixty horses and mules and with three pack loads of provisions. One of the ten Pimas

Kino's Explorations into the Present American Southwest, 1697 and Following

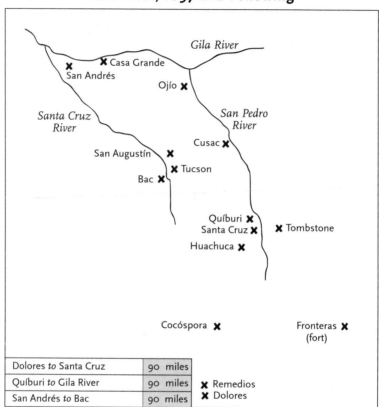

Dolores *to* Santa Cruz	90 miles
Quíburi *to* Gila River	90 miles
San Andrés *to* Bac	90 miles

Fig. 25

was an official at Dolores named Francis the Painter. He was a fine interpreter and catechist like Francis Pintor, who had died with Father Saeta two years earlier at Caborca. Perhaps he had taken the name Francis Pintor when he was baptized.

They headed first for Quíburi, which was ninety miles from Dolores as the crow flies. They went north through Remedios and Cocóspora, where there was a Jesuit. After a few more stops, they arrived at Huachuca, where eighty Pima residents received them hospitably.

Huachuca was about fifteen miles southwest of Quíburi, and at a later time there would be a U.S. fort at Huachuca with the Buffalo Soldiers (African American cavalry). The next morning they traveled to the San Pedro River and stopped at Santa Cruz, a few miles south of Quíburi and across the river from the present-day town of Fairbank. A few miles east of Fairbank is the later mining site of Tombstone, where many movies would be made.

At Santa Cruz there were a hundred people. They had built an adobe house with a timber-and-dirt roof for a future missionary, and they were caring for a hundred cattle, which Kino had sent them. The next day, a Spanish captain arrived at Santa Cruz with twenty-two soldiers and a pack train. This was a diplomatic mission to meet and to see the peaceful nature of the people, but the soldiers were well armed, as they were on the frontier with the Apaches to the east. After greeting one another, they went a few miles north and downriver to Quíburi, where Cacique Coro gave them a big welcome.

At Quíburi, there were a hundred houses and five hundred people. Quíburi was fortified and situated on a bluff with a commanding view of the surrounding countryside. The land was irrigated, and the people grew corn, cantaloupe, watermelon, other foodstuffs, and cotton. They wove the cotton into cloth, dyed it, and made clothes. They wore shoes made of animal skins.

When Kino's party arrived, they found the Pimas celebrating a recent victory over their nomadic enemies. Kino wrote that they found them to be very jovial and friendly, dancing over the scalps and spoils of fifteen enemies, Jocomes and Janos, whom they had killed a few days before. The captain, the sergeant, and many others entered their circle and danced with them.

That evening and the next days, both Kino and Manje spoke about the mysteries of the faith, and the captain spoke about matters of state and war.

When they left the following morning, they were accompanied by Cacique Coro and thirty of his armed warriors. The threat of an Apache ambush was serious, and it would be a ninety-mile trip down the San Pedro to the Gila River. For the first sixty miles north of Quíburi, the San Pedro River was mostly deserted because of hostility between Coro's Pimas and the Pimas on the San Pedro nearer the Gila. All the Pimas on the San Pedro were called the Sabaípuris.

As they traveled, they had scouts out because they were afraid of being ambushed. Nomadic people lived in the mountains to the east of the San Pedro River and north of the Gila. The nomadic people had tents, and when they moved, a team of at least two big dogs dragged poles carrying a tent.

The party had sent messages that they were coming with peaceful intentions. Although Father Kino was now in a new territory, he knew some of the chiefs because they had traveled down to Dolores to be instructed and baptized. The first village they came to was Cusac, with seventy people and twenty houses. It was in a beautiful location with many cottonwood trees by the San Pedro. In the roughly thirty miles from here to the Gila River, there were ten villages with about 100 people in each village, except that the principal village of Ojío, near the Gila and under the Christian cacique Humari, had 380 people and seventy houses.

At Cusac, Kino's party was received with crosses, arches, a swept road, and abundant cooked food. The visitors gave gifts of knives, needles, religious medals, and ribbons—valuable gifts at that time and place, and not too bulky to transport. They also had a bulkier gift of cloth.

There were talks about the faith and about loyalty to the Spanish government. These meetings, conversations, and instructions often went on all night. The travelers then went downstream another five miles to a bigger village, where they were warmly received and where a temporary lodging had been constructed of poles and mats. While Kino was baptizing four infants and some sick people who were in danger of death, Cacique Humari and numerous companions arrived. They had come down on foot from Ojío because there were not yet horses in these villages. All of the villages probably had goats and sheep, but the cattle and horse ranches extended to the south only from Bac and Quíburi.

The next morning after Mass, Cacique Coro and Cacique Humari publicly embraced and were reconciled. Then they all traveled north together, stopping at some villages, until they reached Ojío, where they had a big celebration. The captain gave a ribboned cane of authority to Cacique Humari. There was a long meeting in which many men spoke—the captain, Kino, Manje, Francis the Painter, Cacique Coro, and others.

Having counted about two thousand people on the San Pedro, including children and infants, they decided to continue their exploration down the Gila to meet new people and to see the prehistoric ruin at Casa Grande. Cacique Coro and his thirty warriors went with them, and they kept sentries on duty during the night.

This part of the Gila was new to Kino, although he had been to Casa Grande from Bac three years earlier. After Casa Grande, where Kino offered Mass as he did each day, they continued down the Gila to San Andrés, where the cacique was a Christian who had traveled to Dolores to be instructed and baptized. They had passed two villages of about two hundred people each on this river, and there were four hundred people at San Andrés. Manje mentions that the people had cotton stockings, which were attached to their trousers so that they formed a single garment. The people also had clothing and shoes made from the skins of deer and pronghorns, which are indigenous animals similar to antelopes. Manje also noticed the shining pottery of these people.

The Pimas on these rivers seem to have been better off than the people of Sonora and Sinaloa were. They were certainly better off than the poverty-stricken and mostly naked Pimas who lived in the desert in southwest Arizona.

The party continued to the Santa Cruz River, and turning south, they traveled eighty miles upriver to San Augustín, where there were 800 people in 186 houses. After visiting here, they went on to Bac, where there were 830 people in 166 houses and where the houses were divided into three neighborhoods that formed a triangle. The people at Bac received them joyfully, even treating them to fresh bread baked in an oven that Kino had sent. At Bac, two of the Spanish officers purchased two Jocome captives, a girl of twelve and a boy of ten. From here, Cacique Coro, mounted on a new horse that the party had given him, left with his warriors for Quíburi.

On the way back to Dolores, the travelers stopped two days to work on the big church that was being built at Remedios. They were back at Dolores on December 2, after a journey of thirty days. They had traveled over five hundred miles and had counted almost five thousand Pimas on the rivers. Kino had baptized eighty small children and eight sick adults who were in danger of death.

A few months later, on February 25, 1698, three hundred Apaches attacked Cocóspora. This is hard to understand because Cocóspora is about forty miles west of the fort at Fronteras. The raiders were deep in Pima and Spanish territory. They took a few horses, as well as smaller animals like sheep and goats, and burned the buildings. The Pimas and the Jesuit missionary were in a barricade, and only two Pimas were killed. However, after the raiders left, some Pimas went after them and were ambushed, and nine more Pimas were killed. A combined force of Pimas and soldiers then gathered and went in pursuit. They caught the raiders, killed thirty, captured sixteen, and recovered the horses and other stolen property.

A month later, on March 30, six hundred Apaches, Jocomes, Sumas, and Xanos attacked Santa Cruz on the San Pedro River at daybreak. The raiders came mostly on foot. There were a hundred people at Santa Cruz and a hundred cattle. Four of the Pimas were killed, and the others barricaded themselves in a building. Santa Cruz was only about five miles south of Quíburi, which had a total of five hundred people, but the raiders, who included both men and women, were so numerous that they felt very secure. They made themselves at home in the village, butchered some animals, and started to cook a meal.

Word of the attack reached Quíburi, where many extra people had come from the west in order to trade. Cacique Coro and a large group of well-armed Pimas moved south to Santa Cruz. Facing so many Pima warriors, the Apache cacique proposed that each side choose ten men to fight each other, and the proposal was accepted. The ten chosen to fight for the raiders included six Apaches. The battle consisted of shooting arrows and dodging or deflecting the arrows of one's opponent.

The raiders shot their arrows well, but they were not nimble in avoiding the arrows of the Pimas. Nine of the raiders were killed or wounded, but no Pimas were hurt. In the end, it was one Pima against the Apache cacique. When the cacique was thrown to the ground and killed, the raiders panicked and fled. The Pimas killed fifty-four of the raiders at Santa Cruz, thirty-one men and twenty-three women. Armed with poisoned arrows, the Pimas pursued the enemy for over ten miles, and only about three hundred escaped.

The battle was so extraordinary and the victory so complete that each side was shocked and even frightened. Cacique Coro moved his people to the west for some months before returning to the San Pedro, and the Apaches and their allies asked the Spanish for peace in El Paso and in New Mexico.

In September of the same year, an interesting meeting took place at Remedios, just north of Dolores, which reveals Kino at work. A statue had come to Remedios from Mexico, and Kino turned the dedication of the statue into a religious and civic celebration. The year before, there had been another great victory of the Pimas on the San Pedro against hostile people to the east. So Kino decided to dedicate the statue on the anniversary of this victory. Caciques and their families came from as far away as Casa Grande, and Kino also invited other Jesuits and Spanish officials.

All sorts of things were happening. Old friendships were renewed, and new friendships were made. Kino had an opportunity to preach about the faith. He also made arrangements for a long trip down the Gila to the Colorado River and south on the Colorado to the Gulf of California. A celebration like this revealed the generosity and hospitality of the Pimas at Dolores and Remedios.

Suppose at a celebration like this that a cacique or a member of his family were to be baptized. Kino might ask a Spanish official and his wife to be godparents. In the Spanish culture, the godparents become coparents (*copadre* and *comadre*). It created a familial relationship.

Kino's religious superiors wanted him to explore the Colorado area because Salvatierra was now in California. They wanted to know if supplies could be sent to the Baja overland from the Pimería. Civil officials also wanted him to explore because there were rumors of a quicksilver mine in the area.

Kino, the cacique of Dolores, and seven other Pimas went on this expedition in October, and they took with them a Spanish captain as an official representative of the government. This captain was important because he was an independent witness that the people were friendly, peaceful, and numerous enough to justify missionaries.

This trip produced the first written description of Pápago land, or the Papaguería. The Pápagos are related to the Pimas, and they received Kino's party with kindness. The people of the different villages guided them through the area as they followed the Gila River to the west. On this trip, Kino realized for the first time that the Gila flowed not into the gulf but into the Colorado River. After going south to the village of Sonoita, they went farther west to a mountain. From this high spot, Kino saw that the Colorado flowed into the gulf. It was too hazy to see California.

During the following years, Kino made other expeditions, and he became friends with the Yumas on the Colorado. They were the biggest Indians Kino ever met. He crossed this river one or two times, but he was never able to open up a land route to Baja California. In 1699, Kino asked his superiors if he could go as a missionary to Upper California, but nothing developed from the request.

In October of 1700, Kino rode a thousand miles in twenty-six days. He was fifty-five years old. Also in 1700, he sent two hundred cattle to Baja California by ship. Each year he also sent fifteen mule loads of flour to California. In this year, he asked for a replacement at Dolores so that he could live at Bac. Superiors said yes, and Kino sent seven hundred cattle to Bac. However, he never got to go. The superiors sent another Jesuit in 1701.

In this year, Kino was named local superior, or rector, of a new rectorate in the Pimería, and Salvatierra came for a second visit. He wanted to find a land route to Baja California because shipping supplies to California was too expensive. He got permission from the various officials and obtained some soldiers. Then he sent word to Dolores that he was coming.

It was a big expedition. There were about 150 animals—horses and mules. There were forty mule loads of food and supplies. The personnel included Salvatierra, Kino, Manje, five Californians, ten or fifteen soldiers, and a great number of Pimas. They all met at Caborca, a hundred miles west of Dolores, where the cacique of Sonoita had sent four Pimas to bid them welcome and to act as guides.

On March 11, 1701, they set out from Caborca for the trip north, over a hundred miles, to Sonoita on the international border. As they set out, they were in a good mood because it had rained recently and the desert was full of flowers. They sang on the trail. However, it soon became difficult for the animals. They had to go more than two days without water, and the animals were half crazed by thirst. Finally, the party found some water, and then they reached Sonoita.

From Sonoita, the way became more difficult. The animals again went two days without water until they found some by a poor village. Salvatierra said the land was black from ancient lava, full of boulders, and sandy. The animals were either damaging their hoofs on rough lava beds or sinking to their knees in the sand.

It was at this poor village that they celebrated Palm Sunday on March 20. The next day they left the animals at a water hole. The main party went on, and that evening of the twenty-first, their guides brought them to three springs. They were only a mile from the gulf. From a high spot they could see Baja California curving away from where they stood. They were convinced that the Baja was a peninsula and not an island. After a further attempt to find sufficient water for the animals, they were forced to give up and return.

In 1702, Kino lost four missionaries. Two of them left the area, and one died of sickness after a year at Tubutama. The fourth one, after a year at San Xavier del Bac, caught pneumonia and died.

Kino spent 1704 building new churches at Remedios and Cocóspora. He sold cattle to raise 3,700 pesos, which he used to buy tools and cloth. Workers with their families came from as far as Bac to help build the churches. Besides daily food, Kino paid them with blankets and fabric.

In this same year, Kino and the Pimas of Dolores gave a charitable donation of silver, worth a thousand pesos, in order to adorn the tomb of St. Ignatius in Rome. They sent the silver to the provincial in Mexico City, and they asked him to forward it to Rome. Instead of forwarding it, the provincial used it to buy and to send to Dolores supplies that had not been requested. The provincial was afraid that the Jesuits would be accused of exploiting the Indians.

In early 1705, while Kino was away, a Spanish lieutenant and his troops plundered Dolores. Some Pimas had moved to Dolores from other villages. The lieutenant took ninety of them and forced them to return to their original villages. He also stole grain, goats, and sheep. He said he would return later for the horses and cattle. Almost all of the ninety people returned to Dolores.

This lieutenant later tried to take corn from another village. When the leaders pointed out that they could easily join the enemy in the mountains, the lieutenant reported to his superiors that the Pimas had revolted. This caused a lot of commotion and wild rumors even as far as Mexico. The lieutenant was finally dismissed from the army.

Six other new churches were also being built in the Pimería in 1705. A Pima from Dolores went to Tubutama to oversee the making of the adobe bricks. Pima carpenters from Dolores helped at Magdalena, Caborca, and other places. Kino said that the carpenters were rather expert.

As Kino grew older, Manje, his friend and riding companion, became a general. Manje wrote a valuable book about his explorations in the Pimería. However, in this book he criticized the missions. He said that the missions were monopolizing the best agricultural land and that only the poorer land was left for the Spanish. He said that the Spanish had been defending the area with their property and their lives. He mentioned that the older missions had few Indians left. Where there were thousands, now there were only a few hundred. He recommended that the land be distributed to the Spanish. He also thought that the Spanish should be able to use the *repartimiento* system as in other places. This system meant that the Native Americans would be distributed to work for the Spanish. The system was hedged with laws; for example, it required just wages. However, it was forced labor. It often led to abuse and to the enslavement of the Native Americans.

Manje also criticized the Jesuits for not offering spiritual ministry to the Spanish and to their Indian servants. This was a touchy subject. If the Jesuits ministered to the Spanish, they were accused of usurping the place and rights of the diocesan clergy. If they did not minister to the Spanish, they were accused of negligence. The Jesuit regional superior reacted to all of this with the threat to pull the Jesuits out of Sonora. Since this frightened the Spanish, the governor of Sonora put the general in jail on a trumped-up charge until he modified his opinions.

In 1706, Eusebio Kino made his last two long expeditions. In January, he went with another Jesuit and a group of Pimas to the Gulf of California and down to Tiburón Island. Along this desolate stretch of the coast they met sixteen hundred Indians, some of whom were Pimas but most of whom were Seris and Teporas. The Indians were affable because some of them had visited Caborca and a few had even been to Dolores. Kino baptized some infants and sick adults, and he invited the Indians to move to Caborca since their land was somewhat sterile. They said that they would do so little by little.

In October of 1706, when Kino was sixty-one years old, he traveled about five hundred miles round-trip to the north of the gulf and near the Colorado River in order to meet some new people. On this trip, caciques of the Yumas met with him at Sonoita, where people were caring for a herd of cattle in expectation of a missionary.

During his last few years, Kino was doing pastoral work, writing, and producing maps.

In March of 1711, Eusebio Kino rode over to Magdalena to dedicate a chapel. In the middle of the ceremony he became ill, and soon after he died. Sixty-five years old, he had spent twenty-four years in the Pimería. He is buried at Magdalena, where a monument was recently erected in his honor.

1712–1767

After the death of Kino, there was a decline. Then, after 1730, there was a revival with the coming of Swiss and German Jesuits, but this renewal did not include Kino's parish at Dolores. Dolores and its *visita*, Remedios, were depopulated by epidemics, and Dolores was eventually abandoned.

In 1736, there was a big silver strike at a village called Arizonac in the Pimería, which brought many more Spanish to the area. Some years after this date, a Jesuit reported that twenty-eight of the ninety-two Jesuit mission parishes in New Spain had no government stipend.

In 1749, a colonel arrived from Spain and came to the area intent on gaining wealth. His first act was a campaign against the Seris. He enslaved them and sent many of them to the south. He then appointed a Pima, who had fought with him against the Seris, as native governor of the Pimería. This Pima had a free hand. The colonel was indifferent to the area and did not visit it. There was general disorder in the area, and people became contemptuous of Spanish authority.

The Pima whom the colonel had appointed finally organized a revolt. The rebels killed Father Thomas Tello at Caborca on November 24, 1751. He was from La Mancha, Spain, born September 17, 1720. He entered the Society before he was fifteen years old and he was thirty-one when he died.

A few days later, the rebels killed Father Henry Ruhen at Sonoita. He was born January 16, 1718, and entered the Society when he was eighteen years old. He was from Borssum, Germany. He died when he was thirty-three years old.

One of the unhappy results of this rebellion was that the unity of the Pimas Altos was broken. As time went on, violence continued between the Spanish and the Apaches. Jesuit Michael Sola had an unhappy experience with the Apaches. He was stationed at a village near the fort at Fronteras. After the expulsion of the Jesuits from New Spain, he wrote in Europe about what had happened.

> It happened one time that the Apache head of an Indian band bowed his head. He came to me at sunset. He said that he wanted to talk with me and that he had many things to say. We sat down. He began this way. "Well, Father, here I am. I want to be with you like your other children of the pueblo because my heart has completely changed. Up to now I have been killing, robbing, and doing as much harm as I could. Now I want to change my life and to be subject to you so that you can teach me how I ought to live."
>
> He and his band settled near the fort. His name was Baptist. He had a brother named Peter. Meanwhile other Apaches robbed cattle and horses from the Spanish some forty or more miles away. The Spanish started to complain about the peaceful Indians near the fort. They saw them as possible spies.
>
> One morning I received a letter from the captain asking me to come to the fort as he had some news for me. I went promptly from the mission to the fort, and they rang the bells to announce my coming as is the custom in

these parts. The Indians, men and women, all came into the fort to greet me, unaware of what was to happen.

With the pretext that he was going to rest, the captain separated me from my beloved children. He read me an order from his superior that he should seize the Indians who were at peace with the least bloodshed possible.

"And it was for this that you summoned me?"

He shrugged his shoulders. He said, "I have to obey. Without the coming of your reverence, I would not have been able to seize them without a lot of bloodshed."

He shouted that they should enter to eat corn. They entered. The doors were closed and bolted. The soldiers came from those rooms of the house where they had been stationed. They fell upon the strongest men who were armed. Another group collected the women.

I returned to the mission with the bitter knowledge that I had been used as bait in such an injustice (tiranias) and that I was leaving in that miserable state those whom I look on as my children.[4]

These Apaches were joined to some Seris. The soldiers started to take them to Mexico. One night, after they had traveled some four hundred miles, the soldiers were dancing and drinking. They were near the Mocorito River south of Villa Sinaloa. During the night the prisoners broke free of their bonds, but they could not free Baptist and his brother Peter, who were probably in chains. So they carried them, and all escaped.

In the morning the soldiers went after the fugitives. They had all disappeared except for Baptist and Peter. They killed Baptist and wounded Peter. Peter shouted, "Don't kill me. I'm a Christian." They then took him to Mocorito, where Peter received baptism before dying of his wounds.

Michael Sola was transferred from this area before the expulsion. He ended up an exile in Italy; the other Hispanic Jesuits from this area ended up in prison in Spain.

CHAPTER 11

Baja California, 1697–1767

John Mary Salvatierra was the superior of the next Jesuit mission to Baja California. Three years younger than Eusebio Kino, he was born November 15, 1648, in Milan, Italy, of a Spanish father and an Italian mother (mentioned earlier). After entering the Society in that country, he arrived in New Spain while still a seminarian in 1675, which was six years before Kino arrived. After Salvatierra finished theology, was ordained, and did tertianship, he was sent as a missionary to the Chínipas area, arriving there at the end of 1680, the year of the revolt in New Mexico, while Kino was still waiting for a ship in Spain. During Kino's first two efforts in California, Salvatierra worked as a priest in the Chínipas mission.

The first Jesuit effort in Chínipas had ended in 1632, almost fifty years earlier, with the martyrdom of Julio Pascual and Manuel Martinez near Guadalupe Victoria and upriver from the pueblo of Chínipas. Since that time, the people had intermarried with the Tarahumaras, and they now spoke Tarahumara rather than a dialect of the language. Some of them were Catholics because they had close contacts with relatives in Sinaloa. Jesuits had also visited the area and baptized some children and some sick people who recovered.

The Jesuits described the people as morally superior (just as they had described the Chínipas people at an earlier date). They did not kill or rob. Each had one spouse. *Hechiceros* were rare, as were common drinking bouts. The people lived along a stream or river, where they had sheep.

Two Italian Jesuits had revived the mission in 1676, and Salvatierra, now thirty-two years old, was assigned to Guazápares and Témoris, where he worked for ten years.

Things went well for Salvatierra at Témoris and at other villages, but he had trouble at Guazápares. People from this village had led the plot against the missionaries fifty years earlier. The majority of the people were now Christian, but many men had second wives in another place. When Salvatierra visited the village, the people were unfriendly. In fact, they mimicked and mocked him when he heard confessions and offered Mass. One night there were sudden war cries around his hut, and he thought he was going to die. But, even though frightened, he felt an obligation to visit because there were sincere Christians in the village.

Salvatierra pretended not to know all that was going on in the village because he could do nothing about it. However, one woman kept complaining both publicly and loudly about the infidelity of her husband. The husband finally killed her. The leadership of Guazápares now approached the other villages and proposed doing away with the Jesuits. When the other pueblos rejected the proposal, the Guazápares found themselves isolated.

Then one night there was a noisy drinking bout. The next day Salvatierra informed the people that he was leaving and that the soldiers were coming to restore order. Then he left.

When the cacique went to Salvatierra and sought reconciliation before the soldiers arrived, Salvatierra returned to the village and preached in the church. He spoke of wrongdoing or sin, about sorrow, about penance and punishment, and about reconciliation and God's mercy. As he spoke, saying that he was a sinner, he removed his top garments. The person in charge of punishing crimes then whipped him. The cacique next submitted to this penance. Then the other men and women did the same. When the soldiers came, the man who killed his wife was punished but no one else.

During his time in the area, Salvatierra made a trip to the bottom of the Copper Canyon, which is bigger and deeper than the Grand Canyon. The descent was another occasion for terror.

In 1690, after Salvatierra had spent ten years in the Sierra, the provincial appointed him regional superior, or visitor, for three years of the Jesuit missions in Sinaloa and Sonora. The provincial asked him specifically to investigate Kino and the Pimería because he was hearing contradictory reports about the situation in that area. Kino had been in the Pimería for four years and as yet had done little exploring.

When Salvatierra left the Chínipas area, he did not go to the coast and then north but traveled directly north through the Sierra to visit the upper Tarahumara missions.

The revolt in New Mexico ten years earlier had fostered a rebellious spirit in northern Chihuahua, and two Jesuits had just been killed (mentioned earlier) at remote spots west of modern-day Guerrero. Salvatierra wanted to see the situation and to encourage the Christians in the area. He then went west through the rugged mountains to Sonora and eventually to Dolores to investigate Kino.

So the two Jesuits met—Salvatierra, who was forty-two years old, and Kino, who was forty-five. They rode together a few hundred miles to see the Pimería, including part of Arizona but not as far as Tucson. On the trip, Kino inspired his companion with his vision of a Christian California, and Kino had a convert.

At this time Father Francis Píccolo, Salvatierra's future companion in California, was working in the Tarahumara. Píccolo was six years younger than Salvatierra. Born in Palermo, Sicily, on March 25, 1654, he taught on Malta as a young Jesuit, and on the way to New Spain, he had kind of a world tour. First he went to Rome and then to Spain in order to leave from Cádiz. A pirate ship chased his ship on the Atlantic, and it ended up in Central America. He saw Guatemala City and then came up through New Spain to Mexico.

Píccolo then went to Carichic in the Tarahumara for about ten years. In the beginning, he went through desolation of spirit in trying to learn the language. However, things improved, and he built a stone church at Carichic that is still in use, the most beautiful of the Jesuit churches in the Tarahumara. Píccolo was a person who got things done, and when Kino heard of him, he tried to get him for the Pimería.

After Salvatierra finished his term of office as visitor in 1693, he became rector of the Jesuit college in Guadalajara for three years. Then he was named superior and master of novices at Tepotzotlán. Salvatierra again met Kino in 1696 when Kino visited Mexico, and they still could not obtain permission from the provincial to evangelize California.

Finally, early in 1697, the provincial named the two of them to go to the Baja, and he appointed Salvatierra as superior. Salvatierra met with the viceroy, who said the government would not put up any money for the venture, not even the 350 pesos a year that was paid to each missionary. Salvatierra would have to raise the money himself. He could take soldiers with him, but he had to pay them. He could appoint and remove the captain as well as other officials. However, the Baja would be part of New Spain and under the king.[1]

At this point, Father John Ugarte, thirty-five years old and eight years younger than Píccolo, stepped in to help Salvatierra. He and Salvatierra went begging, and they raised thirty thousand pesos from donations for immediate expenses as well as another thirty thousand to start a pious, or missionary, investment fund to support the work in California.

John Ugarte was born June 22, 1662, in the capital of Honduras. He studied in Guatemala City, and after ordination he was minister at Tepotzotlán. Then he taught philosophy and was superior at San Gregorio in Mexico City. He is described as a big man and very strong.

John Ugarte very much wanted to be part of this new mission effort of 1697. However, he agreed to stay in Mexico in order to raise money, to publicize the effort, to purchase supplies, and to get the supplies to the coast. In 1700, he obtained permission to visit California. He just missed Salvatierra in Sinaloa, where Salvatierra was going north again to Dolores in order to search with Kino for a land route to the Baja. John Ugarte got to California in a leaky boat in March of 1701. He then wrote to the provincial and obtained permission to stay.

So it was in the summer of 1697 that Salvatierra arrived in Sinaloa on his way to Baja California. While he waited for Kino to arrive as well as for the supplies from Ugarte, he decided to visit friends in the Chínipas area.

When it was decided that Kino should stay in Sonora instead of returning to California, the provincial named Francis Píccolo to replace Kino. When Salvatierra received word of the replacement, he decided not to wait. He had a ship and a sloop at his disposal that had been lent by the treasurer of Acapulco.

In crossing the gulf, the ship became separated from the sloop, which was manned by six sailors and carried the meat of thirty butchered cattle as well as good corn. The ship itself sailed on October 10, 1697, with seventeen men on board, seven of which were the captain and the ship's crew. The other ten colonizers, who would be both workmen and soldiers, were a very diverse group. There were three Indians—a Mayo herder, a Yaqui warrior, and a boy from near Guadalajara. The other seven were Salvatierra, a Spanish soldier, a mulatto Peruvian sailor, a Sicilian seaman, a Maltese artilleryman, aPortuguese ranch foreman, and a creole muleteer. The Portuguese was Steven Rodriguez, the future captain of the Loreto garrison who would spend forty-nine years serving in California. Either Salvatierra knew these people personally or others had highly recommended them.

Considering that Salvatierra was a half-Spanish Italian, very few Spaniards went to conquer Baja California for the faith and for the Spanish

Explorations of Salvatierra and Others in Baja California, Beginning in 1697

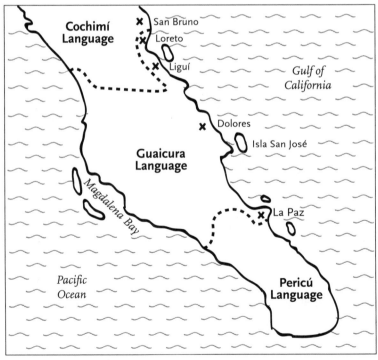

Fig. 26 The Pericú people also inhabited the islands as far north as Isla San José. The Guaicuras lived along the coast past Loreto to near San Bruno. There were some Cochimís at Liguí.

crown. And Salvatierra had promised to do it without government help. Furthermore, although they came with goodwill, these soldier-workers were the nucleus of a new people who would gradually replace much of the indigenous population of Baja California.

The ship landed at San Bruno, where Kino and some of the sailors on the ship had been thirteen years previously, on Kino's second trip. They then sailed fifteen miles south, arriving October 18 at a place which they named Loreto because Salvatierra had a statue of Our Lady of Loreto. This spot would be the headquarters of the Jesuit mission of Baja California.

When the Indians, including women and children, came to see the newcomers, Salvatierra attempted to speak to them. He had the notes of Goñi and Copart about the Guaicura language from the previous expedition. The people at Loreto (then called Conchó) were the Guaicuras. Kino had also made a vocabulary of five hundred Guaicura words when he was at La Paz. There were also Cochimís in the immediate vicinity, and Salvatierra had Kino's notes for this language that Kino had compiled at San Bruno.

In Baja California there were perhaps twenty-four thousand Cochimís, five thousand Guaicuras, and three thousand Pericús. The three languages were not related, nor are the Guaicura and Pericú languages known to be related to any other language. Cochimí, however, is related to the Yuma language on the Colorado River, to the Seri language north and south of the Sonora River along the coast of Sonora, to some of the Pueblo languages of New Mexico, and to the languages of northeast New Spain. Each of the three Baja California languages had many dialects, and the Jesuits found the language situation extremely difficult because any one of the languages could change so much within two or three settlements that it became unintelligible.

At Loreto there were about four hundred Guaicuras who were surrounded by Cochimís. The Cochimís were north of Loreto at San Bruno. There were also a few Cochimís south of Loreto at Liguí, where there was only a little water. To the west of Loreto, the Cochimís were very numerous in the mountains. And some of these were accustomed to living at Loreto in the winter months.

The newcomers spent the first day exploring on foot and by ship along the bay, looking for a safe and level spot with water. The Indians showed them some water holes, and they chose a level area near them and not too far from the shore.

Many mesquite trees (hardwood) grew in the area. They were not very tall, but some had trunk diameters of over six feet, compared to the usual diameter of up to two feet. There were also a few coconut trees.

That night the men slept on the ship, and in the morning of Saturday, October 19, they cleared the spot for the first settlement. Then they unloaded the animals: ten sheep, five goats, four piglets, one horse, and a dog. The Californians were curious about the animals because they had no domestic animals, not even dogs, and something happened that made everyone laugh. The Indian men were naked, and the women wore skirts of woven reeds, which made a rustling sound like corn being shaken together. Attracted by the sound, the piglets ran at the women, grunting the whole time. When the women ran away, they made even more noise, as if calling the piglets with greater insistence. Real corn was finally brought to quiet the animals.

The Spanish unloaded corn, clothing, and other supplies and carried them to the settlement site, a task that took four days. Some of the Californians helped with the work, and they were given *pozole* (cornmeal mush) in return. They demanded more food.

The Californians were engaged in a relentless search for food, consuming whatever they could find. If one group invited another to a festival, they gave all the food they had. So the Californians did not understand the restrained sharing of food by the newcomers. They even wanted to consume the domestic animals before they could escape and run wild. They also thought that the seventeen newcomers were too few to deny them the food.

The Spanish dug a trench around the site and filled it with thorny mesquite branches, mostly to keep people away from the food supply. This action angered the Californians, and Salvatierra asked the ship's captain to leave at the settlement a small mortar that fired stones.

On Monday, October 21, the horse disappeared, and a group went to look for it with some of the Californians. When they found it, it was being butchered by other Californians, who were using rocks as knives. The soldiers took the horsemeat but did not attempt any punishment. This incident meant that for the time being there would be no means of transportation at Loreto except walking.

On Wednesday, everyone was drenched with rain, which was a surprise because they had heard that it never rained in California. On Friday, October 25, they brought the statue of Our Lady of Loreto ashore with salvos from shoulder arms. They said the Hail Mary in Guaicura with the Indians and sang the Litany of Loreto. They carried the statue in procession from the shore and placed it in a tent within the enclosure. Mass was celebrated on Saturday, and after Mass the ship left in order to bring more soldiers, animals, and supplies from the mainland.

On the following Tuesday, October 29, a tall cacique came into camp from San Bruno, asking about specific individuals who had been on the earlier expedition with Father Kino. He was as naked as the other men were, so they could see that a side of his body was being eaten away by cancer. He stayed at the camp and attended the catechism class to prepare for baptism.

The ten newcomers were in a precarious position. The Californians were allowed into the camp if they were unarmed, and although they were unwilling to work, they expected food. They attended a catechism class with Father Salvatierra, and then they were fed. But Salvatierra knew that only the cacique from San Bruno was learning anything, and at the end of the day it was difficult to get the Californians to leave the enclosure.

The Californians held back from overpowering the newcomers because some of their number were against it and because they were uncertain about the return of the ship. Salvatierra attempted to warn them of the deadly nature of the Spanish weapons. They set up a target and had a contest. The Indian arrows only scratched the target, but the bullets from the harquebuses pierced it. Salvatierra took a shot himself, and it was one of the best.

On November 11, the cacique from San Bruno was baptized. His name was Ibó, which meant both "sun" and "day" in Cochimí. The next morning he told the ten that an attack was coming, and it was launched at midday on November 13.

The Californians first called for any Indians to leave the compound, and Ibó and two boys left. About two hundred Californians then attacked in four groups from four different sides, shooting arrows and throwing rocks. Two of the groups were Cochimí and two were Guaicura from four different small tribes. When the defenders attempted to fire the mortar, it exploded, and they were fortunate that no one was hurt.

It was a fierce fight, and it lasted until sundown. The ten defenders had two harquebuses and some muskets, and three of the Californians were killed. Others were wounded, and one of the wounded died later. After the Californians used whistles to call off the attack, there was dead silence for fifteen minutes. Then Ibó returned to the camp, and he was surprised that none of the defenders had been hurt. Actually two of them had been wounded, but this fact was kept from the Indians.

The next day, Californians who had not participated in the battle came to the camp. One of them, to prove he had not fought, offered as a gift a big root that he had found in the mountains the previous day. It was a yucca, from which manioc (also called cassava) is made, a sort of good-tasting, but stringy, bread. The following day, other Californians came who had fought, and the lost sloop with its six sailors and supplies also appeared.

One evening a soldier shot a coyote. When the Indians asked for it, it was handed over, and they consumed it. At this time in Baja California there were many wild animals, but only the mountain lions were numerous. The wild animals included some bears in the north, bighorn sheep, deer, a few wolves, and a few bobcats.

The Cochimís in the north hunted the abundant mountain lions (cougars or pumas), but in the south the different peoples, including the Cochimís, had a superstition against killing them. Partly because of this, the mission livestock would often be overrun by mountain lions, with the lions taking the calves and colts. The Jesuits finally gave up breeding horses and mules, purchasing what they needed on the mainland at high prices. In later years, a mission would always be happy to trade one of its cattle for a dead mountain lion.

On Saturday, November 23, Cacique Ibó received the sacrament for the sick, or extreme unction. By this time his wife and two sons were in the encampment, and Ibó wanted them baptized. However, one of the children was old enough to learn the doctrine and prayers with his mother, so only the younger child was baptized with two other children. Also, some of the Californians, influenced by Ibó's example, took an interest in the religious instruction.

That evening the ship returned. Besides supplies, it brought Father Francis Píccolo and a Tarahumara workman named Ignatius Xavier. During the first two months, the newcomers built mud huts for the church and for places to live. The church was ready in early December, and at Christmas each of the Jesuits said three Masses.

During 1698, the two Jesuits were studying the languages, attempting to teach doctrine, and helping to get things established at Loreto. Salvatierra also spent time writing letters and reports. In Mexico, John Ugarte—in order to keep benefactors informed, to foster interest in the mission, and to attract further donations—published two slender volumes of Salvatierra's letters and reports (1698 and 1699).

Some Californians destroyed a canoe in April of 1698. When soldiers went after them, they were ambushed, and in the ensuing fight three Californians were killed. This incident ended armed resistance to the newcomers.

In June of 1698, all the Californians left Loreto because the delicious fruit of a species of cactus was in season. At this time, the party at Loreto was very short of food, but on June 19, the ship returned with supplies, horses, and seven volunteer soldiers (four Spaniards, a Yaqui, an Englishman, and a mestizo). The soldier-workers now numbered sixteen, making a total of twenty-two people from the mainland at Loreto.

In November, Salvatierra and some companions made a trip north about fifteen miles to San Bruno, which was Kino's old site. For a few miles they had to cut a trail for the animals through a forest of cactus. This site would be a *visita*, or a place where a priest would visit, but it would not have a resident pastor. The party was actually a few miles west of San Bruno at a place called Londó.

After one year, at the end of 1698, there was a fine Christmas celebration at Loreto with much dancing. The California dances were different from the dances on the mainland, and there were about thirty different dances. Some told a story, some were pantomime, some were instructional, and some were humorous. Even young children joined in the dances, and Salvatierra also joined in. He encouraged the soldiers to participate and also to perform the folk dances of their own regions. Moreover, some of the soldiers had musical instruments, and Salvatierra himself played both the guitar and the flute, having studied the flute in a formal way as a student.

By this time, more than a hundred California families were being instructed, but the Jesuits were not yet ready to baptize the adults.

After Christmas, Píccolo explored the coast for about fifteen miles south of Loreto. He found very little water and very few people.

Salvatierra had been sending Californians on the ship that went to the mainland for supplies so that they could see the mainland missions. Some of these Indians were Cochimís, and they told Salvatierra that corn and other plants could be grown in the mountains at Viggé, meaning Highland, which was about seventeen miles in a straight line southwest of Loreto. It was over a pass at eighteen hundred feet and on the west side of the Sierra.

Cochimís from Viggé had visited Loreto, especially in the winter, and some of their children had been baptized. Also, the first adult to be baptized at Loreto after Ibó and his family was a seventeen-year-old from Viggé named Francis Xavier.

When these people invited the Jesuits to establish a mission at Viggé, the invitation was quickly accepted because Salvatierra was desperate to find someplace to grow food. The attempt to farm at Loreto had been a disaster, and it always would be. They did have a vegetable garden, but its produce did not go far, and the only success at Loreto was a later orchard. Also, pasture for livestock was scarce at Loreto.

After John Salvatierra again visited San Bruno in March, Francis Píccolo set out in early May for Viggé with ten soldiers and about ten Californians, carrying a good supply of corn. With horses, they followed an arroyo into the mountains. It was hard going because there were bushes and trees in the arroyo, and at one point water came rushing down. Finally the way became too difficult for the horses, and the captain wanted to turn back because there would be so few of them among so many unknown Indians. When Píccolo said he was going on with the Californians, the soldiers left the horses with four of the Indians and went up the arroyo with the rest. They found a spring and slept overnight.

After Mass the next day, they continued their sweaty and exhausting climb. At one spot, they passed wild grapevines with thick trunks that extended well over a mile. In the afternoon, they knew that something was wrong because they kept going higher and higher into the mountains to where no one could possibly live. When they talked to the guides, they realized there had been a misunderstanding. They had been saying, "Viggé, viggé," which meant "Highland, highland." The guides then led them back toward the settlement, which was actually called Baiundó.

At about 4:00 P.M., as Píccolo described it, a valley suddenly came into view, extensive and delightful to behold, with groves and streams. They saw fruit-bearing cacti, yucca, mescal plants, and fruit trees. All were overjoyed. When the Indians came to welcome them, Francis Píccolo addressed the assembly and explained the reasons they had come. When he started to talk about the faith, he found they could answer many questions, and they could make the sign of the cross because the first convert, Francis Xavier, had been instructing them. The visitors stayed four days and toured the surrounding countryside. Some Indians from the west gave information about the Pacific coast, and when the visitors left, they were able to return to Loreto in one day.

The mescal plant, which Píccolo mentioned, grows only in the mountains, and it was the staple food of those who lived there. Excluding the summer, the mescal plants ripen during eight months of the year, being ripe when the leaves open and reveal the heart of the plant. Women would go together to harvest the plants. Then they would split up, and each woman would cut with a wooden knife eight or nine of these hearts, each the size of a human head. Each woman had a heavy load that she carried in a net down her back, which was also supported by a cord across her forehead. When the women returned after several hours, they baked the mescal. A fire was started, and rocks were heated to a high temperature. The women separated the fire and rocks a little with a stick, placed the mescal hearts in the middle, and covered them with surrounding hot dirt to form a pile, which they left smoldering or baking for more than twenty-four hours.

Mescal is sweet tasting, and there was enough for three days, depending on the number of people. The smaller leaves are also nutritious for chewing and sucking but not for swallowing. The people used the larger leaves to make strings or cords from which they made nets. The mescal plants in California were smaller than those on the mainland. The Californians made no drink from the plant, although something like a wine can be produced. The mescal plant looks almost the same as the maguey, a different species of plant that can be used to make a drink called pulque. However, there were no maguey plants in California.

The Californians also consumed different kinds of seeds, which they sometimes toasted. They put the seeds on a wooden platter with hot coals. Then they shook the platter a little so that neither the seeds nor the platter would burn.

A few weeks after Píccolo's party returned to Loreto, the captain, who had suffered eye infections, resigned for health reasons. The real reason for his resignation, however, was that he objected to the position of the military at Loreto. On the mainland, the soldiers were not expected to do construction and all the other work that Salvatierra expected. Further, although the mainland soldiers were sometimes overworked with escort duty for wagon trains, military and police work, and so forth, they often had enough time to start their own farms or ranches while in the service. At Loreto, they were expected to be full-time soldier-workers who could not obtain land, start a farm, or hunt for pearls. Nor did Salvatierra permit gambling or hard drinking.

Being a soldier at Loreto required dedication and was almost a religious vocation. The soldiers started each day with Mass, and they were expected to be an example of moral living for the Indians. This morality included the just treatment of the Indians and no sexual affairs. The Jesuits expected chaste living from the soldiers and from everyone else.

It was hard duty for the soldiers in California, but it was less dangerous than on the mainland. Salvatierra tried to compensate the soldiers by paying 450 pesos a year rather than the usual 300. Also, the soldiers were charged about 25 percent less than their counterparts on the mainland for horses, military supplies, and food (some staples were free). No money changed hands, but the soldiers had accounts with the treasurer at Loreto. They could save their money or they could buy things at Loreto, and they could place orders when supplies were purchased once a year in Mexico.

At the end of May, Salvatierra made another trip to San Bruno because he heard that the Cochimís were gathering there. The delicious fruit of a cactus was coming into season, and the Guaicuras of Loreto had a standing invitation to participate in the harvest. This high cactus is called the pipe-organ cactus in Arizona, and it gives fruit on the peninsula from June to August. The fruit is sweet, the size of a lemon, and it was called *pitahaya*. It is easy to peel, and it has seeds so small that they can be ignored. But some years the cactus gave no fruit if the weather was too moist.

The Californians divided the year into six parts, depending on the food that was in season. Their hardest time was around May after the mescal season and before the *pitahaya* season.

A different cactus bearing very good fruit was also called *pitahaya*. This fruit is bittersweet, more juicy than the first, and the size of an orange. It is also easy to peel and has very small seeds. This cactus is a bush rather than a tall, freestanding cactus, and it spreads into a thicket. It gives fruit from September to November and is found only on the beaches.

When Salvatierra made the trip to San Bruno, there was tension between the Cochimís and the Guaicuras because a Guaicura had killed a Cochimí at Loreto. The murderer had been identified and had received many lashes. According to rules fashioned by the provincials, a culprit in a mission pueblo could not receive more than six lashes. He may have been punished by the captain, who could order twenty-five lashes for a first offense according to government regulations. In any case, the relatives of the slain Cochimí were satisfied by the punishment, but other Cochimís were not.

At San Bruno, Salvatierra gave an instruction and preached against the worship of the moon. He said it was like honoring a torch but ignoring the person to whom it belonged. The Cochimís thought this humorous, but they were cool toward Salvatierra, partly because of his Guaicura companions. When Salvatierra and some of the soldiers explored the surrounding region, the Guaicuras and the Cochimí renewed their friendship with a nightlong dance. The Guaicuras slaughtered one of the sheep that Salvatierra had brought and gave the meat to the Cochimí women.

Some children were baptized at this time. When the soldiers started looking for the missing sheep, the Guaicuras left and returned to Loreto. When Salvatierra and the soldiers returned to Loreto, the matter of the sheep was not pursued.

On June 1, Father Píccolo and ten of the soldier-workers set off to build a trail to Viggé that horses and other livestock would be able to manage. They went about seven miles, and then the work began with bars, picks, axes, and hoes. They were clearing bushes and levering big boulders out of the way as they ascended the arroyo, and Cochimís from Viggé came to help. At one point they thought they would have to build some bridges, but the Cochimís showed them a trail around the problem areas. After twelve days of very hard labor, they were able to ride their horses to Viggé, where they stayed two days.

During their visit, they climbed a high hill from which they could see both the Gulf of California and the Pacific Ocean. The Pacific is about thirty-five miles from Viggé as the peninsula is somewhat narrow at this latitude. When they left, they were able to return to Loreto without dismounting.

At the end of June, the supply ship returned and brought six more volunteer soldiers, some of whom were adventurers without the dedication of the veterans. Salvatierra decided to accept them, although some would have to be dismissed later for lack of funds. It became the custom to accept soldiers on a trial basis for two years at half pay. In any case, thirty soldiers, as well as some sailors, were now stationed at Loreto, and four of the veteran soldiers had wives who had come from the mainland.

At this time, after one and a half years, they started to build adobe houses, an adobe church, and a temporary adobe chapel. It would take five years to build the church, and even then it would have a thatched roof. They dug a trench for the church foundation and filled it with rock fragments. On this foundation they raised walls of adobe blocks. As they raised the walls they worked in hardwood windows and doorframes of mesquite wood. They had limestone from which they were able to make cement, and there was another material from which they could make an exterior stucco finish, which protected the blocks and made a good appearance.

Eventually they built a three-room Jesuit residence, a building for visitors, a barracks for the soldiers and sailors, a house for the captain and one for the treasurer, a barracks for unmarried Californian women, houses for the married soldiers, and two rows of houses for the Californians. The Californians shared in the work, receiving mostly food as a salary. The labor of the Californians was needed, and their participation gave them a stake in Loreto. Also, by working together, the Californians and the newcomers got to know one another.

For the roof of the church, they later brought cedar beams from the mainland. They also manufactured tiles at Loreto in order to cover at least the church roof. Loreto would eventually look much better than the mission villages of the mainland benefactors. In August, they managed to replace the damaged keel of their ship.

The Jesuits were ready to establish the second mission at Viggé by October of 1699. On October 7, a large party, including Francis Píccolo, fifteen soldiers, five Yaquis, and Loreto Cochimís, left Loreto with a long pack train of horses, mules, and burros loaded with food and tools. They also had goats and two dogs.

When they arrived at Viggé, Píccolo met with the people and said that he had returned as he had promised and that he wanted to construct three small adobe buildings—a church, a house for himself, and a common building. With a lot of help from the Cochimís, they laid out the dimensions, dug trenches for the foundations, set the stone foundations, made twenty-five hundred adobe blocks with the wooden forms they had brought, and raised the walls, which were two adobe blocks thick. All of this construction was done in two weeks, and each building was about the size of a room in a modern house.

Since they now had to wait for the adobe to dry before adding the roof weight of thin tree trunks, adobe mud, and thatch, they decided to explore the thirty-five miles between them and the Pacific Ocean. Taking enough food for eight days, some of them set out on October 24, 1699, with mules, horses, and even some of the goats as an emergency source of food. They took the two dogs to use in rounding up the goats. After traveling seven miles, they came across about a hundred Cochimís with whom they established friendship. When the Spanish offered gifts to the Indians, the Indians also offered gifts to the newcomers, such as food, feathers, and flint stones for making fire. The Indians were also skilled at starting a fire by quickly rotating a stick against other wood.

It took two rough travel days to reach the ocean. The animals were able to make it, although at one point some horseshoes had to be replaced. They now had to find water for themselves and the animals, and places where the animals could graze. They found no water along the coast, but the Cochimís picked out a good place to dig in order to create a water hole. They had a big copper bowl that they filled in order to water the animals.

They explored north along the coast for two days and found neither water nor people before their limited provisions forced them to turn back. The Pacific side of the peninsula, except in the south, was almost uninhabited for lack of water. Most of the Cochimís lived on the western side of the Sierra, extending from about fifteen miles south of Viggé to the far north. Other Indians, Guaicuras and Pericús, lived in the mountains south of the Cochimís.

When the Jesuits went exploring, they sometimes were shown amazing paintings in rock shelters or in caves. The Californians ground rocks to fine powder from which they made colored pigments, mainly red, orange, brown, and black. The paintings, numerous in the mountains between La Paz and Mulegé, are mostly of people and of larger animals such as deer, bighorn sheep, and pronghorn antelope. The paintings, with the human figures facing the viewer and the animals shown from the side, are sometimes high on cave walls or on high cave ceilings where scaffolding would have been needed. When the Jesuits arrived, the people were probably no longer painting because they said that the paintings had been done in earlier times by a race of giants. It is now thought that the paintings were done between A.D. 500 and A.D. 1500.[2]

On the way back to Viggé, Píccolo and his party slaughtered one of the goats and gave the meat to the new people they had met. Píccolo invited them to come to Viggé for instruction. When the Spanish returned to Viggé, they finished the buildings. Since the patron saint of the church was St. Francis Xavier, Píccolo renamed the settlement San Xavier Viggé, and he remained there when the others returned to Loreto.

Two years later, in early December, Salvatierra began the baptism of two hundred well-instructed adults at Loreto. At this time, there were seventy people from the mainland living at Loreto. Loreto had a rather stable population of about four hundred people all during the seventy-year Jesuit period. However, the number of Californians at Loreto gradually decreased in favor of people from the mainland. When the Jesuits were expelled in 1767, there were about three hundred people from the mainland living at Loreto, and another hundred from the mainland lived in the rest of the peninsula.

By 1700, Salvatierra realized that they would not be able to colonize and evangelize Baja California without financial help from the government. They were spending twenty-seven pesos a year, and they were growing little food. His request for government help was a delicate matter, not just because of his promise to do without government aid, but also because he wanted to keep control of the soldiers.

The government started to give six thousand pesos a year in 1702. This contribution helped, but it only paid the salaries of thirteen soldiers. The Spanish government was short of money during the early years of the new century because of the War of the Spanish Succession, another war about the European balance of power.

Salvatierra went to Sinaloa with five Californians in 1700. He was there on business, but they all visited Chínipas. While he was away, Píccolo divided his time between Loreto and San Xavier Viggé.

When Salvatierra returned, he took up his duties, which included visits to the Cochimís near San Bruno. On one trip, he was invited to go into the mountains to visit Comondú, whose Cochimí people were related to those at San Bruno. Father Kino had been through this general area with Admiral Atondo on their earlier exploration to the Pacific. After visiting Comondú, Salvatierra decided to go south through the Sierra, which rises in this stretch to over a mile high, and to surprise Father Píccolo at San Xavier Viggé by arriving from the north (twenty-five or thirty-five miles by trail). After visiting Píccolo, he returned to Loreto. Salvatierra had made a circular trip of about a hundred miles, and it was his first good look at the interior of the peninsula.

Later in the year there was some problem at Viggé. The people rejected the new ways, and Píccolo returned to Loreto.

Three and a half years later, things remained precarious at the mission. To obtain supplies, they were making dangerous trips across the gulf in the launch. In desperation, Salvatierra and five Californians went to Father Kino for supplies. They also went with Kino on an unsuccessful expedition to find a land route to the Baja. At this time, Salvatierra established a ranch and agricultural base at Guaymas, on the mainland north of the Yaqui River. Guaymas only receives six inches of rain a year in comparison to twenty-four inches at Villa Sinaloa. Even if some running water reached the place, it must have been more a collection point for donated supplies than a productive farm.

Salvatierra had been following all of Kino's suggestions. Kino had recommended a small colony at Loreto where he knew there was water, an agricultural base on the mainland, and control over the soldiers. Salvatierra also started with Kino's maps and language notes.

Salvatierra, however, was not a good businessman. He paid twelve thousand pesos for a wreck of a ship that was worth about a thousand and that was later sold for five hundred pesos. Later, he contracted to have a ship built for twenty-two thousand pesos that was poorly constructed. On its first voyage it sank and six people drowned, including a new Jesuit missionary. In general, the ships on the Gulf of California were not very good. Ships were built at places like Acapulco for crossing the Pacific and for trade with South America.

When the ships were worn out, they were sold to entrepreneurs on the Gulf of California.

While Salvatierra was exploring with Kino in March, Father John Ugarte arrived at Loreto. He was the giant from Honduras who had been promoting the mission in Mexico City, and his presence gave new life to the mission. This thirty-eight-year-old brought young energy to the mission, compared to Píccolo, who was turning forty-seven, and Salvatierra, who was fifty-two.

Two more Jesuits came to Loreto in 1701. There were now about a hundred people from the mainland living in California. These included five Jesuits, nineteen soldiers, twenty-four sailors, and eight African and Filipino servants. There were about fifty Native American laborers from the mainland, not counting other Native Americans among the sailors and soldiers.

Here is a picture of the racial makeup of the community at Loreto as things developed over the years. Six or eight skilled workers (sometimes more) maintained the ships and launches. They were carpenters, caulkers, ironworkers, and shipwrights who had little wood to work with except the ten-foot-high mesquite tree. Its hardwood was used for repairing the ships, making door and window frames, and building small cabinets. These workers were mulattoes and mestizos, and some of their descendants became landowners in California after the Jesuit period.

Among the soldiers were carpenters, stonemasons, blacksmiths, cowboys, and tanners. The tanning of animal hides was important because the people needed leather for things like shoes, saddles, saddle packs and straps, harnesses, reins, and so forth. There were twenty-five soldiers at Loreto in the early decades and thirty in later years, but since these soldiers were often away on errands or were stationed at other mission sites, there were usually only eight or ten living at Loreto. These soldiers, who volunteered mostly from Villa Sinaloa and Compostelo on the mainland, tended to be white.

Thirty sailors were stationed at Loreto, although this number fluctuated. The sailors were mostly Filipinos and Indians. The Indians were Yaquis in earlier days and Californians later on. The sailors received half the pay of the soldiers, but the sailors did not have the soldiers' expenses for horses and military supplies.

There was some intermarriage between the Californians and the mainlanders during the Jesuit period. But as time went on, the social structure at Loreto came to reflect the structure on the mainland: whites, mestizos, mulattoes, blacks, and Indians. Some of the families at Loreto had Indian house servants from the mainland because the Jesuits did not permit them to have Californians as servants.

In 1701, Salvatierra started to think that the whole enterprise was impossible. When he proposed that they give up the effort, he had a lot of support, but the determination of Ugarte strengthened the resolve of the others. Toward the end of the year, Ugarte went to San Xavier Viggé, and Píccolo traveled as far as Mexico to beg money for the mission.

When John Ugarte went to San Xavier Viggé, he faced two big challenges: to evangelize the Cochimís of that place and to achieve some sort of agricultural self-sufficiency. He started the evangelization by trying to get the people to attend Mass, rosary, and catechism every day. Initially they were often absent, and they made a joke of everything—including him. At one point, Ugarte became so exasperated at the laughter that he seized the ringleader by the hair with one hand and lifted him into the air with the other. He twirled him around a few times before setting him down. The people were impressed. Another time, after he tried to sober them up with a very vivid description of hell, he heard them talking among themselves. They said that hell must be a good place if it had so much firewood. They thought they ought to leave their own land and go there. He also discovered that they were teaching him the mispronunciation of certain words in order to increase the hilarity. He finally learned the correct pronunciation from the children.

Then Ugarte had to create a productive farm. He had to persuade and cajole people to work who were accustomed to a great deal of leisure. He did it with kind and patient words and with small gifts. He also had to persuade them to help prepare the barren land for seed. Bushes had to be cleared. Ravines had to be filled in with hundreds, even thousands, of loads of dirt and stone. Irrigation ditches had to be dug. The challenge was extraordinary, especially since it was not nearly as lush as the enthusiastic Píccolo had described it.

John Ugarte, as the first farmer, introduced many plants and trees to the peninsula, including beans, squash, corn, melons, bananas, peaches, date palms, figs, and citrus. However, during Ugarte's first years at San Xavier Viggé, there was a drought, and little food was actually grown.

On one occasion, the people became so angry with Ugarte that they decided to fill him with arrows. When a child warned him that they were coming, he jumped under the bed, and they shot the bed full of arrows. They must have just been expressing their resentment at being pushed because they could have killed him at any time.

It was a radical lifestyle change for the Cochimís, and it was the women, more than the men, who were attracted by the more steady source of food. In their former way of life, the people stayed a week or so at a water hole or spring while they searched for food; then they moved on. The burden of searching for food had been more on the women than on the men.

At Viggé they built adobe houses for Ugarte and for themselves, and a school was started for the children, who would later go as catechists to other missions. The people eventually made San Xavier Viggé a garden spot, providing Mass wine for all the missions, helping the other missions with donations of food, and in time trading their products on the mainland for things like tools, tobacco, and chocolate. Their main exports would be wine and dried figs.

John Ugarte also tried to get the people to give up certain superstitions, like the fear of killing a mountain lion. One time he came across a lion that was sleeping not far from the trail. Dismounting, he stunned the animal with a big rock and then killed it with another one. He wanted to ride with the carcass to Viggé so that the people could see that the spirit of the lion would not kill him, but he could not mount his horse with the dead lion because his horse was terrified by the smell. So Ugarte draped the lion over the limb of a tree. He was thus able to mount the horse, and also able to control it as he dragged the carcass from the tree limb. Then he rode back to Viggé.

In September of 1701, the second captain at Loreto gave up his position for the same reasons as the first captain and returned to the mainland. When he left, seventeen of the twenty-nine soldiers resigned and went with him. When Salvatierra asked those remaining to elect their captain, they chose the young Portuguese, Steven Rodriguez, who had arrived with Salvatierra four years earlier.

After five years, in 1702, Píccolo wrote a twenty-page report about the mission for the government. It was later printed in Mexico as *Informe del estado de la Nueva Cristiandad de California*. In the report, he mentioned that one thousand adults and three thousand children were ready for baptism. He also mentioned that the buildings were made of adobe and had straw roofs. This report was so optimistic that it created a wrong impression about Baja California.

During these years, there were occasional conflicts between the colonizers and the Californians. An example of one occurred in June of 1702. A young soldier at Loreto was married to a Californian. When the *pitahaya* fruit was in season, the girl went off to a harvest festival with her pagan mother without telling her husband. The husband went after her. When he got into a confrontation with a Californian, he shot the Californian dead. Other Californians killed the soldier.

This violence created a surge of hostility between the mainlanders and the Californians. Captain Rodriguez rushed squads of soldiers to protect San Xavier Viggé and the *visitas*. There were a few clashes between the Californians and the soldiers, and about four Californians were killed. A corn harvest was lost to fire at San Xavier Viggé.

Although the *pitahaya* in the mountains were in season, there was hunger and even semistarvation that June of 1702 in Loreto. The people did have meat to eat, but their stomachs rebelled at the unvaried diet.

In 1703, Father Kino and the Pimas of Dolores moved a hundred cattle and many loads of grain down to Guaymas, the agricultural base of the California mission, north of the Yaqui River. The supplies could be kept there safely until they could be shipped to Loreto. The Pimas would make the same donation in each succeeding year.

In this same year, two explorations were made to the Pacific coast. Also in 1703, when Ugarte was away from San Xavier, some Christian

Indians of the place were killed by nearby pagan Indians. Urged on by the relatives of the slain Indians, Captain Steven Rodriguez led an expedition against the raiders. At this point the people of the area handed over the leader of the raid. Back at Loreto, Salvatierra wanted to exile the culprit to the mainland, but the captain insisted on his execution.

In August of 1703, the newcomers sailed about seventy-five miles north of Loreto to see a spot called Mulegé, which had been discovered by a mission ship that had been blown off course. The location was near water and the coast, so it was a good site for a mission. The only problem was that a spur of the Sierra ran into the gulf about twenty-five miles south of Mulegé. It cut Mulegé off from Loreto because mules could not climb it.

In 1704, the Jesuit general named Salvatierra provincial of the Jesuits in New Spain for a three-year term. Salvatierra went to Mexico to talk his way out of it, but the province consultors refused to cancel an appointment that had been made by the general.

Area of Baja California Worked by Salvatierra, Píccolo, and Ugarte, 1697–1703

Loreto to San Xavier	17	miles
Loreto to Liguí	25	miles
Loreto to Comondú	26	miles
Loreto to Mulegé	75	miles

Fig. 27

Salvatierra served as provincial for about two years. In August of 1705, he came as provincial to visit California, bringing along Brother James Bravo, who would serve in California for thirty-nine years. Salvatierra had named Ugarte superior of the mission. He now appointed Píccolo regional superior for Sonora, and he named Kino procurator for the Pima mission. This office did not give Kino much authority, but it allowed him to build or to help build churches all over the area.

At this time, the Jesuits had been in California for eight years. Salvatierra would be leaving five Jesuits, so they decided it was time to expand. They would begin missions at Liguí to the south and at Mulegé to the north. Father Peter Ugarte, S.J., John's brother, had come to California the previous year, but he would only remain a few years due to poor health. Peter Ugarte founded the mission at Liguí (also called San Juan Malibat), twenty-five miles south of Loreto. He had the help of other Jesuits, but he lived for some months by himself under a tree. In the beginning he could not get the people to help. When he was preparing the adobe bricks, he got help from the children by making a game out of dancing in the mud. Eventually he was successful, but this mission at Liguí was abandoned after eighteen years.

The mission at Mulegé with the Cochimís was a permanent success. The people at Mulegé were quick to learn the Spanish language, and they later served as interpreters and catechists among the Cochimí people who extended throughout the north of Baja California. The priest who started this mission was successful, but he found the work too hard. He went to work in Sonora, and Father Francis Píccolo went to Mulegé as pastor after he returned from being regional superior on the mainland. At the present time, the remains of the mission archives are at Mulegé.

When Salvatierra left after his visit, five Californians went with him to see Mexico.

In 1706, the government wanted the Jesuits to find a port on the Pacific side for ships coming from the Philippines. Ugarte explored with forty Yaqui soldiers who came from the mainland, but they did not find a port. In this same year, Captain Steven Rodriguez married a young woman from the mainland. In December, Salvatierra and the five

Californians returned from Mexico after Salvatierra, now fifty-eight years old, was replaced as provincial at his own request.

It was about this time that Ugarte moved five miles south of Viggé and started over. There had been a drought during Ugarte's first five years at Viggé. The new site, inheriting the name of San Xavier Viggé, had more water because it was at a lower altitude and drained more mountains.

In 1708, Father Julian Mayorga, thirty-eight years old and from Spain, arrived at Loreto. After studying the language for some months, it was decided that he should found a new mission at Comondú, which had the same latitude as Loreto and was halfway between the gulf and the Pacific Ocean. Salvatierra and Ugarte went with him to help build a rude chapel and a hut. They also attempted to make friends with the people who lived there. Father Mayorga was at Comondú for twenty-eight years until his death. During that time he instructed and baptized 1,736 people. They had a school for boys and one for girls, and a hospital. Before the expulsion, the last Jesuit at Comondú built a stone church with arches. The present village of Comondú is a little more than a mile south of the old mission pueblo.

During the first ten years in California, the Jesuits did not mention any diseases. Then in 1708, they reported that half of the people at Loreto, Viggé, and Comondú died from smallpox. It was a devastating blow, and the enthusiastic construction work at the new mission of Comondú came to a halt and was intermittent thereafter.

Father Clement Guillén, from Zacatecas in New Spain, came as a missionary in 1714. After studying Cochimí, he revived the mission at Liguí that Peter Ugarte had founded. By 1715, the Jesuits had four hundred cattle in Baja California. They took little meat from this herd because they wanted the animals to increase. After eighteen years, they were still trying to establish a food supply independent of the mainland.

During the early years, they often went hungry or on half rations. The Jesuits wrote of rabbits, ducks, deer, and wild sheep. Even so, the game must have been sparse because of the scarcity of water and pasture. The gulf was full of fish and oysters, and they did some fishing, but they never developed a big, efficient fishing enterprise. Not just the colonizers but also the Californians often went hungry. However, even in hard times Salvatierra was generous in sharing food with visiting Californians, much to the annoyance and fear of others at Loreto. When they did get food from the mainland, it was often spoiled because of long delays or because it got wet on the way over.

John Salvatierra tried to establish friendly relations with the Guaicuras at La Paz in 1716. These people were enemies of the Spanish because pearl fishermen had mistreated them and because the admiral had shot a canon at them on Kino's first expedition.

Salvatierra had encountered a ship with six Guaicuras on board who were probably being forced to dive for oysters. He ransomed the six men and brought them to Loreto. He decided to return them by ship to La Paz and try to establish friendly relations. After they landed at La Paz, they met some Guaicuras who fled at the sight of the strangers. Some Native Americans from Loreto ran after them and caught up with the women, who defended themselves by throwing rocks. The Loreto Indians retaliated and killed some of the women. This second tragedy at La Paz cemented hostile relations. When Salvatierra returned the six Guaicuras and offered gifts, the gifts were rejected, and the Guaicuras left. Friendly relations were not established.

While this was going on at La Paz, Father Francis Píccolo was at Mulegé, not quite halfway up the gulf coast, where he had been for seven years. Boy catechists had gone from Mulegé to other villages to tell the people about the things they had learned at Mulegé. In November of 1716, Píccolo sent word to the northwest that a group from Mulegé was coming to visit. With loaded supply horses, Píccolo and five companions traveled five days northwest, seventy miles in a straight line from Mulegé, to a river that flowed through fertile land and made occasional ponds as it moved west toward the Pacific Ocean. The river water was plentiful enough that Píccolo was surprised when told that the river sank into the ground some miles before reaching the Pacific and that the ponds toward the Pacific did not hold freshwater.

When they arrived at the river, two of the horses jumped into a deep pond. One of them perished before it could be rescued, and some of the corn and wheat flour was lost. Since the water was cold, the chocolate could be dried without damage.

People came from miles around to meet the visitors. The local people brought fresh fish, cactus fruit, and something like dates, and the visitors from Mulegé provided corn dishes, tortillas, and chocolate.

Píccolo's group stayed eleven days along the river. A man named Cloud came to meet Píccolo, and Píccolo's companions described him as the viceroy of the area. He gave Píccolo some strings of artistic blue shells. When the boy catechist was introduced to him, Cloud said that he was happy to meet him because of the fine way he spoke to his people. He gave the boy two small strings of beads. Píccolo gave Cloud some corn and tobacco and also a cane, which was an acknowledgment of his authority. Cloud also asked for wheat seeds. The people were not farming, but they told Píccolo that in the north the land was fertile and populous and that the people planted corn.

Those coming to meet Píccolo only stayed two or three days. There must have been a north wind because the mostly unclothed Cochimí were uncomfortably chilly (in early December), and they were also hungry, even with the two corn meals a day that could be provided. Cloud invited Píccolo to visit his village, which was toward the Pacific Ocean, but Píccolo decided to return to Mulegé because he was short of supplies.

Píccolo spent three more years at Mulegé, and for eighteen months, beginning in 1717, he had the help of a great, newly arrived missionary, Father Nicholas Tamaral, thirty years old, from Seville, Spain. Tamaral also studied Cochimí during his time at Mulegé.

At this time, Salvatierra was called to Mexico to consult with the viceroy. Although suffering from kidney stones, he decided to go. He took Brother James Bravo, the treasurer at Loreto, along as a companion. Bravo was later ordained a priest. He built the stone church at Loreto and served a total of thirty-nine years in California.

Salvatierra's condition worsened on the journey, and he died at Guadalajara, sixty-eight years old, on July 18, 1717. After the funeral, James Bravo went on to Mexico to meet with the viceroy and to present Salvatierra's proposals. This meeting was important because the viceroy was new and deciding on his policies. Also, the War of the Spanish Succession had been over for a few years, and Spain was no longer draining all possible money from the colony.

The viceroy refused the request to finance the construction of a college at Loreto. He also refused to donate to the mission a salt flat on an island just off Loreto, which would have been a source of money for the mission. The island had no freshwater, so it sustained neither people nor animals (with the exception of rodents and snakes), but it had the biggest salt pan, or flat, on the peninsula. The salt was pure, unmixed with sand or dirt. People visited and took blocks of the salt.

The viceroy took under advisement the suggestion that the Spanish establish a port with another garrison of twenty-five soldiers at Cabo San Lucas, on the southern tip of the peninsula, in order to receive ships from the Philippines on their way to Acapulco. He also gave 4,000 pesos so that the mission could buy a ship. He agreed to pay 18,276 pesos a year for the salaries of the sailors, the twenty-five soldiers, and other employees, but the Jesuits in California would continue to receive no stipend. Captain Steven Rodriguez was paid 600 pesos, and the other soldiers received 450. The viceroy asked that the Jesuits find a port on the Pacific side.

In 1717, the Jesuits had been in Baja California for twenty years, and that year there was a rare hurricane that lasted for three days and did major damage. It destroyed many adobe buildings, and John Ugarte spent twenty-four hours on a rock.

When James Bravo returned to California, he brought Father Sebastian Sistiago, about thirty-four years old and from near Oaxaca in New Spain. Sistiago had held the Chair of Fine Arts at the Colegio Maximo and would make a fine contribution during the next thirty years.

John Ugarte was now superior, and in 1718 he brought from Durango a weaver with an Irish name, Anthony Moran. Moran was paid five hundred pesos a year to teach the people how to spin and weave wool into cloth. Up until this time they had been importing the cloth from which the women made clothes.

Since the government had asked the Jesuits to find a suitable port on the Pacific side, Ugarte assigned Captain Steven Rodriguez and Father Clement Guillén to lead an expedition to explore Magdalena Bay, about 170 miles north of the southern tip of the peninsula. The bay was known, having been charted as early as 1602, but it had never been approached by land.³ The bay, now considered one of the great harbors of the world, is about ninety-five miles in a straight line southwest of Loreto, but about 160 by trail. Protected by two long islands, the main part of the harbor is fifty by fifteen miles. The Pacific gray whales visit in the harbor during February and early March.⁴

Rodriguez and Guillén left Loreto on March 3, 1719, with twelve soldiers and seventeen Indians. Since they would be meeting mostly Guaicuras, two of the Indians were Guaicura interpreters from the interior of the peninsula. Clement Guillén, forty-two years old, had spent five years in the country and was an excellent linguist, but he may not have known Guaicura since he was stationed at Liguí, where the language was Cochimí.

They went south to Liguí and then southwest into the mountains. They traveled south through the mountains until they were opposite the bay, and then went west about forty miles to the bay. They made only six miles a day because they had to clear a path for the animals almost the entire way. Since they were meeting small groups of Guaicuras almost every day, it took time to make friends, give gifts, and obtain guides for the next stretch of the journey to water holes or to the next settlement. They also had to find pasture, and they were looking for good spots for future missions.

When they got to within thirteen miles of the bay, they stood looking at mudflats and sand dunes, which were broken by inlets from the bay. The captain pulled the party back five miles to establish a camp where there was water and pasture. Early on March 26, he sent a squad of soldiers with the interpreters to look for water and pasture closer to the coast.

The squad traveled many miles and slept overnight at a spot where there was pasture but no water. In the morning, they reached the bay, saw the gray whales, and, exploring along the bay, found some Indians by a water hole. Making friends through the interpreters and giving gifts, they received water in return, but the well was too deep for the animals. The Indians lent them some baskets with which to water the animals, but the baskets could not hold the water. They traveled back that day but had to camp overnight. When the squad reached camp in the morning, after forty-eight hours on the trail, the animals were stumbling from lack of water.

These expeditions were often slowed down by the deteriorating condition of the animals. The horses and mules often had to pick their way over rocks. Their hides became stuck with thorns. Often the pasture was not lush grass but scrubs and bushes, some of which had thorns. Donkeys made out better than horses and mules, but they were not as useful.

The captain sent another squad the next day, but they returned that night without having found water or pasture. The captain then decided to return to Loreto, and they traveled back in two weeks, half the time of the outward journey.

Also in 1719, John Mugazábal, who had been a soldier in California for fifteen years, became a Jesuit brother. Many of these Jesuits lived into advanced old age. For example, John Mugazábal lived to be seventy-six, and Clement Guillén lived to be seventy-one.

John Ugarte, now fifty-seven years old, decided to build a ship. Ugarte and the Californians had built a prosperous establishment at San Xavier Viggé with two thousand sheep grazing on the mountain-sides. But it had been a huge effort, and they had actually established three different sites.

It was mentioned earlier that, after working hard to build up San Xavier, the people had endured a five-year drought. They found a spot five miles to the south where there was more water. So they started over, even building a stone church. Water was collected in a ditch and distributed to the fields. Things were going well until there were another four years without rain. This time the people moved west. They found a place where the water bubbled out of the ground, ran for a bit in an arroyo, and then disappeared into the ground. This was a difficult place to get to with the mules, so the people had to make a path by filling in a ravine with hundreds of loads of dirt, stone, and rocks. Then they had to fill in another ravine with thousands of loads of dirt and stone in order to obtain a level field. This field was going to be a vineyard, and it eventually yielded forty-eight large earthen vessels of wine a year.

Jesuit Expansion among the Cochimís

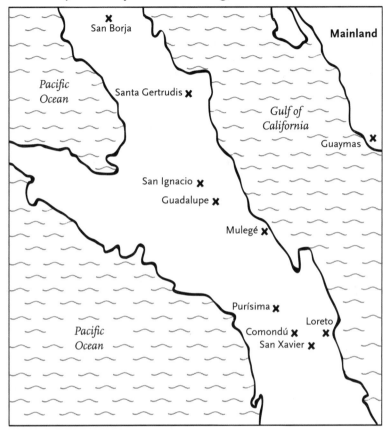

Fig. 28

What was the result of all this work? With sufficient rain, all three places were very productive. This area on the western slope of the Sierra produced corn, wheat, cotton, and wine for the five missions that existed during those years. Sometimes the people made donations to other locations, especially new missions. Sometimes they sent food to Loreto for use by others but received a credit so that they could obtain goods from Loreto or make purchases once a year from Mexico City. Sometimes they sold their products on the mainland.

The mission villages in California were smaller than those on the mainland. For example, on the mainland a mission pueblo might have a hundred families, compared to a hundred people in a *ranchería* on the peninsula. On the mainland, a Jesuit might care for one pueblo and three or four *visitas*, but on the peninsula a Jesuit might care for a smaller mission village along with eight or more *rancherías*.

There was more violence in California than on the mainland, where each nation lived rather peacefully within itself. On the peninsula, the smaller groups were often in conflict over food or over a wrong that had been suffered.

When Ugarte decided to build a ship in 1719, he thought he would have to bring almost everything from the mainland. But the Californians knew where there were good trees in the mountains about 120 miles to the north, south of the river that Píccolo had visited. Ugarte went to look at the trees with an Englishman, William Strafford, who had a long career in the area as a ship's captain and who worked for the Jesuits on two occasions for about a year as commander of the launch.

The two of them saw giant poplars with white bark, six feet in diameter and over sixty feet high. The trees were in deep ravines, only about twenty miles west of Mulegé on the coast, but a good forty-five miles by trail. It was the middle of September when they stood looking at the poplars. Strafford thought it would be impossible to get the logs from the mountains to the coast, but ten months later the ship was built.

Francis Píccolo, now sixty-five, had been pastor at Mulegé, and Ugarte transferred him to Loreto to be pastor and acting regional superior. At Mulegé, the new pastor was Sebastian Sistiago, who had been training there since his arrival in California more than a year earlier. Substituting for Ugarte at San Xavier Viggé was Nicholas Tamaral, who had arrived almost three years earlier and who had trained at Mulegé and Viggé.

Three lumberjacks came from the mainland and went up to the area with Ugarte, Strafford, Sistiago, and some of the Californians, where they lived in huts for four months near the future mission of Guadalupe. They had mules, horses, and oxen, and the Cochimís of the area pitched in to help. They felled trees, fashioned some parts of the ship, and built a trail so the oxen could drag the logs to Mulegé. When the oxen turned out to be insufficiently trained, the men used rollers and horses, and Ugarte wrote that each person did the work of three men.

The men had insufficient food, sometimes eating mescal, during the four months it took to get the wood to Mulegé. At Mulegé, with carpenters and ironworkers from the mainland, they again lived in huts for six months while they built the ship under the direction of William Strafford. During this time, Ugarte was able to feed his workers very well, even though the missions were short of food, due to the generosity of Píccolo at Loreto and the people of Viggé. The workers were without chocolate and sugar for only one short period, and they even received wine and brandy.

They finished the ship in mid-July. Named the *Triumph of the Cross,* it was launched in September, and it was a great ship. Ugarte used it to explore the north coast of the gulf. The ship, called a sloop, crossed the gulf seventy times during the next twelve years and made many more crossings after that. The Jesuits used it for twenty-five years. This is a little surprising because so many of their earlier ships had ended up wrecked after a short time. It was probably the finest ship built in the gulf area up to that time, and it was certainly the first ship ever built in California. It was built by a priest and some natives in a place where, as Ugarte once put it, a nail was looked upon as a precious jewel and even a board was a treasure. The ships were careened at Acapulco every second year.

After the new sloop was in the water in September of 1720, Regional Superior John Ugarte took stock of the whole situation. They had two fine ships, and there was good money coming in from the government for the salaries of the sailors and soldiers. There were five missions and nine Jesuits. There was the Guaicura mission of Loreto, where the spoken language was actually mostly Spanish. The other four missions were the Cochimí pueblos of Liguí, San Xavier Viggé, Comondú, where Jules Mayorga was pastor, and Mulegé on the coast, where Francis Píccolo had been pastor. Mayorga and Píccolo had been at their posts about ten years, and there were well-trained Cochimí catechists at both places.

Ugarte had five experienced missionaries, including himself, and the four new Jesuits looked promising. The newcomers included a young Spaniard named Nicholas Tamaral, who was turning a *visita* of San Xavier into a lush farm. Oaxacan fine-arts professor Sebastian Sistiago was speaking Cochimí like a native after two years. John Mugazábal, the former soldier and new brother, was known to be responsible and to get on well with the Indians, and the latest arrival, Everard Hellen from Prague, was studying Cochimí and seemed competent.

As for the Californians, the Cochimís in the north were receptive and kept asking for missionaries. The Guaicuras in the south were not receptive, and some were hostile. It would have been easier just to go north with the Cochimís, but the government wanted a port in the south or on the Pacific side for the ships coming from the Philippines.

Ugarte and the other Jesuits had a planning meeting. They would attempt to go both south and north. They would establish a new mission with the Guaicuras at La Paz, which was two-thirds of the way down the coast from Loreto. It was rather distant, and they might have to establish a mission midway between Loreto and La Paz. However, the principal move would be to the north through the central mountains to establish two more missions with the Cochimís. Ugarte assigned the more experienced Jesuits to the Guaicuras, Bravo to pastor at La Paz, and Guillén to establish *visitas* with the Guaicuras to the west of Liguí.

Ugarte assigned the new and less experienced Jesuits to the Cochimís. Nicholas Tamaral would establish the Cochimí mission of Purísima, north of Comondú, which he had been visiting from Viggé. Everard Hellen would establish the mission of Guadalupe at the place from which the ship's lumber had come, south of the river that Píccolo had visited. Hellen would serve there for sixteen years and would eventually produce a Cochimí grammar, which was useful but was never published.

Here is a summary of the situation, from south to north, on the eve of the expansion of 1720.

- James Bravo would be the new pastor at La Paz and would evangelize to the south.
- Clement Guillén would remain at Liguí, and he would evangelize the Guaicuras across the peninsula.
- John Ugarte would remain at San Xavier Viggé as pastor and regional superior.

- Francis Píccolo and Brother John Mugazábal would be at Loreto.
- Jules Mayorga would remain at Comondú.
- Nicholas Tamaral would found a new mission at Purísima.
- Sebastian Sistiago would remain at Mulegé.
- Everard Hellen would establish the new mission of Guadalupe.

The move to La Paz was a big operation by land and sea. On November 11, 1720, eighteen people—Guillén, three soldiers, and fourteen Native Americans—left Liguí with eighteen horses and pack animals for the 125-mile trip (about 160 by trail) south along the gulf to La Paz. From the start the way was difficult, with the animals picking their way across rock-strewn beaches, circling marshes, and ascending and descending hills and summits. On the fourth day, getting over two summits, some of the mules fell and rolled over, and other mule loads came unpacked. Sometimes a load had to be unpacked and carried so that a weaker mule could climb a summit. And sometimes the men had to force the animals to follow the trail because they kept trying to avoid rocks and thorny bushes.

On the sixth day, the group discovered a deposit of gypsum, which was used to make whitewash and perhaps the exterior stucco.

Sometimes the men met small groups of people who acted as guides to water holes, but often they had to dig for water. Almost halfway through their journey, they found good water at a place called Dolores, which Guillén thought was an apt site for a mission. It was halfway between Loreto and La Paz, and he and the people of Liguí later moved to this spot.

The Sierra runs south close to the gulf shore, and sometimes it intrudes into the gulf. When the men were about forty miles from La Paz, they were forced west into the mountains. They now had to deal with higher hills and even canyons, and water was harder to find. They sent out squads to search for passes, which then had to be cleared of rocks and spiny bushes.

When they were twenty miles from La Paz, they found flint stones, which were used to make fires and to fire flintlock weapons. Everyone loaded up with these stones because they were scarce on the peninsula.

Principal Settlements of Southern Baja California

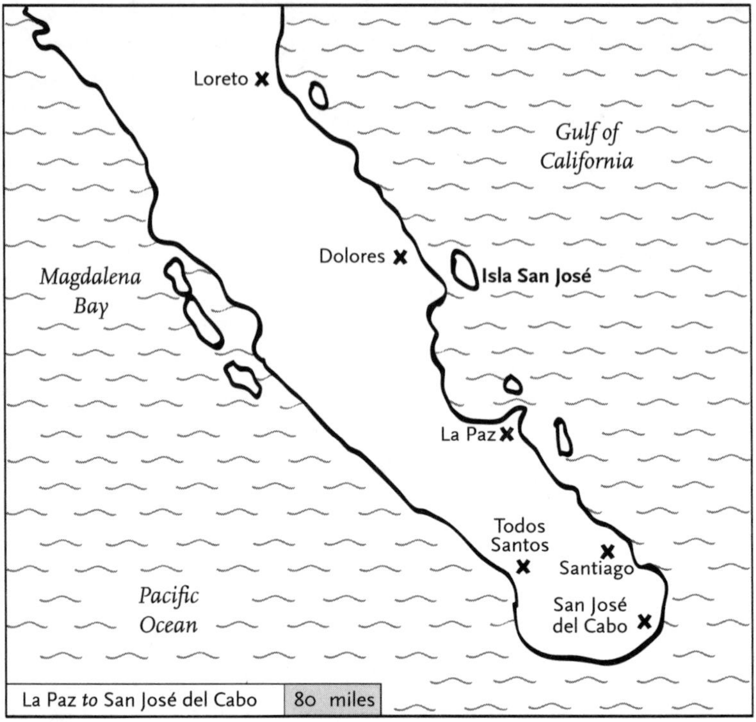

Fig. 29 Some of the mission pueblos were a few miles from these modern towns.

They had just run out of food when they made it to the beach north of La Paz. They had been on the trail for twenty-five days and had covered six miles a day. They were very relieved when they saw the mission sloop because it meant they would be able to eat.

Eighteen others sailed down on the *Triumph of the Cross,* including John Ugarte, James Bravo, and sixteen Native Americans, mostly men. They arrived three days before Guillén's party. One of the Indians was John Diaz, originally from the mainland, who had been part of the crew of a pearl-fishing ship. At one of the island stops, the local people had surprised and killed the crew and captured the ship. Sparing the life of John Diaz, the people forced him to show them how to sail the ship. When Diaz later escaped, the Guaicuras found him and gave him shelter, and after some time Diaz got a ride on another pearl-fishing ship up to Loreto.

La Paz has one of the best harbors in Baja California and had always attracted the Spanish. Two islands on the outer edge of the bay form the harbor. Eusebio Kino and Admiral Atondo were here for a few months before their longer stay at San Bruno. This is the place where the admiral shot the canon at people eating corn and where Loreto Indians had killed a few local women.

When Ugarte's party sailed south, they stopped at San José Island, halfway down, in order to return two boys, about eleven years old, who had been picked up as hostages at an earlier date by the captain of one of the Loreto ships when the people had attacked his ship. The boys had been treated well at Loreto, and now they were going home.

Ugarte's party landed at San José on December 2, 1720, made friendly contact with the people, and returned the boys. On December 3, they landed at La Paz.

For a month, the Guaicuras avoided all contact with the Loreto party. The people from the islands often came to visit, but they were enemies of the people at La Paz. Sometimes they had to come to the peninsula just to obtain water. They came from the islands in large canoes, one of which could hold twenty-two people. The Pericús were the only Californians with good canoes because they had better trees to work with. The other Indians had a few canoes, but they usually fished from rafts.

The people on the islands were part of the Pericú people at the southern end of the peninsula. These island people were friendly and a little humorous. For example, a person might pick up a chair, thank the newcomers profusely for their gracious generosity, and then start to walk off with it.

The newcomers at La Paz kept trying to make contact with the Guaicuras. They went on trips, and they took canoes and a launch along the shore, but the Guaicuras avoided all contact. Finally, at the end of December, a cacique allowed them to approach. A Jesuit and John Diaz, the indigenous man from the mainland who had lived here, approached him. When the cacique saw John Diaz, he gave a shout, and there was much embracing. Good relations then followed.

It was mentioned that James Bravo was the first pastor at La Paz, and he was there for eight years. In working south, Ugarte wanted him to establish *visitas* in preparation for more missionaries. Bravo did get as far as Santiago and San José del Cabo, which are at the end of the peninsula.

Clement Guillén's land party stayed a little over a month at La Paz, helping to get things established and exploring both south and west. On the trip south from Liguí, Guillén had noticed a good spot for a mission, halfway between Loreto and La Paz. Guillén had been at Liguí, south of Loreto where there was little water, and Liguí, like the whole coast, was often attacked and plundered by people from the islands. So it was decided that Liguí would become a *visita* and that a new mission would be established at this place, now called Dolores, north of San José Island and about seventy miles from both Loreto and La Paz.

Ugarte wanted Guillén to persuade the islanders to settle at Dolores, and he also wanted Guillén to evangelize across the peninsula to Magdalena Bay, which was directly opposite Dolores and San José. It was a difficult assignment because Dolores itself was a relatively poor place with a limited amount of water and was somewhat isolated from the other missions. Also, Guillén and the Cochimís from Liguí were moving to a place where there were Guaicuras in the mountains and Pericús on San José. However, over several years Guillén did these things with good success.

On January 10, 1721, Guillén's party left La Paz in order to return to Liguí. Guillén kept a diary of the whole trip, and he hardly mentioned meeting any people on the trip south from Liguí, although they did find local people who acted as guides. For the trip back, they decided it would be easier to go through the mountains, and going that way, they continually met small groups of people. The Pericús, who surrounded the Guaicuras at La Paz, were in the mountains north of La Paz. North of them were the Guaicuras and then the Cochimís. There were enough people in the mountains that the travelers felt threatened. At one place they saw a smashed cactus, which was a sign of hostility or even a declaration of war, but at another place they were invited to race, which was a sign of friendship. They returned to Liguí in two weeks, or half the time of the outward journey.

Ugarte was asked by the government to explore the northern end of the Gulf of California in 1721, and in that same year a new Italian missionary arrived whom Ugarte assigned to Santiago. The people at the southern end of the peninsula were not purely indigenous. Some people around Santiago looked like the descendants of northern Europeans with their beards and fair skin. Farther south, near the future San José del Cabo, some people looked like the descendants of Africans. Europeans and Africans had been in the Americas for over two hundred years, and many ships had sailed past the end of the peninsula. Pirates probably stopped or even lived there. Spanish ships from the Philippines could have been there, and whites, Africans, or Filipinos could have left these ships. In any case, culturally and linguistically, all these people were Native Americans.

In May, Ugarte set out on the *Triumph of the Cross* with a launch and a canoe to explore the northern end of the gulf. There were twenty-eight in the party, and over half were Filipinos. The others included one Peruvian, one Yaqui, five Californians, and six Europeans. The Europeans included an Irishman and the Englishman, William Strafford, who was the pilot.

Starting from the islands on a latitude level with the Sonora River, the gulf extends north more than two hundred miles to the Colorado River. It was a rough trip for Ugarte. He was fifty-nine years old and suffered severe pain from rheumatism during the voyage.

Going north from the Sonora River on the mainland side, they found almost unbroken desert all the way to the Colorado River, which was in flood. The river, which today no longer reaches the gulf, came into the gulf in two arms, full of mud and debris. The water of the gulf at the northern end was black from lava rocks and mud. It was a desolate place.

On the California side the situation was better. Water drained from the lengthy Sierra San Pedro Mártir, and nearby Cochimís had shelters and attractive pottery. Still, there was no good port along this coast.

The tide in the area rose and fell much more than in other places. Also, the islands, extending across the gulf at the Sonora River, were treacherous with sandbars and fast currents. Everyone was convinced by the trip that California was not an island and that there was no passage to the Pacific.

While Ugarte was exploring, Francis Píccolo was acting regional superior at Loreto. Now sixty-five years old and with infections in both eyes, he felt useless and even finished. In a dictated letter, he requested free room and board from the provincial for two sons of Captain Steven Rodriguez so that they could attend the tuition-free Colegio Maximo in Mexico City. He said that the boys deserved the room and board because of the generous service of their father. He also mentioned that their mother had acted as a nurse since her arrival in California, turning her home into a hospital. She also taught sewing, embroidering, and reading to the Indian girls and women.

The two boys did attend the Colegio Maximo. One remained in Mexico as a diocesan priest, and the other achieved a bachelor's degree and later succeeded his father as captain of the Loreto garrison.

In 1722, the Jesuits complained to the government in Madrid about Spanish officials who were coming to California and carrying off livestock and farm products as taxes. Madrid agreed that no official could do this in the future unless he had written authorization from the viceroy or the highest authority in Guadalajara.

In this same year, there was a destructive plague of locusts, which originated in the southern mountains and swept north. The Californians toasted, ground, and consumed them, with the result that an epidemic swept the land with high mortality.

During the first thirty-five years of the Jesuit presence in California, this was the only year that the locusts came. But in the next thirty-five years the locusts came nine times—four successive years in the forties, two successive years in the fifties, and three successive years in the sixties just before the expulsion.

When the locusts swept north, they mostly missed the missions of Comondú and Purísima. They consumed all tender leaves but did little damage to ripe wheat and corn, and the mescal plant was the least damaged of all edible plants.

The locusts avoided the beaches where one of the *pitahaya* cactus species was located, but in the interior of the peninsula they hit an area with one swarm after the other. With tender plants gone, the livestock went hungry and decreased in number by half. All sorts of methods were used to fight the locusts, but the methods met with little success.[5]

There is data about purchases in Mexico City for the California mission in 1725. Over twenty thousand pounds of goods were purchased for nineteen thousand pesos and were transported to the gulf on 130 mules.

By 1725, Clement Guillén was regional superior. Guillén and Sistiago alternated as regional superior for twenty-two years between 1725 and 1747. They were both from New Spain and noticeably fine linguists. In a letter to the viceroy, Guillén recommended that a *presidio* (fort) be established in the south in order to protect both the mission villages and the port where ships from the Philippines stopped. He mentioned the violence that existed among the people and how difficult it was for the twenty-five soldiers, mostly at Loreto, to maintain order in such a vast area. If someone was murdered, the Californians expected the soldiers to punish the murderer. If the soldiers did not, then the people themselves would seek vengeance.

The people lived in small, isolated groups. It was rare that people went more than a half day's journey from their home *rancheria* in search of food. On the other hand, two people at La Paz said they could understand the Guaicura dialects across to the Pacific. If people did go on a long journey, they wore footgear made of three layers of deerskin in order to protect their feet from the heat of the sun-baked rocks.

When the people became Christian, it meant peace in the land and an end to war, abortion, and infanticide. However, the population did not go up but declined. The principal reason for the decline was the new diseases, but the Jesuits mentioned in puzzlement that the Christian families usually had only a few children.

In 1728, a new Jesuit established the mission of San Ignacio on that river that Píccolo had visited. It would produce more food than any other mission on the peninsula, although the fields were in a low spot that was susceptible to floods.

By this time, the California mission as a whole had become self-sufficient in food production. Wine and brandy were traded on the mainland. Each mission also had an income of about 400 pesos a year. The Jesuits in California were not receiving the 350 pesos a year from the government, but they were being supported by the Pius Fund in Mexico. It was estimated that 10,000 pesos were needed to found a mission village. This money was invested so that it would produce 400 or 500 pesos a year.

As time went on, many people in New Spain grew to resent the wealth that was being built up by the church in general and by the Jesuits in particular, even if the church and the religious orders were responsible for social services, education, and the missions.

Francis Píccolo died on February 22, 1729. He was seventy-four years old and had been a missionary for forty-two years. During his California years, he moved around, supervising the agricultural base at Guaymas on the mainland, serving a term as regional superior in Sonora, going to the mainland for supplies, and going to Mexico on business. He explored, founded missions, and then handed them over to others.

By 1730, Nicholas Tamaral had been at Purísima for ten years, and the place was becoming prosperous. There was a dam to hold and distribute the water of a stream. There was a vineyard of 280 vines, fifty-five pomegranate trees, thirty-nine fig trees, some lemon trees, sugarcane, wheat fields and cornfields, cultivated cactus plants, a truck garden, a flower garden, and other tropical fruits. They did not have much live-stock at Purísima, but later, at the time of the expulsion, there were twenty-two hundred sheep and goats, as well as a hundred other animals such as milk cows, oxen, mules, and horses.

This all sounds too good to be true because the place is not known as being that productive. There may not have been enough water for all Tamaral was attempting to do.

This was the workday schedule at Purísima: After being awakened by the bell for the Angelus, the people gathered in the church to visit and to sing a prayer they called the Alabado. Some then left to prepare breakfast and to take food to the sick and the homebound elderly while the others attended Mass. After Mass and breakfast, people went to work, making cloth, farming, or working on the stone church that Tamaral had started. After lunch they took a two-hour siesta. After working from 2:00 P.M. until 5:00 P.M., they said the Angelus and ate supper, after which they met in the church for the rosary and singing or choir practice. The men and women then separated to study and discuss the Christian doctrine, and after that they retired. This routine was broken by Sundays, holy days, and fiestas.

Once a week, other people came to Purísima from the countryside for instruction, religious celebrations, and fiestas. These people had to be fed and cared for. The parish extended to the Pacific Ocean, and some people only came every two months. By 1730, two thousand people had been baptized at Purísima, and 340 marriages had been contracted.

In 1730, Nicholas Tamaral, now forty-four years old, volunteered to turn Purísima over to another Jesuit and to begin again in the south where the challenge was so much greater and where there were no experienced Jesuits. It would mean learning another language, and he was assigned to San José del Cabo.

On December 29, 1730, John Ugarte, who was sixty-eight years old, died at San Xavier. His last years had been difficult. For ten years he had sores on his legs that would not heal. He had rheumatism and he also had an asthmatic cough that disrupted his sleep. The three founders were now gone, and almost half of the Jesuits' seventy years in Baja California were over as well.

During these years, new missionaries continued to come to New Spain from Europe, and they wrote home about what they saw there. The luxury of the churches, the wealth of the Spanish, and the destitution of the indigenous amazed one young German. He described the native people in Mexico as very poor, possessing nothing except what they earned by hard labor. They received two reals (eight reals to the peso) a day for hard work. They were barefoot, and their sole garments were pants and a rough jacket. They slept on the bare earth, and their primary nourishment was corn. Drunkenness was common on the weekends.

In September of 1734, there were three Jesuits and six soldiers in the south. One soldier guarded La Paz. Father William Gordon, thirty-seven years old and from Aberdeen, Scotland, was a new missionary and the pastor at La Paz, but he was away substituting at another parish. La Paz was a place that no Indian group really claimed, and the people from La Paz were living to the south at Todos Santos.

There were two old soldiers without guns with Father Lorenzo Carranco, thirty-nine years old and from Cholula, New Spain, who had been pastor at Santiago since 1726. There were no soldiers with Father Nicholas Tamaral, forty-eight years old, from Seville, Spain, and the pastor for four years at San José del Cabo after his ten years at Purísima.

There were three armed soldiers with Father Sigismund Taraval, thirty-four years old and from Todi, Italy. Taraval had had a few years of experience with the Cochimís when he replaced Nicholas Tamaral at Purísima. During his few years at Purísima, Taraval visited an island off the Pacific coast, probably Cedros, where he saw new species of deer and rabbits. The deer were small and the rabbits were huge. He had become the pastor of Todos Santos the previous year.

So there were three priests and six soldiers in the south when the clouds of rebellion began to gather. The rebellion was centered in Santiago and in a pagan village near San José del Cabo. In Santiago, Father Lorenzo Carranco had appointed a Christian named Botón as governor, but Botón continued to live as a pagan. Carranco removed him from office, and Botón was whipped. Meanwhile, in a pagan village near San José del Cabo, a leader named Chicori was detaining a young girl, who was under instruction, as one of his wives. Nicholas Tamaral had confronted Chicori and was apparently unsuccessful in having him release the girl.

After Botón moved to Chicori's village, the two of them conspired to do away with the Jesuits and the soldiers. Over a period of several months, they successfully recruited others into the conspiracy, both pagans and Christians, and they put together an effective plan. They would first attack La Paz, kill the soldier, take what supplies were available, and then move south to the other missions.

Both Lorenzo Carranco at Santiago and Sigismund Taraval at Todos Santos knew that something was wrong. They warned Nicholas Tamaral at San José del Cabo, but he did not take the warning seriously. After attacking La Paz and killing the soldier, the rebels entered Santiago on October 1, 1734. They killed Lorenzo Carranco and the two old soldiers, destroying the houses, the church, and the cross and taking whatever supplies would be useful. Many of the people of Santiago joined the rebels. On October 3, they killed and beheaded Nicholas Tamaral at San José del Cabo.

At Todos Santos, some miles to the west on the Pacific coast, the people received word about what had happened. Sigismund Tavaral wanted to defend the pueblo, but the three soldiers just started to pack up, and many Indians followed their example. In the evening, some sixty or seventy started to trek the fifty miles north to La Paz. The refugees included women, children, and old people, and Tavaral went with them. They walked all night, fearful of being ambushed, and the pace was slow because of the children, old people, women with babies, and some pregnant women. Some men went ahead as scouts. They had mules to carry corn and church objects. The next day the refugees did not stop to sleep or eat. They walked on during the day without water, very anxious to reach La Paz, and two of the mules collapsed from the heat and their heavy packs. They reached La Paz that evening, doing the fifty miles in twenty-four hours. They now had water, but they did not stop to eat and rest because they were still fearful. When they found a canoe, some went to an island near La Paz.

Back at Todos Santos, some people joined the rebels, but others refused and attempted to defend the pueblo. The rebels attacked Todos Santos, and forty-nine Christian Indians were killed. Regional Superior Clement Guillén ordered all the Jesuits to gather at Loreto. He incorrectly feared that the rising would be general. The Cochimís finally went to Loreto and asked Guillén to allow the Jesuits to return. The soldiers from Loreto clashed with the rebels near Dolores, and Dolores, seventy-five miles south of Loreto, was secured.

For over thirty-five years, there had been heroic effort and success in California, but now the Jesuits were in the unhappy position of requesting the government to put down a rebellion. Twenty soldiers in Loreto were joined by 115 Yaquis (each paid half a soldier's salary) from the mainland. There were also Californians from San Xavier and other places. They formed an army and occupied La Paz, and from La Paz they made excursions to Santiago and San José del Cabo.

The rebels attacked La Paz three times and were driven off. Early in 1735, a ship from Manila arrived at San José del Cabo. Eight sailors were killed when they landed in a boat from the ship. Finally, the governor of Sinaloa, Manuel Huidobro, came over with some soldiers, but he was not energetic. Things dragged on into 1737 before there was an end to the fighting.

1740: The Yaqui Rebellion

In 1740, an uprising among the Yaquis was more or less instigated by Manuel Huidobro, who had been named governor in 1734 of the newly united provinces on the mainland. He and his staff were hostile to the Jesuits and wanted them removed from the area. He welcomed any complaints from the Indians against the Jesuits, and he sent a delegation of Yaquis to the viceroy in Mexico City to complain about the Jesuits and to request their removal. He also appointed a Yaqui who had been with him in California to be governor of the Yaqui Nation.

Huidobro was attempting to undercut the Jesuits' authority and perhaps to take more control himself through his Yaqui appointee. But the strategy did not work.

There were now a growing number of Spanish in the area, and everyone was discontented. Some Spanish wanted Indian property and more workers for the mines. Some Yaquis wanted authority over the Yaqui villages. The Jesuits wanted better government for the area, and the local Spanish government wanted the Jesuits to leave.

In the spring of 1740, a band of Yaquis took 150 cattle from some Spanish cowboys, whom they sent fleeing. When other Yaquis and Mayos joined them, they attacked two ranches, taking property and leaving many dead. Then, well over a hundred in number, they attacked a mine site, obtained silver worth forty thousand pesos, and left many dead.

They then entered the Yaqui mission villages and took supplies. Some of the Jesuits were manhandled, but all were allowed to leave. The uprising then became general among the Mayos and Yaquis.

On the Fuerte to the south, the governor had forced many Indians to work in the mines. Then, when he sent men in to survey the lands along the river, the Indians thought he was about to confiscate their property. So they rose in rebellion and joined the Yaquis and Mayos.[6] As the governor barricaded himself in a Spanish town, the Indians scoured the country-side, robbing, killing, and taking women and children prisoners. The governor blamed the Jesuits for the insurrection that he himself had provoked and that was now aimed at him and the Spanish settlers.

A Spanish captain, Augustine Vildásola, finally came down from a northern fort, fought two big battles with the rebels, and ended the insurrection. Probably a total of three hundred Spanish died in the insurrection, and perhaps over two thousand Indians. Vildásola became governor, and the Jesuits sent new priests to the Yaquis. After these events, the Indians came and went with more freedom in order to work in the mines. The requirement to work three days on the mission land was relaxed or abandoned. The villages no longer produced big farm surpluses, and there was much less help for the missions in California.

This insurrection happened in 1740, and it marks the beginning of the end of the Jesuit missions. In 1751, the Upper Pimas (mentioned earlier) revolted for reasons very similar to those of the Yaquis. Then in 1767, the Jesuits were expelled, and the missions were secularized. This meant having diocesan clergy as well as paying taxes to the government and tithes to the church.

The Indian villages were becoming marginalized as more Spanish moved to the area. In a sense, they had always been marginalized, since they were not permitted to do mining or pearl fishing, but the communal agriculture had been successful. Now, less bound by communal work, the Indians were freer to work their own land. Some did well and sold their surplus outside the mission, but other families fell into poverty. Indian families left the missions to improve their lot, and many ended up bound by debt to the haciendas and mines.

There is a description of the mission villages on the Sinaloa River in 1744.[7] Some of the villages are described as Spanish, which means Spanish-speaking people of different racial backgrounds. A few of the northern Indians lived as equals in these Spanish villages, but most of the northern Indians in this area were servants to the Spanish or workers in the mines and on the haciendas.

After the expulsion, the Yaquis continued to do well or at least better than other nations. They retained their land, which was the most productive in the gulf region, and no mines were developed in their immediate area. Moreover, their labor was needed in the mines, and they managed to avoid the new taxes. The diocesan priests who replaced the Jesuits were sympathetic and supportive.

In California during the 1740s, there was a changing of the guard among the Jesuits. In 1744, Father James Bravo died at age sixty-one, as did a German Jesuit of thirty-eight years after eight years in California. In 1746, Captain Steven Rodriguez, about eighty years old, died, as well as a German Jesuit, forty-three years old, after about ten years in California. In 1747, Sebastian Sistiago, the veteran from Oaxaca and about sixty-three years old, retired to Mexico because of poor health. In 1748, Clement Guillén, from Zacatecas and seventy years old, died at Loreto. Both Rodriguez and Guillén were blind for about two years before they died. Guillén had spent most of his missionary life as pastor at Dolores, south of Loreto, and it was about the poorest mission in California.

Captain Steven Rodriguez had served in California for forty-nine years, and his service was not recognized by the government. Requests to the viceroys to have his military commission confirmed were ignored because the viceroys resented the authority of the Jesuits in Baja California. Later requests for a military pension were also ignored, as civil authorities thought that Rodriguez was too subservient to the Jesuits. Another point of view is that he and his wife shared the Jesuits' religious ideals. Rodriguez was very generous in helping to establish each mission. He acted as supervisor and stonemason for the foundations of the adobe churches as it came time to build each one.

In 1741, a soldier named Manuel de Ocio was stationed in the north at San Ignacio. When great quantities of oysters washed up along the north shore of the peninsula, Indians brought pearls to San Ignacio, and Ocio arranged to trade goods for the pearls. The pearls in the gulf were not really of high quality, but he collected hundreds of pounds of them.

He resigned his commission, sold the pearls in Guadalajara, and came back in a ship to gather more pearls. He later traded supplies for pearls with other fishermen, purchased many properties in Guadalajara, and brought a crew to the south of Baja California to mine silver. Mining for gold and silver was never significant in Baja California, but there were now independent Spanish settlers in the south.[8]

Another change at this time was that the number of soldiers was raised from twenty-five to sixty, with thirty in the south and thirty in the north. For eighteen months, the presidio in the south was independent of the Jesuits, but there was so much trouble that the viceroy finally put it under Jesuit authority. The lieutenant in the south was now theoretically under the captain at Loreto, but he acted with independence in alliance with Manuel de Ocio and the other Spanish.

In 1743, Bernard Rodriguez was confirmed by the government as captain of Loreto while his blind father, Steven, was still alive. After his confirmation, the Jesuits gave up their right to name the captain.

Three times during the 1740s, epidemics swept through the south. The missions in the south were consolidated at Santiago and Todos Santos, and there was a great decrease of native people in the south.

It was about this time that the Cochimís started to develop small businesses in the mission villages, making and selling hats, rope, stockings, and other articles. Until this time the Californians' freedom of movement had been restricted, but once they started the small businesses, they had more freedom to travel for business or social reasons.

One of the replacement Jesuits in the 1740s was Father Michael Barco, thirty-eight years old, from Placencia, Spain, who arrived in 1744. He started to build a stone church with a vaulted roof at San Xavier Viggé, and it was worked on intermittently for fourteen years until its completion in 1758. It is the most beautiful of the Jesuit churches in Baja California.

Barco was expelled with the other Jesuits in 1767. After lengthy imprisonment in Spain, he was exiled to Italy, where he contributed to linguistic publications and wrote *Historia natural y crónica de la Antigua California,* which has been translated into English. He died in 1790, eighty-four years old. About a mile from San Xavier is another church with unfinished stones, which probably dates to the time of John Ugarte.

Before the expulsion, two fine organs were brought from Mexico for Loreto and San Xavier Viggé.

Another magnificent colonial church at San Ignacio in the north was started by Father Joseph Rotea, born in Mexico City in 1732. He came to San Ignacio in 1758, when he was twenty-six years old. During his years at San Ignacio, he was continually building. A stone dam was destroyed by flood and had to be rebuilt, and it was a big job. In 1760, he opened two schools for boys and girls, and he began the church. After the Jesuits were expelled, the Moorish-style church was completed by a Dominican pastor.

A third attractive stone church was built at Comondú. In Baja California, the first captain used to go to a mission to help when a new church was started. He stayed as they laid out the boundaries of the church, dug the footings, and filled them with rock fragments. He got it started.

Going from south to north, here are some statistics about the California mission in 1744, when there were seventy Spanish or mainland families in California.

We have no data for Santiago, but there were 300 families in twelve settlements at La Paz and its *visita* of Todos Santos. At San Luís Gonzaga, a new mission west of La Paz, there were 180 families in three settlements. At Dolores, a poor place, there were 200 families in eight settlements. At Loreto, where the spoken language was Spanish, there were 45 Indian families. At San Xavier Viggé, there were 115 families in various settlements.

At Comondú there were 150 families. Purísima had 156 families in various settlements. Mulegé had 95 families. Guadalupe, with livestock but almost no workable land, had 200 families in four settlements. San Ignacio, with its very abundant harvests, had 300 families with another 100 at a dependent mission.

North of San Ignacio, there would be three later missions, Santa Gertrudis in 1752, San Borja in 1762, and Santa María in 1767, with the last being about 150 miles south of the Colorado River. These last missions had big populations, but at these higher latitudes the living conditions continued to be harsh. It was cold, and there was limited water and almost no wood. There was little native food in the mountains except for the mescal plants. The main foods at this more narrow part of the peninsula were shellfish, fish, and turtles, which were brought to the missions from both the gulf and the Pacific Ocean.

In 1750, Father Lambert Hostell, forty-four years old and from Munster-Eifel, Germany, was regional superior. He was stationed at Dolores, where Guillén had been pastor and where the people still could not support themselves. He wrote that everyone was a Christian from Dolores across to the Pacific and south to the cape. He said there were six thousand California Christians, and he quoted Father Ferdinand Konschak (better known as Consag) that there were really no rivers on the peninsula. This Ferdinand Konschak, from Varazdin, Croatia, and forty-seven years old, was the most eminent Jesuit explorer, geographer, and cartographer of Baja California.

The pope gave permission for Jesuit regional superiors to administer the sacrament of confirmation in 1756. Bishops had visited Sinaloa and Sonora to administer the sacrament, but it had never been administered in California. With regard to the other sacraments, it was the custom in those days for people to confess and to receive the Eucharist at least once a year at Easter. On the mainland, many Jesuits hesitated to give communion to the Indians even at Easter, yet in California much more frequent communion was encouraged. Sebastian Sistiago had encouraged this practice and had written often to defend it.

In the 1760s, a Filipino, Gaspar Molina, was the architect and builder of two small sailing ships at Loreto.

One of the colonial Jesuit historians mentioned that in 1762, the Jesuits had fifty-four mission schools in New Spain.[9]

In 1762, five years before the expulsion, almost eight thousand people lived at the mission villages in Baja California. Almost three thousand of these were at two new missions fairly far to the north, opposite the Sonora River. At the end, in 1767, there were sixteen Jesuits in California. One of these Jesuits, Wenceslaus Linck, estimated that there were twelve thousand baptized Indians in Baja California at the time of the expulsion.

A group of Jesuits at St. Ildefonso who wanted to modernize the curriculum in the colleges met in Mexico City in 1763. The majority of the group were young, American born, and outstanding scholars. Two of the Jesuits in the group were F. X. Alegre and F. X. Clavijero. Both were from Vera Cruz, and both were later major historians of the Society. The group proposed adding programs in Italian, French, experimental physics, mathematics, and chemistry. The provincial accepted the plan, and the new programs were begun at the Colegio Maximo even though the University of Mexico had not yet agreed to grant degrees for these subjects.

The group also wished to reform the method of teaching. They wanted the students to do more reading and research instead of just memorizing their class notes. When the Jesuits were expelled, the colleges continued under new administrators, but there was little follow-up to the modernization.

The seventy-year effort in California was from 1697 to 1767. It took some time for the expulsion order to reach California and for the Jesuits to be assembled, so they actually left the peninsula on February 5, 1768.

During their years in California, the Jesuits never published a grammar and vocabulary of Cochimí or of the other California languages. Earlier, superiors had asked Sebastian Sistiago to prepare a book for publication, but he was a perfectionist and never finished the job. After the expulsion, Jesuits in Italy preserved details about the California languages that were later published.

Although only fifty-five Jesuits served in Baja California, this mission is a significant chapter in the history of the Society, partly because, from a human point of view, it made little sense. For a seventy-year period, the Jesuits poured men and money into a barren land where there were few people and where those people were the poorest imaginable. However, they believed that these people had the right to live both in this world and the next, and they hoped that they would be the beginning of a new Christian civilization in California. The fifty-five Jesuits do not include Kino and his companions in their earlier effort, nor do they include five who came and remained for only a few months.

At the end, there were sixteen Jesuits at fourteen mission stations. The sixteen include six from Spain, two from New Spain, three from Germany, three from Bohemia, one from Austria, and one from Alsace.

At the time of the expulsion, many Californians in all of the mission pueblos spoke Spanish. Seventy years after the expulsion, no people in Baja California still spoke the original languages. Part of the population probably died out, and part probably became ladinos.

The Jesuits left Baja California in February of 1768, and the Franciscans came to replace them one month later. From now on, the civil government and the soldiers would be in charge, not the missionaries. One year later, the Franciscans, with Spanish and Indians from both the mainland and the peninsula, began founding pueblos in Upper California. The leaders of the expedition acknowledged that their best soldiers were those from Baja California with their well-trained horses.

The move north was partially financed by the Pius Fund in Mexico. Supplies and people went from Baja California through the northern missions, with Jesuit maps of the area farther north, to San Diego, which was founded in July of 1769. At San Diego, the male Indians were naked and spoke a Cochimí language, but the Cochimís from Baja California could not understand them. The newcomers moved on to Monterey, and they founded San Francisco in 1776. The Dominicans replaced the Franciscans in Baja California.

Here are the missions that were established by the Jesuits during their seventy years in Baja California.

- Loreto, 1697—250 miles from the bottom of the peninsula
- San Xavier Viggé, 1699—17 miles southwest of Loreto
- Santa Rosalia de Mulegé, 1705—75 miles north of Loreto (the ship was built here)
- Liguí, 1705—24 miles south of Loreto, abandoned after twenty years
- San José Comondú, 1708—25 miles west of Loreto
- Guadalupe, 1720—125 miles north of Loreto (the logs for the ship came from here)
- Purísima, 1720—45 miles north of Loreto
- La Paz, 1721—150 miles south of Loreto

- Dolores, 1721—75 miles south of Loreto
- Santiago, 1721—215 miles south of Loreto
- San Ignacio, 1728—135 miles north of Loreto
- San José de Cabo, 1730—235 miles south of Loreto
- Todos Santos, 1733—200 miles south of Loreto, the only mission on the Pacific coast
- San Luís, 1737—80 miles south of Loreto
- Santa Gertrudis, 1752—170 miles north of Loreto
- San Borje, 1762—250 miles north of Loreto
- Santa María, 1767—310 miles north of Loreto and 270 miles south of San Diego

CHAPTER 12

The Expulsion, 1767–1768

On the evening of Wednesday, June 24, 1767, the viceroy of New Spain opened a package of instructions from King Charles III of Spain. The king ordered the viceroy to arrest all Jesuits in New Spain, to take them to the port of Vera Cruz, and to exile them to Europe. The viceroy was to seal and take possession of all Jesuit papers and records. Each Jesuit could take his prayer books and whatever else was absolutely necessary for the journey. No Jesuit, even if old or sick, was to be left in New Spain. The king also sent an official, Joseph Gálvez, as special commissioner for the expulsion.

There were no charges, and the king never gave a reason for the order. However, it was the time of the Enlightenment in Europe, and the spirit of the age was secular and antireligious. Also, since the Jesuits were supporters of the pope's authority, expelling the Jesuits would weaken the pope.

The viceroy had a difficult assignment—to arrest and exile 688 priests, brothers, and seminarians, many of whom had been born in New Spain and had relatives in influential positions. He was also about to undermine the only organized system of higher education in the country while schools were still in session.

Neither the viceroy nor the Jesuits thought of defying the king. Spain's government of the colony had been paternalistic rather than autocratic (at least during earlier Hapsburg times). People felt loyalty to the king and had affection for Spanish culture and institutions. There were no revolutionary movements among the white people at this time, even though there had always been considerable antagonism between the Spanish born in Europe and those born in New Spain.

The viceroy had another problem because Thursday, June 25, was one of the longest days of the year. So he moved with officers and soldiers at 4:00 A.M. on Thursday morning before people were up. The soldiers demanded entrance to the Jesuit houses in Mexico City and read the expulsion order. They arrested the Jesuits and occupied their residences, churches, and schools. There were 164 Jesuits in Mexico City, including seminarians, the provincial staff, teachers, pastoral workers, some graduate students, and some who were retired or sick.

After the arrest of the Jesuits, notices were posted in the plazas and main streets that informed people of the expulsion. The people were exhorted to be silent and to obey the great monarch who occupied the throne of Spain. They should neither discuss nor give their opinion about the high affairs of state. The viceroy also arranged for the departure of the boarding students at St. Ildefonso.

On June 28, three days after the arrest, the viceroy took the Jesuits in carriages to the Shrine of Our Lady of Guadalupe for a last visit before leaving for Puebla, Jalapa, and the port of Vera Cruz. Great crowds—friends, students, former students, and relatives—greeted the Jesuits in these places.

Jesuits from Tepotzotlán, Puebla, Querétaro, Celaya, Guanajuato, and León had also been arrested and were on their way to Vera Cruz during the last days of June. At Jalapa, the Jesuits were moved from the carriages to horses and mules because the way down from Jalapa to Vera Cruz was so perilous.

They all arrived at Vera Cruz at the beginning of the summer, in the rainy season and at the time of suffocating heat and disease. In early July, there were 400 Jesuits out of the 688 in the province at the port. Under guard, they were placed in the Jesuit college, in different monasteries, and in private houses. Besides these 400 at Vera Cruz, another 100 were missionaries in northwest New Spain, and the other 188 were mostly at colleges in different cities.

Other Jesuits arrived during the summer. The novitiate continued to function in Vera Cruz, and classes were set up for the other seminarians. That summer, there was an epidemic that involved a lot of vomiting, and most of the Jesuits became infected. At least thirty-four died that summer in Vera Cruz. Among this first big group of exiles, another nineteen died in an epidemic in Havana, eleven died of disease or neglect on the high seas, and nine died just after reaching port in Spain.

Fifty-five of this group were shipped out in July, but the rest had to wait until the autumn. In October, 210 were dispatched on seven different ships, and in November, 265 sailed in six ships. They were going first to Havana, where they would be joined by 1,000 Jesuits from Panama and South America.

The government only had trouble with the expulsion in four cities at the center of the country where there were large numbers of Native Americans.

San Luís de la Paz was the Otomí pueblo that had been founded in the time of Gonzalo de Tapia. On the morning of Thursday, June 25, many people were at Mass because they were celebrating each day of the octave of the Feast of Corpus Christi. The commissioner (not Commissioner Joseph Gálvez) waited until evening before reading the expulsion order to the Jesuits, and the Indians became suspicious that something momentous was about to happen. They took up arms and surrounded the Jesuit establishment, and the commissioner took refuge in the school. The Jesuits accepted the expulsion order and were able to calm the people, but pamphlets were printed and disseminated that denounced the king, the expulsion order, and the Spanish government in Mexico City. The Jesuits left two weeks later on July 7.

On July 13, Joseph Gálvez arrived at San Luís de la Paz with troops from the capital. He threatened the Indian officials and forced them to give a list of those who had led the opposition to the government. The commissioner then arrested the accused, tried them before a military court, and hung four on July 20, one of whom was a widow named Anna María Guatemala. Then he destroyed the houses of the condemned and exiled their families from the pueblo. Neither the family members nor their descendants could ever return to San Luís de la Paz. The commissioner then left for San Luís Potosí, where he arrived on July 24 and found that the Jesuits were still in residence.

At San Luís Potosí, the Native Americans, probably Otomíes, had been in a state of rebellion since May because of new taxes. In the middle of June, a quarrel between a soldier and an Indian led to the public tearing apart of a Spanish flag.

On June 24, the mayor of San Luís Potosí opened the expulsion order and discovered that he was named commissioner for the expulsion of the Jesuits. He called for help and carriages from an hacienda. But when he left with the Jesuits on Friday, June 26, the Feast of the Sacred Heart, they were stopped by Indians outside the city and forced to return to the college. There was some rioting on this day, the prison was opened, gunpowder was taken from a government warehouse, and shops were looted.

On July 9, the mayor tried again to leave with the Jesuits but was again stopped. On July 24, Joseph Gálvez arrived with troops. He was angry with the Jesuits because they had not left on their own. He immediately put them in carriages and sent them to Vera Cruz with an escort of seventy soldiers. He then began reprisals, hanging fifty people, whipping many, and sending two hundred to prison.

On October 16, Gálvez arrived at Guanajuato, where the Indians were in a state of rebellion and where the Jesuits had left the city on their own after receiving the expulsion order. The commander executed 9 rebels, gave two hundred lashes to 5, sent 11 to exile (at least from the city), and imprisoned 164 (30 for life).

At Pátzcuaro, the people were angry and defiant because of taxes, and the expulsion of the Jesuits had intensified their anger. Joseph Gálvez arrived at the city on November 14 and executed thirteen people.

In punishment for the protests and riots, Joseph Gálvez had hanged a total of 76 people, whipped 74, sentenced 664 to prison, and exiled 110, not including the families of the exiled, who also had to leave their homes. These people were all Indians, and in order to pay for the military action, Gálvez took part of the Jesuits' California Pius Fund.

It took six days for the expulsion order to reach the city of Chihuahua. The two or three Jesuits in the city left on their own, and the governor sent orders to the nineteen Jesuits of the Tarahumara mission that they should assemble at Chihuahua. The Jesuits came in during July. They stayed at their own residence in the city, and the governor treated them with consideration and permitted visitors. At the end of July, the nineteen Jesuits left for Mexico City and Vera Cruz with the governor and some soldiers. They avoided large population centers as they had been ordered to do. Two of the Jesuits fell sick during the journey, and they were left temporarily with a Franciscan community.

The seventeen Jesuits from the Tarahumara arrived east of Mexico City in the middle of September. When they asked if they could visit the Shrine of Our Lady of Guadalupe, their request was sent to the viceroy, who gave permission. They stayed two days at Guadalupe, where huge numbers of people came from Mexico City to see them.

They left the shrine on September 26, and it took them a little over two weeks to reach Vera Cruz, where they were held for a month. After they boarded a ship at Vera Cruz on November 10, a storm came up. They remained on board in the harbor for eleven days, and three of the Jesuits became sick, apparently from tainted food, and were returned to shore. On November 21, they sailed for Havana, where there were now fourteen Tarahumara missionaries. On the short trip to Cuba, they became sick, and five of the fourteen died, apparently from food poisoning. In Havana, nine Tarahumara missionaries were grouped with other Jesuits from Peru and Argentina, and they all sailed into exile two days before Christmas 1767.

It was on November 30, 1767, five months after the promulgation of the expulsion order in Mexico City, that the new governor of California arrived at Loreto. He was very uneasy because he had heard that the Jesuits in California had power and wealth (four million pesos) and that the Indians had gunpowder, ten thousand guns, and a ready willingness to defend their land.

The Jesuits in California knew that the expulsion was coming because their brothers in Sinaloa and Sonora had already been arrested. The Jesuit superior in California was Father Francis Ducrue, who later wrote an account of the expulsion. When he heard that the governor had arrived, he came down the next day from Guadalupe to Loreto, where he formally acknowledged the authority of the governor.

The governor waited one more day before informing the four Jesuits who were at Loreto that they were dispossessed and about to be exiled.

Taking the keys, he took command of the garrison and asked to see the books. With disappointment he learned that the mission had seven thousand pesos and that part of this was owed to the soldiers for salaries. In the warehouses were supplies worth sixty thousand pesos, not counting food, which at that time was scarce.

A few things in the churches had value, but there were no mines and no pearls. The Jesuits had always been forbidden by the provincials to fish for pearls because the whites were hostile to any serious economic competition from the Jesuits and the Indians. The provincials had even forbidden any Jesuit in California to have a pearl in his possession, and no pearl could be used to adorn a church statue nor for any other purpose.

It took a few months for the governor to become familiar with the situation and for the Jesuits to wind up their affairs. There was an epidemic in one of the villages. On January 19, some Franciscans arrived to replace the Jesuits, and they faced a formidable challenge. They did not know the languages, and they would function without the former authority of the Jesuits and without the income of the Pius fund.

The Indians were angered by the expulsion and were anxious about the future. The Jesuits urged them to be loyal and obedient to Spanish authority and to accept what was happening.

There were sixteen Jesuits at Loreto—fifteen priests and one brother. On February 3, a final Mass was celebrated at which Father Ducrue preached. Almost all the people at Loreto received communion. In order to avoid possible trouble, the governor arranged for the Jesuits to embark before daylight on the morning of February 4, 1668, but the whole town was there to see them off. Father Ducrue spoke: "Good-by, beloved California. Good-by, beloved Indians. Our hearts will be here until death. Weep not for us for we have been found worthy to suffer something for Jesus Christ."[1]

The Jesuits were taken across the Gulf of California to the port of San Blas, where they saw many Otomí prisoners from San Luís de la Paz. The Otomíes were imprisoned there after the riots, and many had already died miserably. A Jesuit was asked to attend to a prisoner who had asked to go to confession. He found him a mass of blood and bones as he was being beaten daily.

The California Jesuits started across New Spain on mules and horses. They were kept in out-of-the-way places and were not allowed to communicate with anyone except outside Guadalajara. For part of the journey they were in carriages, but they had to descend on horses from Jalapa to Vera Cruz, where they arrived on March 25, forty-four days after leaving San Blas. They were kept isolated for almost three weeks until they went on board ship April 13 with nine soldiers and forty Indian prisoners who were being taken to Havana. They recognized among the prisoners some Indians whom they had seen at San Blas.

They were twenty-four days at sea before they reached Havana, where they were imprisoned about ten days. Their books and other possessions were taken, and they were left with their breviaries. The trip from Havana to Spain took fifty days.

In Spain, the sixteen California Jesuits were separated and imprisoned in very crowded cells. After eight months, the German Jesuits were released due to the intercession of the Austrian ambassador. They left on a Dutch ship and made their way through Belgium to Germany. After that, the Hispanic Jesuits from Baja California were exiled to Italy.

Father Francis Ducrue ended his account as follows: "One last word for our beloved Indians. Will the reader pray that God preserve and strengthen them in the faith so that the labor and sweat of their missionaries may not be without fruit, and that we will see them there in heaven?"[2] Father Ducrue spent twenty years in Baja California. Eleven years after returning to Europe, he died in Munich, the city of his birth.

There were 688 Jesuits in New Spain at the time of the exile. A total of 101, including the ones mentioned earlier, died on the trip to Spain from mistreatment, food poisoning, and disease.

Sinaloa and Sonora

A commissioner, not Gálvez, arrived at Villa Sinaloa in early September of 1767. He closed the school and sent word that the Jesuits were to gather at Guaymas on the coast where the California Jesuits had a farm. Guaymas was starting to become a town but with only a few scattered houses.

The first Jesuits to arrive came in canoes down the Yaqui River and then traveled north along the coast about thirty-five miles to Guaymas, where they were imprisoned in a circular barn. They were held eight months at Guaymas while the affairs of the mission were wound up and other Jesuits came in. It was during their months at Guaymas that the California Jesuits were expelled to Spain. When a very old Jesuit, Joseph Palomino, died after seven months at Guaymas, a band of Yaquis came for his body, which they carried to the Yaqui village of Huiribis for burial.

In May, the fifty Jesuits at Guaymas were sent south in an over-crowded ship to San Blas. It should have been a journey of six days, but for some reason they were held three months on the ship. Scurvy became so bad that they thought they would die. The captain of the ship put them ashore at Puerto Escondito in Baja California, and they received some relief. As they continued to San Blas, a severe storm blew up, and again they prepared for death.

After a few days at San Blas, they were ordered to start the rugged 150-mile climb to Guadalajara. Provided with horses and with mats for sleeping, the fifty Jesuits left San Blas with armed guards. The first day of travel was through swamps full of crocodiles. Since the horses could not make it through the mud, most Jesuits dismounted to lead the horses. They were often up to their waists in water, and everything they had became soaked. During the next days, they were sleeping on wet mats or on the damp ground.

Modern Road Map of Guadalajara Area

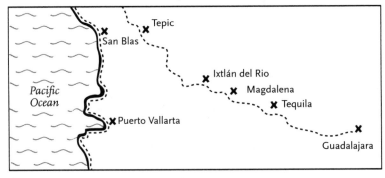

Fig. 30

At Tepic, they were not allowed to rest but were pushed on to Tetitlán, by which time some were so weak and sick that they had to be tied to their horses. From Tetitlán, they went to Ahuacatlán, where they began to die. Twenty of the fifty Jesuits died on this climb to Guadalajara.

Today there is a dirt road from San Blas to Tepic, the state capital of mountainous Nayarit, and a paved road from Tepic to Guadalajara. Today, more or less parallel to the paved road is a dirt road that must be the old trail.

The Jesuits contracted an unknown tropical disease, perhaps from going through the swamp. The bug or virus then incubated for several days. Many were racked with fever as they approached Ahuacatlán on the dirt road about ten miles west of Ixtlán del Rio. Three died at Ahuacatlán and were buried there. Their bodies and tongues turned black before they died, and the corpses continued to sweat after death.

As they came into Ixtlán del Rio, the fever was raging. Twelve died and were buried there, and the rest were pushed on toward Magdalena. Two died on the way and were buried in a ravine. One of these Jesuits was from New Orleans. Two more died in Magdalena, and the last of the twenty deaths occurred in Tequila.

Here are the twenty who died.

At Ahuacatlán:
- Henry Kurtzel, forty-six, German. Considered a very holy person, he was pastor at Movas, east of the Yaqui River, with the Lower Pimas.
- Sebastian Cava, thirty-five, Spanish. A gentle person, he was at Vaca on the Fuerte River.
- Joseph Watzet, forty-seven, German. He was at Yécora, just north of Father Kurtzel's village.

On the way to Ixtlán del Rio:
- Pio Laguna, thirty-four, from Chiapas, New Spain, of delicate health. He attended the very dangerous mission of Baceraca in the foothills of the Sierra.
- Peter Díaz, thirty, from Mexico City. A charitable and joyful person, he had just arrived at Atil in the Pimería.

In the village:

- Nicholas Perea, seventy-two, from Zacatlán, New Spain. He was a missionary for forty-two years.
- Francis Villaroya, thirty-four, from Aragon, Spain. He was successful at Banamichi on the San Miguel River, a tributary of the Sonora River.
- Michael Fernandez, sixty-six, from Tlalpujahua near Mexico City. He spent thirty-six years at Ocoroni.
- Lucas Marino, fifty-six, from Cantabria, Spain. He spent his life at Navajoa on the Mayo River.
- Alexander Rapicani, sixty-six, German. He was pastor at Batucos in Sonora.
- Francis Pascua, thirty-five, from Oaxaca, New Spain. Considered very holy, he had an excellent command of the Opata language and worked just three years at Arivechi, west of the Yaqui River. People said he raised a little girl from the dead.
- Joseph Ronderos, fifty-one, from Puebla, New Spain. He spent six years at Comondú in Baja California and sixteen years with the Lower Pimas at Bamoa on the Sinaloa River.
- Francis Hlawa, forty-three, from Prague, Czech Republic. He spent sixteen years with the Pimas.
- John Nentuig, fifty-five, Czech Republic. A mathematician, he was with the Pimas at Guasaves. He wrote a book about Sonora that has been translated into English.
- Joseph Liébana, about thirty, from Málaga, Spain. He spent a short time at Bacadeguatzi to the east in the foothills of the Sierra.

Buried in a ravine on the way to Magdalena:

- Maximilian Leroy, forty, a Belgian who came to New Spain from New Orleans. When the French government secularized the Society or made it illegal to be a Jesuit, he could have joined another religious order or become a diocesan priest. Since he wished to remain a Jesuit, he went to Sonora and was a priest to the Yaquis.
- Ramón Sánchez, thirty-two, from Pamplona, Spain. He was at Tecoripa, west of the Yaqui with the Lower Pimas.

At Magdalena:

- Manuel Aguirre, fifty-three, from Pamplona, Spain. He had an excellent command of the Opata language. His *Doctrina Cristiana y Pláticas en Opata* was published in Mexico two years before the expulsion by the bishop of Durango. He was superior of the Sonora mission at the time of the expulsion.
- Fernando Berra, thirty-two, from Marfíl, New Spain. He had just arrived at Bacoburito, Sinaloa, in the foothills of the Sierra. Gonzalo de Tapia had made contact with the Bacoburito people in the very beginning of the mission.

At Tequila:

- Bartholomew Sáenz, fifty-three, from Cordova, Spain. He was at Banamichi on the Sonora River.

The twenty who died included seven from Spain, seven from New Spain, three from Germany, two from the Czech Republic, and one from New Orleans.

Thirty Jesuits made it to Guadalajara. They were taken across to Vera Cruz and sent by way of Cuba to Spain. They were imprisoned for three months in Havana and then for ten years in the port of Santa María, across the bay from Cádiz in Spain. Nine died at Santa María, and the remaining non-Hispanics were eventually rescued.

One of those who died at Santa María, in 1779, was James Sedelmayr. His Pima vocabulary and grammar manuscript was apparently lost. Among those rescued was Ignaz Pfefferkorn. When he was back in Germany, he wrote the book about Sonora that was mentioned earlier and that has been published in English.[3]

In 1773, the pope gave in to pressure from the Bourbon kings and suppressed the Jesuits as a religious order. The decree of suppression was read to the Jesuit prisoners at Santa María. They did not know what to think because it seemed that the pope was approving the hatred of their persecutors.

This group from Sinaloa and Sonora was the last from New Spain to reach Spain. The earlier Jesuits from New Spain had been sent on to Italy, but the government suddenly feared that exiled Jesuits would give information about Baja California to the enemies of Spain. So the government imprisoned this last group of Hispanic Jesuits (about fourteen who survived the prison at Santa María) for the rest of their lives. They were sent to monasteries in remote parts of Spain, where they remained prisoners but where conditions were better. The last member of this group, Anthony Ventura, died in 1806 after thirty-nine years of prison life. No other Jesuits were kept permanently in prison except for five who arrived rather late from the island of Chiloé off the coast of Chile.

The work of the colonial Jesuits in New Spain was a work of service and love for Christ and for the people of North America. Extending over two hundred years, the work began with a bloodbath on the York River in Virginia and ended with a death march from San Blas to Guadalajara.

AFTERWORD

In the early nineteenth century, the Jesuits were restored as a religious order by the pope. The order began to grow once again, and to spread around the world.

Today, there are 516 members in the Jesuit Province of Mexico, including 132 seminarians and 52 brothers. Their number has been steady for at least ten years because, although they are accepting fifteen or more novices a year, some members are dying and others are leaving. The total includes twenty-nine from other provinces who are almost all studying in Mexico—novices, scholastics, and tertians.

The 516 also includes 19 working in the "foreign missions"—one in Uganda, one in Russia, one in Germany, one in Korea, two in Japan, six in the United States, and seven in Central and South America.

In Latin America, the Jesuits have always done a lot with their personnel, and this is true today in Mexico. It was different in the United States, where our high school and college communities used to be very large.

In order to present an overview of the work of modern Mexican Jesuits, let us start with their five universities and six high schools. Their principal university is the Universidad Iberoamericana in Mexico City with 10,600 students, almost 1,000 of whom are in graduate programs. The faculty is almost 2,000, including 15 Jesuits. There are other Jesuits as administrators and chaplains. The Iberoamericana has branches with college and graduate students in Puebla (5,057), Torreon (2,370), and Tijuana (1,466). The fifth university is in

Guadalajara with 7,398 students.

The six high schools are in León, Puebla, Guadalajara, Tampico, Torreon, and Tijuana. The school in Tijuana has just 245 senior high students and is attached to the branch of the Iberoamericana in that city. The other five schools each have about 2,000 students, including grammar school children. For example, in León there are 1,166 in elementary school, 644 in junior high, and 520 in high school, for a total of 2,330.

Besides the above there is a trade school in Puebla with 619 students, mostly in grammar school. There are probably other grammar schools associated with Jesuit parishes, and there is a boarding school with 85 students in the Tarahumara Indian mission.

The theologate in Mexico City carries the historic colonial name of Colegio Maximo. There are a total of thirteen scholastics in three years of theology, and another six doing pastoral work in various cities and preparing for comprehensive examinations. The other seminarians are studying in Guadalajara, with the novices at a place nearby.

Beyond the educational apostolate, the work becomes more diverse. For example, there are four Jesuits at a retreat house in Cuernavaca, south of Mexico City. One of them also teaches church history at the diocesan seminary, and at least one helps at a parish.

There are three on an island in the Gulf of California. One works in a prison, one is director of an industrial school, and one is doing pastoral work.

There is a community of three in Xalapa, near Vera Cruz. One works for the archdiocese and is counselor at the public University of Vera Cruz in Xalapa. The second is doing pastoral work and the third is teaching theology at the diocesan seminary. There are other small communities like these in other cities.

The largest concentrations of Jesuits are in Mexico City and in Guadalajara. They are involved in province administration, in education, in our seminaries, in national religious organizations, in human-rights advocacy, in theological reflection, in pastoral work, retreat work, and social work, in radio and TV, and also in publication. There are also Jesuit nursing homes in these two cities.

There are nineteen Jesuits with the indigenous in the State of Chiapas, which borders on Guatemala. They are in two towns and in the city of San Cristóbal de las Casas in the north central part of the state. Some of them have been there for a very long time. They are doing pastoral and educational work and staffing a Center for Indigenous Rights. Two of them are composing a grammar and a dictionary, and also a translation of the Bible into the Tseltal language.

There are eight Jesuits doing pastoral and social work with Nahuatl-speaking people south of Vera Cruz, near the city of San Andres Tuxtla, which is near the Gulf coast.

Seventeen Jesuits are in the Tarahumara area of the Sierra Occidental, where the larger towns are Spanish speaking and where there are also diocesan priests at work. The Jesuits are doing pastoral and social work in about five parishes.

There is an elderly Jesuit from Guadalajara, Luís Verplancken, who has done impressive things in service to the Tarahumaras. He works out of Creel, a stop on the railroad line through the Sierra, and north of the Copper Canyon. He has developed a clinic or small hospital for the Tarahumaras, who are not charged for care. Sisters of Charity are the nurses, and there are six doctors. After medical school, doctors must serve two years or so in a poor area. The hospital has recently been enlarged and remodeled.

Many of the patients are infants and small children, who are often brought in close to death from sickness and malnutrition. Four or five hundred are restored to health each year. There is a garden behind the hospital. The adult Tarahumaras are permitted to go outside even when they are still sick. If this were not permitted, they would not stay.

There is a boarding school with eighty-five Indians. Father Verplancken also has heavy equipment for digging wells.

There has been a severe drought in the Sierra in recent years. Begging the money, Luís has often purchased yearly for the Tarahumaras two or three hundred tons of corn and beans in the United States or Mexico. The Tarahumara is the only colonial mission to which modern Jesuits have returned. But here and in other places, the work continues.

For the past eighteen years there have been Jesuits high in the Sierra Oriental at Huayacocotla, a hundred miles north of Puebla, where the majority of the people are Otomíes, Tepehuanes, and Nahuatl speakers.

From the beginning, along with pastoral work, there has been a radio with music, educational programs, and information about health care (especially of children), community events, and legal services. The radio signal reaches about a hundred communities, but it has helped form a larger community of the nearest forty. Thirteen of the communities have developed two carpentry cooperatives and a sawmill.

Nine years ago, the Jesuits moved lower in the Sierra at the invitation of the people to a place in which almost all of the people were indigenous of the three language groups mentioned above. There were caciques (rural bosses) who were trying, and are still trying, to expropriate the land of the indigenous. In one three-year period, thirty-four indigenous were murdered. In 1986, the leader of the assassins was successfully prosecuted and received a prison term of thirty years.

At present, there is a team of three Jesuits and five laypersons, and they also have the assistance of three lawyers. The work continues at the two sites, including the one with the radio. The lawyers give lectures about the law, especially agrarian law, and many cases have been won, even though the ownership of their own land by the indigenous is still threatened.

The Mexican Jesuits of today speak not of serving the indigenous but rather of accompanying them. They say that accompanying the indigenous must include respect for their cultures, and that they have learned the true meaning of Christian unity from the way that the indigenous work, celebrate, struggle, and worship together.

This is actually an accompaniment that began over four hundred years ago in Florida, in Virginia, and on the coast of the Gulf of California. And it is an accompaniment that looks ahead into the next millennium.

NOTES

Chapter 1: John Segura, S.J., and Companions, 1540–1571

1. The Jesuits had established many foreign missions before they reached a Spanish colony in 1566. The early missions were in India (1542), Japan (1549), Brazil (1550), West Africa (1553), Ethiopia (1555), and Ceylon (1556). The first Jesuit entered China in 1556. All of these missions were established during the lifetime of St. Ignatius of Loyola. After the Jesuits reached Florida in 1566, other Spanish missions were founded in Peru (1568), Mexico (1572), the Philippines (1581), Paraguay (1587), and Colombia (1598).

2. St. Augustine was founded in 1565, which was the same year that the Spanish established themselves in the Philippine Islands. They went to the Philippines from Acapulco, New Spain.

3. The details about the death of Peter Martinez differ in the early accounts. See Gerard Decorme, S.J., *Mártires Jesuítas de la Provincia de México* (Guadalajara: Buena Prensa, 1957); Félix Zubillaga, S.J., ed., *Monumenta Antiquae Floridae, 1566–1572* (Rome, 1946), documents 41, 43.

4. The sources for the first three chapters are as follows: Félix Zubillaga, S.J., ed., *Monumenta Mexicana*, 8 vols. (Rome: Institutum Historicum Societatis Jesu, 1956–1991). This eight-volume work covers the first thirty-five years, from 1570 to 1605. The volumes contain mostly letters from the generals to the Jesuits in New Spain as well as the yearly reports from New Spain. The volumes are well organized and indexed, with each document starting with a summary, and with good introductions for each volume. Clifford M. Lewis, S.J., and Albert J. Loomie, S.J., *The Spanish Jesuit Mission in Virginia, 1570–1572* (Chapel Hill, N.C.: University of North Carolina Press, 1953); Gerard Decorme, S.J., *La obra de los Jesuítas mexicanos durante la época colonial,*

1572–1767, 2 vols. (Mexico: Antigua Librería Robredo de José Porrúa e Hijos, 1941); Jerome Vincent Jacobson, S.J., *Educational Foundations of the Jesuits in Sixteenth-Century New Spain* (Berkeley: University of California Press, 1938); Peter Masten Dunne, S.J., *Pioneer Jesuits in Northern Mexico* (Berkeley: University of California Press, 1944).

5. Also in the spring of 1568, the first Jesuits arrived in Lima, Peru—four fathers and four brothers.

6. John Segura's companions were Father Luis de Quirós, Brother Gabriel Gómez, Brother Sancho Zaballos, Brother Pedro Mingot de Linares, Cristóbal Redondo, Gabriel de Solís, and Juan Baptista Méndez. The boy who survived was Alonso de Olmos.

Chapter 2: Mexico City, 1572–1576

1. A family of languages is a group of languages that seem to have a common origin. The Uto-Aztecan languages are called a phylum, meaning a family of families of languages. Some of the Uto-Aztecan languages in the United States are the Pima and Pápago languages in Arizona, some of the Pueblo languages of New Mexico, the Comanche language of east Texas, as well as the Hopi, Ute, Paiute, and Shoshone languages. The Navajo and Apache languages are not Uto-Aztecan. These two peoples came down from western Canada before 1500. The Navajo learned farming from their indigenous neighbors. The Apaches were hunters and gatherers. The Apaches were centered in west Texas and New Mexico, but they raided across Arizona into northern Sonora.

2. There continues to be disagreement about the size of the population before the Spanish conquest within the borders of present-day Mexico. However, extensive archaeological work has been done in the Nahuatl-speaking area of central Mexico. It shows a rapid increase in population during a few centuries before the conquest. Before the conquest there were about 920,000 people in the valley of Mexico and about 3.33 million in the Nahuatl-speaking area of central Mexico. See Michael E. Smith, *The Aztecs* (Cambridge, Mass.: Blackwell, 1996).

3. C. E. Marshall, "The Birth of the Mestizo in New Spain," *Hispanic American Historical Review* 19 (1939): 161–84.

4. Lake Texcoco was actually only the part of the lake around the island. Other parts of the lake had different names. A great deal of food was grown south of the island, where the water was fresher, on built-up mounds that looked like floating islands. Since the Spanish language has no *sh* sound, the Spanish used the letter *x* for the *sh* sound in the indigenous languages. Examples are

Uxmal (an ancient Mayan city in the Yucatán), Texcoco, and Tlaxcala. However today the *x* in these words has the sound of *s*. In a few place-names, the letter *x* has the sound of the English *h*. Examples are Oaxaca, Mexico, and Texas.

5. Tacuba is now within Mexico City. Part of the lake still exists between Mexico City and Texcoco.

6. The hospital also probably had mental patients. The original name of the hospital was the Immaculate Conception.

7. Gonzalo Aguirre Beltrán, "The Slave Trade in Mexico," *Hispanic American Historical Review* 24 (1944): 414.

8. There were seven dioceses in the country in 1572: Yucatán, Chiapas, Oaxaca, Puebla, Mexico City, Pátzcuaro, and Guadalajara.

9. Colin M. MacLachlan and Jaime E. Rodríguez, *The Forging of the Cosmic Race* (Berkeley: University of California Press, 1980), 197. The authors take the estimates from Gonzalo Aguirre Beltrán, *La Población Negra de México*. The estimates are for 1570 rather than 1572.

10. Peter de Gante arrived two years after the conquest in August of 1523. In 1526, he started a school for the indigenous in the city of Texcoco. This school was moved to Mexico City and expanded to include the orphanage. Gante trained fifty catechists. The students put on tableaux and sang Christian songs in Nahuatl at any festival in the region. There was a year of Latin. The students also built a church, which for many decades was the best church in the city.

11. Robert Ricard, *The Spiritual Conquest of Mexico, 1523–1572,* trans. Lesley Byrd Simpson (Berkeley: University of California Press, 1966).

12. Tlatelolco is also the place where Friar Bernardino Sahagún lived while he wrote his great book, *Historia general de las cosas de Nueva España* (more like an encyclopedia and only printed in modern times), about Mexican history, religion, and customs—one column in Nahuatl and another in Spanish. With the help of Indian scholars he wrote the history of the people, including the story of the conquest from their point of view. The book describes their religious beliefs in detail. The first draft of the book was done at Texcoco, with the Indians supplying the information as well as advising on the correct use of Nahuatl. With other Aztec scholars the book was rewritten at Tlatelolco and rewritten again at the Franciscan residence near the Zócalo. During his lifetime Sahagún had five books published in Nahuatl: a grammar, the Gospels, the theological virtues, sermons, and a life of St. Bernardino of Siena. He also produced the only Nahuatl hymnal, which was printed during the colonial period. Sahagún died in 1590 when he was ninety-one years old. A good biography of Sahagún is Luis Nicolau d'Olwer, *Fray Bernardino de*

Sahagún, 1499–1590, trans. Mauricio J. Mixco (Salt Lake City: University of Utah Press, 1987).

13. Agustín Churruca Peláez, S.J., *Primeras Fundaciones Jesuitas en Nueva España, 1572–1580* (Mexico City: Editorial Porrúa, 1980), 265.

14. Ricard, 406–14. The Franciscan books were mostly in Nahuatl, Otomí, and Tarascan. The Dominican books were in Nahuatl, Mixtec, and Zapotec (the last two languages are spoken in Oaxaca and are related to Otomí). The Augustinian books were in Nahuatl and Huaxtec. The Huaxtec language was spoken north of Vera Cruz along the Gulf of Mexico. It is an interesting language because it is related to the Mayan languages in the Yucatán. The Huaxtecans must have been separated from the Mayans by an expanding Uto-Aztecan population around Vera Cruz. Ricard in his *Spiritual Conquest,* listing books published up to 1572, does not mention anything published in Mayan. The Gospels had been translated into at least three languages— Nahuatl, Tarascan, and Mixtec. In these languages there were also the Epistles and Gospels for the Sundays of the year and for major feast days. The published books were for the missionaries and for the people, but sacred Scripture was only for the priests. Especially after the Council of Trent, the Catholic Church, fearing heresy and the private interpretation of the Bible, did not want vernacular language Scripture in the hands of laypeople.

15. The college building in Pátzcuaro now houses the Museo Regional de Artes Populares. The hospital building is now called the House of the Eleven Courtyards. Fine arts and crafts are sold there.

16. The historical manuscript of John Sánchez was published only in modern times. See Juan Sánchez Baquero, S.J., *Fundación de la Compañía de Jesús en Nueva España, 1571–1580,* ed. Félix Ayuso, S.J. (México: Editorial Patria, 1945).

Chapter 3: Tepotzotlán, 1576–1584

1. Herman W. Konrad, *A Jesuit Hacienda in Colonial Mexico: Santa Lucía, 1576–1767* (Stanford, Calif.: Stanford University Press, 1980). Charles W. Polzer, S.J., and Thomas E. Sheridan, *The Presidio and Militia on the Northern Frontier of New Spain,* vol. 2, pt. 1, *The Californias and Sinaloa-Sonora, 1700–1765* (Tucson: University of Arizona Press, 1997).

2. The Jesuits published three Nahuatl grammars. After Rincón's in 1595, there was *Arte de la Lengua Mexicana,* by Horacio Carochi, in 1645. In 1758, Ignatius Paredes published an expansion of Carochi's grammar.

3. *Cacique* is an Indian word from the Caribbean that means "chief" or "governor." In modern Mexico the word refers to a rural political boss.

4. Anthony Sedeño arrived in the Philippines two years before Matteo Ricci established a Jesuit residence in Zhaoqing, China.

5. John Tobar left other Nahuatl manuscripts. One was an explanation of the Mexican calendar. Another was about the origin, history, and religion of the Indians and was published in 1972. He is thought to be the author of a third Nahuatl manuscript about the apparition at the Sanctuary of Our Lady of Guadalupe. It is an important manuscript because it is so early, and it had been preserved at the Colegio Maximo. It differs in a few details from the traditional account of the apparition. It mentions not many roses but a flower. It has the bishop saying to Juan Diego, "Perhaps you were dreaming or were drunk," which is not in the other early Nahuatl manuscript. The benefactor of the Colegio Maximo, Alonso de Villaseca, had given generously to the sanctuary, which today is called a basilica. He was laid out there for three days after his death in 1580. This also indicates the early date of the devotion. For more information about these matters, see Churruca Peláez, 210–11 n. 9, 373–81.

6. Modern Mexicans speak of the six jewels (cities) of the ancient civilizations and the four jewels (churches) of the colonial era. The six jewels are Uxmal and Chichén Itzá near Mérida in the Yucatán, Monte Alban and Mitla near Oaxaca, Palenque near the Gulf of Mexico, and Teotihuacán near Mexico City. The four jewels are Santa Prisca in Taxco, the Sagrario Metropolitano in Mexico City, the Jesuits' San Francisco Xavier at Tepotzotlán, and Santa Clara in Querétaro.

Chapter 4: Gonzalo de Tapia, S.J., 1584–1594

1. The principal sources for this chapter are Decorme's works; Zubillaga, *Monumenta Mexicana;* W. Eugene Shiels, S.J., *Gonzalo de Tapia, 1561–1594, Founder of the First Permanent Jesuit Mission in North America* (New York: United States Catholic Historical Society, 1934); Thomas H. Naylor and Charles W. Polzer, S.J., *The Presidio and Militia on the Northern Frontier of New Spain, 1570–1700* (Tucson: University of Arizona Press, 1986).

2. Philip Wayne Powell, *Soldiers, Indians, and Silver, 1550–1600* (Berkeley: University of California Press, 1952). This is a good book about the Chichimec War.

3. The Jesuit general was Claudio Aquaviva. He was general for almost thirty-four years, from 1581 to 1615. He dealt with the crisis of priests leaving. He sent the visitor in 1590 to deal with any problems in the province, to get the missions started in the north, and to appoint the new provincial. Aquaviva then directed the mission effort during its formative period. He died just before

the setback to the mission effort in 1616 by the Tepehuán rebellion.

4. Zubillaga, *Monumenta Mexicana,* 4:242, 255, 348.

5. The description of the weather of Villa Sinaloa is based on data for a five-year
. period in the twentieth century. During this five-year period, the town of El
Fuerte on the Fuerte River, the next river to the north, received only half the
rain of Villa Sinaloa. This data is given in Ralph L. Beals, *The Aboriginal
Culture of the Cáhita Indians* (Berkeley and Los Angeles: University of
California Press, 1943), 8.

6. The two letters are in the reports of 1592 and 1593 from New Spain to Rome.
Zubillaga, *Monumenta Mexicana,* 4:350–54. This article and the previous one
are reprinted in *The Jesuit Missions of Northern Mexico.* This book is vol. 19 in
a series called Spanish Borderland Sourcebooks, published by the American
Museum of Natural History. See also Shiels, 121–24.

7. Zubillaga, *Monumenta Mexicana,* 4:547–60.

8. Ibid., 3:651–59.

9. Ibid., 5:6–10.

10. Ibid., 5:446–47.

11. Shiels, 171.

Chapter 5: The Tepehuanes, 1590–1616

1. The sources for this chapter are Decorme's works; Dunne, *Pioneer Jesuits in
Northern Mexico;* Luis González Rodríguez, *Crónicas de la Sierra Tarahumara*
(Mexico City: Secretaria de Educatión Pública, 1987).

2. Zubillaga, *Monumenta Mexicana,* 5:458.

3. Ramirez was the first Jesuit on the northern plain, and he may have seen some
buffalo. The buffalo range extended down to Durango, or at least it had in the
past.

4. In April of 1598, two Jesuits from New Spain went with a newly ordained
bishop to establish the order in Colombia, South America. The Jesuits in
Colombia were under the Jesuits in Peru. Seven schools were started by
1643, and an independent Jesuit province was established in 1696. The
Jesuits in Panama were also members of the Province of Peru. In going to Peru
the Jesuits had to cross Panama, which was a dangerous place with yellow
fever and other diseases. In the 1700s, the Jesuits in Panama made an effort
to establish mission villages in the jungle. The missions were not successful
because of the hostility that the native people had for the Spanish. When the
Jesuits withdrew from the mission villages, the bishop of Panama decided to
use the available personnel to establish the University of Panama. A Peruvian
Jesuit told me that at the time of the expulsion, his province had more mem-

bers buried in Panama than they had buried in Peru.

5. This and what follows is from Zubillaga, *Monumenta Mexicana*, 6:627–39. Each year the local Jesuit communities reported to the provincial about what had happened. In Mexico City these reports were copied or summarized and sent to the general in Rome.

6. Ibid., 639–40.

7. González, 146.

8. Decorme, *La obra*, 2:76.

Chapter 6: Sinaloa, 1594–1614

1. The main sources for this chapter are Peter Masten Dunne, S.J., *Pioneer Black Robes on the West Coast* (Berkeley and Los Angeles: University of California Press, 1940); Charles W. Polzer et al., ed., *The Jesuit Missions of Northern Mexico* (New York: Garland Publishing, 1991); Juan Nentvig, S.J., *Rudo Ensayo: A Description of Sonora and Arizona in 1764*, trans. Alberto Francisco Pradeau and Robert R. Rasmussen (Tucson: University of Arizona Press, 1980); Charles W. Polzer, S.J., *Rules and Precepts of the Jesuit Missions of Northwestern New Spain* (Tucson: University of Arizona Press, 1976).

2. See Max L. Moorhead, "The Soldado de Cuera," in *The Spanish Borderlands: A First Reader*, comp. Oakah L. Jones (Los Angeles: L. L. Morrison, 1974).

3. In 1611, the first French Jesuits arrived in Canada, although a permanent mission was not established until 1625. It was in 1634 that the first English Jesuits arrived in southern Maryland.

Chapter 7: Sonora, 1614–1767

1. Decorme, *La obra*, 2:316.

2. Ibid., 2:327.

3. In 1618, three priests and two brothers established a residence in Mérida, Yucatán.

4. Basilio's grammar was expanded and republished by other Jesuits in 1737. It was reprinted in 1890. Other Jesuit grammars, which are not mentioned in the text or in the notes, are an Opata grammar by Natal Lombardo in 1702; *El arte de la lengua Tepeguana: con vocabulario, confesionario, y catecismo* by Benito Rinaldini in 1743; a Cáhita grammar by James Paul Gonzales around 1745; *Tarahumarishes Worterbuck* by Matthew Steffel in 1751; and an Otomí grammar by Francis Miranda in 1759 (the only published Jesuit grammar that was not about a Uto-Aztecan language).

After the expulsion, Father Francis Ducrue published *Specimen Lingua California* (in a journal by Von Murr) in Europe. Besides the grammars, the Jesuits published other books relating to the missions both before and after the expulsion, including catechisms, homilies, histories of the missions, and the lives of deceased missionaries.

Father Bartholomew Castaño published a brief Spanish catechism in 1644. Translations were published in Nahuatl, Tarascan, and Otomí.

There is no mention that the Jesuits translated sacred Scripture into the native languages as the Franciscans had done before the Council of Trent. This means that at Mass the Jesuit had to sight-read Scripture from Latin into the native language. However, the published homilies may have been a cover to get at least the Bible stories into the native languages.

5. Theodore E. Treutlein, "The Economic Regime of the Jesuit Missions in Eighteenth-Century Sonora," *Pacific Historical Review* 8 (3:1939): 289–300.

6. Theodore E. Treutlein, "The Jesuit Missionary in the Role of Physician," *Mid-America* 22 (2:1940): 120–41.

Chapter 8: The Tarahumaras, 1611–1767

1. Besides the works of Decorme and González, this chapter is based on Peter Masten Dunne, S.J., *Early Jesuit Missions in Tarahumara* (Berkeley: University of California Press, 1948).

2. Decorme, *La obra*, 2:250.

3. González, 261–68.

4. Dunne, *Tarahumara*, 121, 145.

5. Ibid., 121, 150, 151.

6. Charles W. Polzer, S.J., *Kino: A Legacy* (Tucson: Jesuit Fathers of Southern Arizona, 1998), 128, 138.

7. The poison from an arrow could kill a person in four hours, but an antidote made from certain roots or leaves was available. The warriors would take the antidote with them into battle. If a person was wounded, he would chew the root, clean the wound as best he could, and apply the moist pulp to the wound.

Chapter 9: Chínipas, 1626–1638

1. González, 44–45.

Chapter 10: Eusebio Kino, S.J., 1681–1711

1. The sources for this chapter are Polzer, *Kino: A Legacy;* Herbert Eugene Bolton, ed., *Rim of Christendom* (New York: Russell and Russell, 1960); Herbert

Eugene Bolton, ed., *Kino's Historical Memoir of Pimería Alta* (Berkeley: University of California Press, 1948); Ernest J. Burrus, S.J., *Kino and Manje: Explorers of Sonora and Arizona* (Rome: Jesuit Historical Institute, 1971); Ernest J. Burrus, S.J., *Kino Reports to Headquarters* (Rome: Institutum Historicum Societatis Jesu, 1954).

2. In 1961, Ernest J. Burrus edited and had published in Mexico City Eusebio Kino's *Vida del P. Francisco J. Saeta, S.J.: Sangre misionera en Sonora*. It was reprinted in 1971 by the Jesuit Historical Institute.
3. Ibid.
4. Decorme, *La obra*, 2:459–60.

Chapter 11: Baja California, 1697–1767

1. Sources for this chapter are Peter Masten Dunne, S.J., *Black Robes in Lower California* (Berkeley: University of California Press, 1952); Ernest J. Burrus, S.J., ed., *Jesuit Relations, Baja California, 1716–1762* (Los Angeles: Dawson's Book Shop, 1984); Ernest J. Burrus, S.J., ed., *Ducrue's Account of the Expulsion of the Jesuits from Lower California, 1767–1769* (St. Louis: St. Louis University Press, 1967); Harry W. Crosby, *Antigua California* (Albuquerque: University of New Mexico Press, 1994); W. Michael Mathes, trans., *Clemente Guillén, Explorer of the South: Diaries of the Overland Expeditions to Bahía Magdalena and La Paz, 1719, 1720–1721* (Los Angeles: Dawson's Book Shop, 1979); Juan María de Salvatierra, *Selected Letters about Lower California*, trans. Ernest J. Burrus, S.J. (Los Angeles: Dawson's Book Shop, 1971); Miguel del Barco, S.J., *The Natural History of Baja California* (Los Angeles: Dawson's Book Shop, 1980); Miguel del Barco, S.J., *Ethnology and Linguistics of Baja California* (Los Angeles: Dawson's Book Shop, 1981).
2. Harry W. Crosby, *The Cave Paintings of Baja California* (La Jolla, Calif.: Copley Books, 1984).
3. Magdalena Bay was known at an early date. In 1602, Captain Sebastián Vizcaíno sailed from Acapulco in order to map the California coast. His expedition landed at Magdalena Bay, explored for a week, made charts of the bay, and found no decent water. The expedition continued north and made charts of the bays of San Diego and Monterey in Alta California.
4. Guillén's party saw the gray whales at the end of March. These giant mammals arrive in February, most of them for a week or so, to either mate or to give birth to twelve-foot-long, 2,000-pound calves. They then return 5,000 miles in four months in order to feed during the summer off of Alaska.
5. Also in 1722, the Jesuits established a residence in Havana, Cuba. The Havana college was founded in 1728, and the church was dedicated in 1755.

At the time of the expulsion, there were sixteen Jesuits and two colleges in Cuba.

6. Ernest J. Burrus, S.J., and Félix Zubillaga, S.J., *Misiones Mexicanas de la Compañía de Jesús, 1618–1745* (Madrid: Ediciones José Porrua Turanzas, 1982), 47–53.

7. Ibid., 97–113.

8. There are many details about Ocio in Crosby's *Antigua California*. This is a big book about the Jesuit period in Baja California. It is full of fascinating information.

9. The historian is Francis Xavier Alegre, S.J. Born in Vera Cruz, he taught mathematics in Havana, and then he taught in Mérida, where he developed a course in the philosophy of law. When the provincial selected him to write a history of the province because its 200th anniversary was approaching, he moved to Mexico and set to work. A few years later, when he had just about finished, the expulsion occurred. Thinking that his work was lost, Alegre rewrote it from memory in Italy as best he could. However, his original manuscript was not lost, and it was published at a later date.

Chapter 12: The Expulsion, 1767–1768

1. Decorme, *La obra*, 1:473

2. Ibid., 475.

3. Ignaz Pfefferkorn, S.J., *Sonora: A Description of the Province,* trans. Theodore E. Treutlein (Albuquerque: University of New Mexico Press, 1949).

ILLUSTRATIONS